The Doctrine of Atonement for Building Human Rights in Malawi

Copyright 2019 by Rev Dr. J. Thipa

All rights reserved. No part of this publication may be reproduced, stored in a retrieval system, or transmitted in any form or by any means, electronic, mechanical, photocopying, recording or otherwise, without prior permission from the publishers.

Published by
Kachere Series
P.O. Box 1037, Zomba
ISBN: 978-99908-0-255-9

The Kachere Series is represented outside African by African Books Collective, Oxford (orders@africanbookscollective.com)

Layout & Cover Design: Josephine Kawejere

The Doctrine of Atonement for Building Human Rights in Malawi

Rev. Dr. Joseph Andrew Thipa (MA, DTh)

Editorial Advisor:

Prof. Uledi Kamanga

Kachere Book no. 70

Kachere Series

Zomba

2019

ABSTRACT

This study is a critical investigation of a theological basis for believers and the Church of Central Africa Presbyterian in Malawi to support a culture of human dignity and human rights, and specifically in the light of the classic Reformed doctrine of atonement, as reflected in the works of Calvin and Barth and also the Westminster Confession. It is argued in this study that the very essence of public recognition and consistent implementation of human rights is far reaching when understood in the light of the Reformed view of the atonement.

In fact, in important and influential studies on human rights in ecumenical Reformed circles, the support for human rights is normally based on other doctrines. This study, however, argues that Jesus' earthly life, sayings or parables in the Gospel narrative are all integral to the atonement process according to classical Reformed understanding, and are of great importance and relevance as a transformative power for the renewed life of the Reformed Christians in Malawi. It is argued that such a transformative power is capable of leading Reformed Christians in Malawi to a different view concerning their reception and building of a human rights culture in Malawi.

Other Reformed Christian responses to human rights do provide an excellent overview of the liberating power of Christ's cross and resurrection, and how believers may understand and affirm their vocation in light of this. However, the claim of this dissertation is that a fuller and more faithful understanding of the atonement will assist Reformed Christians in Malawi to see more clearly the importance of a culture of human rights specifically for the more faithful practice of their own Reformed faith and piety.

For that reason, the research study has two research questions.

The main research question investigates the relationship between the classic Reformed doctrine of atonement and human rights. The secondary question inquires about the implications of the classic Reformed doctrine of atonement for the promotion of human rights in Malawi. Hence, the research study comprises of five chapters.

Chapter 1 introduces the problem being research, whilst Chapter 2 argues for a more faithful understanding of the Reformed view of the atonement. Chapter 3 provides the necessary background for the Church of Central Africa Presbyterian and its involvement in political change, and its response to the introduction of human rights and freedoms in Malawi. Chapter 4 discusses human rights in Malawi, in light of the Reformed doctrine of the atonement. The last Chapter (Chapter 5) summarizes and makes conclusions.

ACKNOWLEDGEMENTS

I take this as an opportunity to thank some people and institutions for their support in the writing of this dissertation.

My wife Agnes, my daughters Patricia and Grace, and my grandchildren Edna, Lonjezo, Vincent and Memory, I thank you all for your being proud of me. You always encouraged me and were confident that I could make it. I do not forget my very dear friend, the late Mr. Adrian Martin Kazambwe, who was always there for me, anytime I ran into difficulties of life. It is unfortunate that I am finishing this research study when the Lord has already called you home.

Prof. Dirk Smit and Prof. N. Koopman, it was a privilege to work under your supervision. You all worked very hard and tirelessly. Thanks for your insight and the advice you offered me along the way. I would, also, like to thank the following - Rev. Daniel Gunya, Rev. T.N. Maseya, Rev. M. Kansilanga, Rev. J.J. Mphatso and the Very Rev. Silas Ncozana - for their support and love. You all allowed God to use you when you, indiscriminately and in your different capacities and positions, gave me an opportunity to go for advanced studies in theology.

The financial assistance of the Presbyterian Church in Canada (PCC), through Blantyre Synod of the Church of Central Africa Presbyterian in Malawi, towards this research is hereby acknowledged. Opinions expressed and conclusions arrived at are those of the author and are not necessarily to be attributed to the PCC.

Kachere Series
P.O. Box 1037, Zomba, Malawi
Kachere@globemw.net
www.kachereseries.org.

This book is part of the Kachere Series, a range of books on religion, cul-ture and society from Malawi. Other related Kachere titles so far are:

Boston Soko, *Nchimi Chikanga: The Battle against Witchcraft in Malawi*
Rhodian G. Munyenyembe, *Christianity and Socio-Cultural Issues: The Charismatic Movement and Contextualization in Malawi*
Andrew C. Ross, *Colonialism to Cabinet Crisis: A Political History of Malawi*
James Tengatenga, *The UMCA in Malawi: A History of the Anglican Church*
Isaac C. Lamba, *Contradictions in Post-War Education Policy Formulation and Application in Colonial Malawi 1945-1961: A History Study of the Dynamics of Colonial Survival*
Uledi Kamanga ed., *Society and the Arts: Studies in Gender, Literature and Language*
Sheikh Imuran Shareef Mahomed, *Majlis Al-Shŭrá Consultative Assembly: Past and Present Application of the Principle of shûrâ in Islamic Governance*
John M.K.Mtitima, *Powers of Culture: Dilemma of the Black Race*

The Kachere Series is the publication arm of the Department of Theology and Religious Studies of the University of Malawi

Series Editors: M. Mbewe; Dr. I. S. Mohammad; Dr. J. Thipa; Dr. H. Mvula; Dr. J. Mawerenga, Dr Fr. Chaima, Mr R. Mdoka

TABLE OF CONTENTS

CHAPTER 1

THE PROBLEM: REFORMED FAITH AND HUMAN DIGNITY 4

INTRODUCTION   **4**

BACKGROUND OF PROBLEM   9

RECENT WORKS ON REFORMED FAITH AND HUMAN DIGNITY   10

THE RESEARCH PROBLEM   22

HYPOTHESIS   28

STRUCTURE OF ARGUMENT   33

CHAPTER 2

THE CLASSIC REFORMED VIEW OF THE ATONEMENT   **37**

INTRODUCTION   **37**

ATONEMENT   38

ANSELM'S VIEW OF THE ATONEMENT   47

JOHN CALVIN'S VIEW OF THE ATONEMENT   53

DEATH OF JESUS   59

JUSTIFICATION   69

SUMMARY   107

SUMMARY AND EVALUATION 168

CHAPTER 3

THE CLASSIC REFORMED VIEW OF THE ATONEMENT IN CONTEMPORARY MALAWI 169

INTRODUCTION 169

BACKGROUND 170

THE CHURCH OF CENTRAL AFRICA PRESBYTERIAN'S VIEW OF THE ATONEMENT 171

JESUS' ACTIVE OBEDIENCE AND THE CHRISTIAN LIFE 192

CONCLUSION 199

CHAPTER 4

HUMAN RIGHTS IN MALAWI IN THE LIGHT OF THE CLASSIC REFORMED VIEW OF THE ATONEMENT 201

INTRODUCTION 201

HUMAN RIGHTS IN MALAWI 209

JESUS' LIFE, IN THE GOSPELS, AND A PATTERN OF LIFE FOR THE REFORMED CHRISTIANS IN MALAWI 214

JESUS' PATTERN OF LIFE FOR BELIEVERS AND HUMAN 217

SUMMARY AND EVALUATIONS 234

CHAPTER 5

CONCLUSION 236

INTRODUCTION 236

CONTRIBUTION OF NEW KNOWLEDGE BY THE 255

BIBLIOGRAPHY 258

ABSTRACT

This study is a critical investigation of a theological basis for believers and the Church of Central Africa Presbyterian in Malawi to support a culture of human dignity and human rights, and specifically in the light of the classic Reformed doctrine of atonement, as reflected in the works of Calvin and Barth and also the Westminster Confession. It is argued in this study that the very essence of public recognition and consistent implementation of human rights is far reaching when understood in the light of the Reformed view of the atonement.

In fact, in important and influential studies on human rights in ecumenical Reformed circles, the support for human rights is normally based on other doctrines. This study, however, argues that Jesus' earthly life, sayings or parables in the Gospel narrative are all integral to the atonement process according to classical Reformed understanding, and are of great importance and relevance as a transformative power for the renewed life of the Reformed Christians in Malawi. It is argued that such a transformative power is capable of leading Reformed Christians in Malawi to a different view concerning their reception and building of a human rights culture in Malawi.

Other Reformed Christian responses to human rights do provide an excellent overview of the liberating power of Christ's cross and resurrection, and how believers may understand and affirm their vocation in light of this. However, the claim of this dissertation is that a fuller and more faithful understanding of the atonement will assist Reformed Christians in Malawi to see more clearly the importance of a culture of human rights specifically for the more faithful practice of their own Reformed faith and piety.

For that reason, the research study has two research questions. The main research question investigates the relationship between the classic Reformed doctrine of atonement and human rights. The secondary question inquires about the implications of the classic Reformed doctrine of atonement for the promotion of human rights in Malawi. Hence, the research study comprises of five chapters.

Chapter 1 introduces the problem being research, whilst Chapter 2 argues for a more faithful understanding of the Reformed view of the atonement. Chapter 3 provides the necessary background for the Church of Central Africa Presbyterian and its involvement in political change, and its response to the introduction of human rights and freedoms in Malawi. Chapter 4 discusses human rights in Malawi, in light of the Reformed doctrine of the atonement. The last Chapter (Chapter 5) summarizes and makes conclusions.

ACKNOWLEDGEMENTS

I take this as an opportunity to thank some people and institutions for their support in the writing of this dissertation.

My wife Agnes, my daughters Patricia and Grace, and my grandchildren Edna, Lonjezo, Vincent and Memory, I thank you all for your being proud of me. You always encouraged me and were confident that I could make it. I do not forget my very dear friend, the late Mr. Adrian Martin Kazambwe, who was always there for me, anytime I ran into difficulties of life. It is unfortunate that I am finishing this research study when the Lord has already called you home.

Prof. Dirk Smit and Prof. N. Koopman, it was a privilege to work under your supervision. You all worked very hard and tirelessly. Thanks for your insight and the advice you offered me along the way. I would, also, like to thank the following - Rev. Daniel Gunya, Rev. T.N. Maseya, Rev. M. Kansilanga, Rev. J.J. Mphatso and the Very Rev. Silas Ncozana - for their support and love. You all allowed God to use you when you, indiscriminately and in your different capacities and positions, gave me an opportunity to go for advanced studies in theology.

The financial assistance of the Presbyterian Church in Canada (PCC), through Blantyre Synod of the Church of Central Africa Presbyterian in Malawi, towards this research is hereby acknowledged. Opinions expressed and conclusions arrived at are those of the author and are not necessarily to be attributed to the PCC.

CHAPTER 1

THE PROBLEM: REFORMED FAITH AND HUMAN DIGNITY

INTRODUCTION

The Reformed faith, also known as the Reformed tradition, was born out of what is called the Protestant Reformation, which occurred during the medieval era when the Christian church became more and more distorted. Jack D. Kinneer (www.opc.org/new_horizons/NH99/NH9902b.html) says that "truths taught in the Bible were obscured and ideas and practices without biblical warrant came to prominence: This led to a movement by Christians to reform the faith and practice of the medieval church. It is from this effort at reform that the name comes: the Reformed faith." Christian members to the Reformed faith itself are, therefore, called Reformed believers or Christians.

Human dignity is about "recognizing that human beings possess a special value intrinsic to their humanity and as such are worthy of respect simply because they are human beings (https://cbhd.org/category/issues/human-dignity). Thus every human being, regardless of age, ability, status, gender, ethnicity, etc., is to be treated with respect. https://cbhd.org/category/issues/human-dignity."

This study investigates a theological basis for Christian believers and churches in Malawi to support a culture of human dignity and human rights, specifically in the light of the classic Reformed doctrine of atonement. The need arises from the self-understanding of the Reformed faith and tradition, and from the contemporary experience in church and society in Malawi.

Within ecumenical Christianity, and especially within the worldwide Reformed tradition, there have been several attempts to provide a theological basis for human rights. Different Christian traditions argue for a theological basis for human rights different ways, based on their own self-understanding and vision. Through several well-known documents and studies, Reformed bodies and churches have done the same – including the World Alliance of Reformed Churches and the (now) Reformed Ecumenical Council[1]. It is, however, important to note that the Reformed documents usually provide a theological case for human dignity and human rights founded on some other convictions and articles of faith, other than the doctrine of atonement. This doctrine is in fact at the heart of the Reformed faith, piety and life; therefore one would expect it to play a crucial role in any attempt towards theological grounding and justification.

The contemporary experience of the Reformed faith members in Malawi has demonstrated that this seeming absence of the doctrine of atonement in the discourse of the Reformed faith on the practice of human rights constitutes a major stumbling block towards their participation in building human rights in contemporary Malawi. It is probably fair to claim that many Reformed Christians in Malawi tend to support a human rights culture, and would indeed love to do so from the perspective of their faith as well. But their own understanding of the doctrine of the atonement, which they regard as the heart of their faith commitment, seems to contradict human rights. In short, it often seems to them that the Reformed notion of the atonement contradicts the very foundation of a human rights culture. The Reformed notion of the atonement has it that Christian believers do good works out of grace alone from God and that they cannot claim them as being done by them. The Reformed notion of atonement, grace alone, rejects awarding of merit on the Christian believer.

This research, therefore, is an attempt to bring clarity in this seeming conflict. Is it impossible for the Reformed faith to ground

---

[1] At the time when the study was done, the body was still called The Reformed Ecumenical Synod. It is now in the process of uniting with the World Alliance of Reformed Churches forming a new World Communion of Reformed Churches.

its support for human rights in its central doctrine of the atonement? And is it indeed correct when Reformed faith in Malawi feels that the doctrine of atonement contradicts its need to support a culture of human dignity and rights?

These are not simple questions, and they most probably have relevance in the Reformed world far outside Malawi as well. Grounding human rights in the the classic Reformed doctrine of atonement tends to meet differing Christian responses within the Reformed tradition and churches. This is partly due to differing views regarding ethical approaches to the understanding of "God's justice and mercy" in his Son Jesus Christ. Dirk Smit (2009: 103) comments that there are different theories of justice that complement and often contradict one another within the Protestant and Reformed faith. Not everyone within the Reformed tradition, who supports justice necessarily understands or accepts justice in the form of human rights.

However, this research limits itself to the understanding of justice as the practice of a culture of human rights. But what is the Reformed tradition? Who speaks for the Reformed tradition? And where does one find the doctrine of atonement according to the Reformed faith and tradition? In this regard, this research specifically focusses on the atonement views expressed by Anselm of Canterbury, John Calvin, the Westminster Confession of Faith, and Karl Barth. This approach affirms the classic Reformed view of the atonement that this research applies to the Church of Central Africa Presbyterian in Malawi, later in Chapter 3 of this research.

The argument why such a focus is seen as legitimate and sufficient will become clearer as the this study progresses. However, very broadly it can already be claimed that the study uses Anselm of Cantebury's view of the atonement because it is from him that the Reformed tradition draws alternatives of punishment or satisfaction for its view of the atonement, through John Calvin. Here, Anselm's view of the atonement has something to do with God's justice (*iustitia*) that has as its fundamental sense the moral rectitude of God's creation order. Anselm conceives of

God as to have originally created human beings compatible God's own nature and dignity. Therefore, human beings were originally created of true reflection to God in accordance with God's moral justice. As such, human beings are capable of finding their true good, and capable of realizing God's purpose. When human beings disobeyed and dishonoured God by sin, their true relation to God and the genuine moral order of God's world were all disordered. But human beings must satisfy God's honour (which they were not capable of doing when they sinned) and restore themselves back to their original status compatible with God's own nature and dignity as spiritual creatures of God. Therefore, God by his gracious work and mercy in Jesus Christ he satisfied his own honour on behalf of all sinful human beings. In Jesus, God rectified the moral ordering of his creation to become as originally established at creation. This moral ordering of creation reflects the divine will and nature, and hence, extending to the relationships between human persons and God, and amongst human persons themselves (Smit 2009: 103).

The study further uses John Calvin's view of the atonement because the Reformed tradition owes much to him for his notion of "double grace". Calvin affirms that believers, in their salvation by God, are both reconciled to God through Christ's blamelessness and empowered by Christ's Spirit to be capable of cultivating blamelessness and purity of life. Such leads to a new life, which is characteristic of the Reformed tradition. Here, Calvin's view of the atonement deals with any possible conflict between the divine justice and mercy, or between the wrath of the Father and self-sacrificial grace of the Son. He intends to express that the church should be pastoral in its dealings with people; in that it should serve the rhetorical function of leading human persons to experience gratitude, to delight in the sovereign and free grace of God [Smit, 2005 (a)]. This life of grace and gratitude has concrete ethical implications in Calvin's thinking, and that human beings correspond to God, the bountiful parent, as grateful sons and daughters (Gerrish 1993: 41).

The study also uses the *Westminster Confession of Faith* because of its connection with the Church of Central Africa Presbyterian in Malawi through the Church of Scotland who owns it. The Church of Scotland established two Christian mission stations in Malawi between 1875 and 1876[2] as Presbyteries of Livingstonia and Blantyre. Later, the two presbyteries became the Synods of Livingstonia and Blantyre, which united in 1924 to become one Church of Central Africa Presbyterian. In 1926 the Synod of Nkhoma, which was established in Malawi by the Dutch Reformed Church of South Africa, joined the unity of the Church of Central Africa Presbyterian. The *Westminster Confession of Faith's* view of the atonement has it that God's justice changes sinners into a state of grace, freeing them from a natural bondage under sin [9 (iv)]. Thus, by God's grace alone, a sinner is enabled to freely will and do that which is spiritually good.

The study uses Karl Barth's view of the atonement because he argues more forcefully and positively than any other theologian that creation is already the work of the free, fatherly grace and mercy of God (Leith 1993: 70, 189). Barth also tends to reaffirm the Reformed faith in his discussion of "justification" and "sanctification." But he interestingly carries it forward to explain how justification may be superior to sanctification, and sanctification superior to justification. Here, Barth's view of the atonement has something to do with justification by faith alone (*sola fide*), which is based upon the humility of faith (CD IV/1 627). Therefore, humility of faith eliminates pride of human effort, exalts what God has done (e.g. in Jesus Christ), and admits that the human person cannot keep the law or measure up to God's standard, and that only God can measure up to God's own standard on behalf of the human person. However, Barth is quick to point out that justification ought to be traceable through what it does in the sanctified life of the believer. Therefore, human works

---

[2] Two missionary groups came to Malawi, one from the Free Church of Scotland (1875), and the other from the Established Church of Scotland (1876).

as such cannot be regarded with contempt or indifference, or rejected because they have meaning and truth. That is, once a person has been justified, he or she has to undergo sanctification for moral transformation for righteousness, which leads to setting up righteousness in one's daily works. This interrelatedness of justice and sanctification, in Barth's thinking on atonement, paves the way for developing a soteriological rationale for the involvement of Christian believers in the quest for the fulfilment of human rights.

This research study affirms the Reformed view of the atonement based on Anselm, Calvin, the Westminster Confession of Faith, and Barth that articulate about God's justice and mercy.. They all agree that God, in his Son Jesus, restored the moral ordering of creation to become genuine and original as it was first established by God at creation. Human beings had disordered God's moral ordering of things because of their disobedience and dishonour of God. God's original moral ordering of his creation reflected his divine will and nature that extended to the relationships between human persons and God himself, and amongst human persons themselves. God thus changes human persons by his justice into a state of grace, freeing them from a natural bondage under sin. And this life in the state of grace and freedom from sin is a life of freedom for the quest for justice in the world.

BACKGROUND OF PROBLEM

The study is set within the Reformed tradition and churches. However, within the Reformed tradition and throughout history, there has not been a single authoritative theological position regarding the theories and practices of social, economic and legal justice [Smit 2005 (a)]. Hence, there has not been a single authoritative ethical approach on God's justice in relation to God's mercy in light of the classic Reformed view of the atonement. Therefore, all claims concerning practices of social, economic and legal justice are and must be modest and contextual, to reflect specific traditions, experiences and perspectives.

Again, the research is set within the classic Reformed view of the atonement's major aspects – God-centredness, Bible-basedness, Justification by Faith Alone, Salvation by Jesus Christ Alone and Structured by the Covenant. They all tend to create misunderstandings that often and easily lead to denial of the life of Jesus Christ and the Christian discipleship as an integral part of our Reformed faith, let alone, making the task of developing a human rights language and culture for the contemporary Church of Central Africa Presbyterian in Malawi more difficult.

Nevertheless, this study approaches God's justice and mercy with the contemporary Malawian view of the classic Reformed doctrine of atonement in mind. Along the way, the research addresses the following questions: What does the contemporary Malawian Church understand by the classic Reformed doctrine of atonement? What is the relationship between the classic Reformed doctrine of atonement and human rights in the contemporary Malawi context? What implications does the classic Reformed doctrine of atonement have, if any, in the building of a human rights culture in contemporary Malawi?

RECENT WORKS ON REFORMED FAITH AND HUMAN DIGNITY

Andrew Heywood (2002) describes human rights as rights to which people are entitled by virtue of being human. Whilst George W. Forell (1978:39) says that human rights are the stuff of declarations and manifestos, which are in effect, heralds of entitlements and protections that eventually must receive a guarantee from the law. Forell adds on to say that human rights are universal in the sense that they belong to all human persons rather than to members of any particular state, race, religion, gender or other group, and hence, they are fundamental in that they are inalienable. Indeed, they function as standards that judge the policies and behaviour of governments, corporations and other agents of power over the lives of people.

In this direction, the Reformed faith goes beyond speaking about personal and individual ethics, to speak about the honour of God (Latin: *soli Deo Gloria*), interwoven with human beings' salvation and well-being. Here, John Calvin would affirm that where God is known, human beings are also treated with human dignity and cared for. The issue of Human dignity/rights, here, would call into question the accepted value systems and cultural stereotypes, which mirror power relationships that are unjust (e.g. between men and women). Here, we must keep in mind that human dignity is something persons have, not something they must earn or someone grants them[3]. Definitely, human rights are very important for the social, economic and political development of humanity. That is the reason why the General Assembly of the United Nations passed the *Universal Declarations of Human Rights*.

The *Universal Declaration of Human Rights* is the primary international articulation of the fundamental and inalienable rights of all members of the human family. They were adopted by the United Nations General Assembly on December 10, 1948, after the Second World War. They include the following civil and political rights: the right not to be subjected to torture, to equality before the law, to a fair trial, to freedom of movement, to asylum and to freedom of thought, conscience, religion, opinion and expression (National Coordinating Committee for UDHR50, *Questions and Answers*, Question 1). They also include economic, social and cultural rights such as the right to food, clothing, housing and medical care, to social security, to work, to equal pay for equal work, to form trade unions and education. As such, the *Universal Declaration of Human Rights* has become a cornerstone of customary international law.

In addition, world governments are legally required to respect the principles outlined in the *Universal Declaration of Human*

---

[3] In a very important recent study, the Reformed philosopher Nicholas Wolterstorff argued precisely this claim in great detail over against theories of justice based on right order, rather than on inherent natural rights.

Rights by applying its principles. It is very encouraging that constitutions of many nations that got their independence after the United Nations adopted the document have made direct reference to the *Universal Declaration of Human Rights*. Dozens of legally binding international treaties are based on the principles stipulated in the *Universal Declaration of Human Rights*. The United Nations, itself, cites the document as justification for its numerous actions, including acts of the Security Council.

All rights in the Universal Declaration of Human Rights are and must be regarded as equally important, although there are some differences of opinion about how to realize the rights and freedoms. The separation of the various rights stipulated in the *Universal Declaration of Human Rights* into two legally binding international Covenants show some of these differences in approach and implementation. Many Western nations argued that economic, social and cultural rights are difficult to justify. For instance, if an individual lacks adequate food, clothing or shelter, it may be difficult in a court of law to determine who is responsible for the circumstances. As such, it was recognized that the Universal Declaration of Human Rights encompasses both "positive" and "negative" rights (National Coordinating Committee, *Questions and Answers* Question 5). The positive rights (e.g. the right to education) requires action by someone to ensure a specific right, while negative rights (e.g. the right not to be subjected to torture) demand that someone avoid doing something. With reference to the *Universal Declaration of Human Rights,* therefore, the two largest Reformed bodies - the World Alliance of Reformed Churches and The Reformed Ecumenical Synod (now Council) – gave a Christian response by producing two respective statements on human rights which this research uses.

In 1970, the World Alliance of Reformed Churches[4] met in Nairobi and called for the *Christian Declaration on Human Rights,*

---

[4] This body is now called World Communion of Reformed Churches (WCRC).

which is a study of the *Theological Basis for Human Rights and Liberation*. The Christian Declaration on Human Rights is aimed at broadening the base of liberation of people from things that keep them in bondage to include the poor and the powerless, ethnic minorities and women. This would be done by improving the theology meant for promotion of human rights and dignity.

The Reformed Ecumenical Synod, mentioned above, produced the *RES Testimony on Human Rights*, a study of the entire area of human rights in their theological, historical and contextual scope. The RES Testimony on Human Rights was produced for the Reformed Ecumenical Council members and others who are concerned about human rights in the hope that it would facilitate a better understanding of the issues involved (*RES Testimony on Human Rights* 1983: foreword). It is meant to stimulate the people of God to take appropriate steps to promote human rights within the perspective of the Gospel's message of justice and love.

The Reformed Christian response on human rights is vital because it will encourage Christians in the Reformed tradition and churches (including the Church of Central Africa Presbyterian in Malawi) to participate in building human rights in their countries. The Church of Central Africa Presbyterian in Malawi[5], popularly known as "General Synod", is a member church of the World Communion of Reformed Churches (WCRC).

Even though there is the Reformed Christian response to human rights available, but this is in form of scanty scholarly literature about grounding of human rights in light of the Reformed view of the atonement. The scholarly literature themselves do not include much about the everyday life of Jesus Christ on earth. For example,

---

[5] The confession of faith upon which this church is founded and built are contained in the following books of confessions:- The Nicene Creed, The Apostles' Creed, The Westminster Confession of Faith, The Westminster Larger Catechism, The Westminster Shorter Catechism, The Confession of Faith of Netherlands, The Heidelberg Catechism, The Belgic Confession of Faith, The Canon of Dort, The Church of Central Africa Presbyterian's Confession of Faith of 1924.

Jesus' ethical examples for believers' renewed life, as narrated by the Gospels are not available in the scanty scholarly literature about grounding of human rights. Instead, the scholarly literature only provide an excellent overview of the liberating power of Christ's cross and resurrection in the incarnation of God for the reconciliation of the world, and how in light of this, believers may understand and affirm their vocation (Miller 1977:145-146). Yes, the scanty scholarly literature affirm that by the Holy Spirit of God believers are called to express solidarity with those who bear a human countenance, more particularly, a willingness to stand up for those whose fundamental rights and freedom are robbed. As such, it can be concluded to say that the World Alliance of Reformed Churches does not ground human rights on the classic Reformed doctrine of atonement. Instead, the World Alliance of Reformed Churches ground human rights only in some other Reformed doctrines, like human beings created in the image of God, covenant responsibilities, and vocation, as they appear in the *Theological Basis of Human Rights* (Miller 1977:145; *RES Testimony on Human Rights* 1983:44). Using starting points such as 'God-centred', the Reformed tradition and churches were able to come up with a *Theological Basis of Human Rights* as we have them today.

The *Theological Basis of Human Rights* critically explain about 'God creating man and woman in his own image' (Genesis 1:27) by which the Reformed tradition and churches understand humanity's image of God as human beings in whatever they relate to in this earthly world (Miller 1977:145). Here, Human life in its wholeness expresses itself in three basic complementary identities: male-female, the individual-society or human life-ecological context. The Reformed tradition and churches, therefore, affirm the equal dignity and interdependence of man and woman. Neither man nor woman is more in the image of God than the other is. From the beginning, God puts both man and woman at the pinnacle of creation so that neither sex is exalted nor is it depreciated. In so doing, the Reformed tradition and churches affirm the equal validity and interdependence of personal rights (freedom and dignity) and social rights (justice and community). Life will only be real and meaningful with individual's support for society, and society's support for an individual, even though every individual has much to live to in oneself. An individual human being should affect others positively, just as seasoning brings out the best flavour in food. Moreover, God declared at creation that it was not good that a man should live alone, but that he needed a woman for a complete and meaningful life in God. There is need for equal dignity, equal worth and equal treatment between individual and society for a proper and just up keeping of every society.

Also, the Reformed tradition and churches affirm the equal dignity and interdependence of the present generation and future generations in the stewardship of creation. Whatever the present generation is all about now, it does affect future generations greatly. For example, if the present generation was to cut down all trees in the forests today, without replacing them with new ones, this would lead to deforestation – and hence, future generations will not have the chance to own forests that will give beauty to creation besides providing them with timber and firewood.

Again, the Reformed tradition and churches affirm humanity's creation in the image of God, which makes humanity to stand in covenant relationship with God – and hence, carries with it covenant responsibilities in human stewardship of creation (Miller 1977:145; The Reformed Ecumenical Synod 1983:44). This is the basis of the right of human beings to rule over the earth and their right to community with non-human creation. God chose man and woman to be God's stewards to nourish and till the natural world and not to destroy or plunder it. Therefore, man and woman should continuously be responsible to God for the maintenance and up keep of the natural world for their survival and well-being.

As such, the Reformed tradition and churches do understand and affirm in general that it is God's right – that is, his claim on human beings – which prompted him go through the process of atonement, which is the very source of the right and dignity of being human. In the atonement all humans need to live in a way that sees the present time as the time at which God calls them to live responsibly toward him and toward one another.

In the Reformed tradition, the call on the churches to give first priority in their study to the theological basis of human rights should not be treated as exceptional or as the first of its kind in the time of the Reformation. John Calvin included a theology of revolution in his theology, and sought to reform the theology, church and society of his time, and therefore, he took his point of departure in theological presuppositions (Miller 1977:8; *The Ecumenical Review* 1999). In Calvin we find the most important approach to social-ethical questions during his time of the Reformation. Karl Barth, too, has written on ethics of reconciliation with the heading, *"fiat iustitia"* (Barth 1981: 198; Webster 1995: 13)

Some take Calvin's attention to the law – particularly as seen in his exposition of the Ten Commandments as the moral law – as the best framework for understanding his own ethics. Still, others see his depiction of the Christian life as dying of oneself and rising from the dead with Christ, of discipleship and sanctification, as the best statement of his own ethics (Smit 2009: 75). Overall, Calvin's point of departure affirmed the Holy Scriptures as the ultimate norm also with regard to the formation of human life in community and society.

On God's law, Calvin conceives of it as far-reaching and going beyond the Ten Commandments given to God's chosen people, namely to all people – and hence, the natural law (Calvin, *Institutes* 2.7.1). Natural law is a philosophy asserting that certain rights are inherent by virtue of human nature, endowed by nature (https://en.wikipedia.org/wiki/Natural_law). For Calvin the natural law is important for civil justice and public order, but ultimately all human social institutions should also come under the criticism of the Word of God. Calvin created room for an approach to social ethics in which the social aspect is not reduced to the individual and that the existing social, political and public institutions should no longer simply be accepted as given and unchangeable (Smit 2009: 103). The Reformed faith, therefore, should call into question (by way of human rights and the doctrine of atonement) of the accepted value systems and cultural stereotypes, which mirror unjust power relationships. Therefore, human beings should spend their whole life in the legitimate service of God, in the practice of justice, purity and holiness. God's law prescribes the observance of justice and equity towards neighbours as the means by which human beings can affirm their honour and fear of God.

Calvin, therefore, encourages human beings to look for what is actually commanded by God behind what is forbidden by law or behind prohibition and negative; human beings should positively look for the "principle" (Smit 2009: 92). For example, the commandment, "Thou shall not kill," forbids human beings to injure or hurt a brother or sister, but at the same time it demands them to aid their neighbour's life by every means. The commandment, "Thou shall not kill," therefore, requires a sincere desire to preserve the life of brothers and sisters (Calvin, *Institutes* 2.8.39). Human beings are, therefore, called to affirm, protect and serve the life of entire human race, to which we belong (Smit 2009: 92). Human beings ought to hold their neighbour sacred as both the image of God and our own flesh (Calvin, *Institutes* 2.8.40). As their flesh, human beings must cherish their own flesh through refraining from crime of murder. For Calvin, plotting, wishing, designing anything for neighbours' injury is all guilt of murder. Therefore, all human beings have dignity and are sacred because they are the image of God (Smit 2009: 92).

Calvin describes the eighth commandment, "Thou shall not steal," as calling human beings to render every person their due, and forbids human beings to long after other people's goods (Calvin, *Institutes* 2.8.45). For Calvin, taking possession of goods with the semblance of justice and sycophancy or taking goods away under the pretence of donation or by an action at law, are different kinds of theft. Therefore, what human beings obtain, possess and enjoy, perhaps fully legal in terms of human laws, may in fact be the result of social and economic injustice, even theft and oppression in the eyes of God ((Smit 2009: 307). Calvin urges human beings to duly obey the commandment, "Thou shall not steal," to let it be our constant aim to faithfully lend them counsel and aid to all their neighbours, and therefore, assist them in retaining their property (Calvin, *Institutes* 2.8.46). That is, human beings are called to practice social compassion and economic justice, through what we think and through what we do (Smit 2009: 307).

In this direction, Calvin warns human beings not to retain their human proneness to excessive self-love but "in the love of God and neighbour" (Calvin, *Institutes* 2.8.54). That is, the love of a neighbour should never be subordinate to self-love. The parable of the Good Samaritan, in Luke 10:36, warns against limiting the precept of love to own connections (Calvin, *Institutes* 2.8.55). The entire human race, without exception, must embrace one feeling of charity and love. Therefore, human beings' love for a neighbour should not be restricted to those whom human beings prefer to love, and their respect for other human beings and dignity should not depend on their actions or their being acceptable according to a set criteria of evaluation and judgment (Smit 2007: 307). Moreover, God loves every person, in spite of who a person is. Here, Calvin stresses that human beings are bound to love their enemies just as their friends (Calvin, *Institutes* 2.8.57). As Christians, human beings are under the law of grace, and therefore, engrafted into Jesus Christ by whose grace he frees human beings from the curse of the law, despite their unworthiness and sinfulness, and by whose Spirit human beings have the law written in their hearts.

On our obedience to parents, rulers, masters and superiors of every description, Calvin urges us to respect and honour them, as long as they do not instigate us to transgress the law of God. The law of God is a call to justice, and therefore, triumps all human authority and power (Smit 2007: 307). That is, when custom, tradition or culture wishes to restrict this piety of worship and justice, we should be willing to resist these voices of authority, for Jesus is the only Lord.

Therefore, Calvin conceives of the Christian life as resting on the knowledge of God the Creator and the knowledge of God the Redeemer. That is, God not only created human beings, but he continues to provide them with everything for existence. God does this by his Holy Spirit through whom he invites human beings into the society of Christ and holds them therein (Smit 2007: 313). It is by the work of the Holy Spirit that human beings receive the grace of Christ and its benefits and effects in their lives. Therefore, it all sums up together for human beings to say that they belong to God because he is their Creator and Redeemer.

Since human beings belong to God, they are called to lives of self-denial, searching for justice and righteousness in their relations with others and godliness in their relations with God (Smit 2007: 310). For this fact, human beings are called to take up their cross and follow Jesus Christ. They should accept their sufferings and cross, whilst trusting in the power of God, learning patience and experiencing God's comfort and consolation (Smit 2007: 311). Again, human beings are called to mediate on the future life, not to escape the present, but precisely to come to a right and proper estimation of the present life, and to receive orientation, perspective and proper priorities (Smit 2007: 312). Also, human beings are called to enjoy and appreciate the wonderful gifts of God in this life, so that they can delight, sustain and support themselves, and enable and empower themselves to live their daily lives of service, love and well-doing (Smit 2007: 312).

Karl Barth, in his *"fiat justitia,"* thinks about "the command of God the Reconciler" in a typically Reformed way – the Christian life. He finds the heart of the Christian life in Prayer, Invocation and Calling upon this God, and therefore discusses this life by reflecting on the different petitions of the Lord's Prayer. Unfortunately, he only finds time to deal with the first petition, hallowed be thy name, under the heading "Zeal for the honour of God" (Barth

1981: 153-167) and the second petition, "thy kingdom come," under the heading "The struggle for human righteousness" (Barth 1981: 233-259). He paraphrases the thrust of what is to follow in his opening sentence in his usual way.

> "Christians pray to God that he will cause his righteousness to appear and dwell on a new earth under a new heaven. Meanwhile they act in accordance with their prayer as people who are responsible for the rule of human righteousness, that is, for the preservation and renewal, the deepening and extending, of the divinely ordained safeguards of human rights, human freedom, and human peace on earth" (Barth 1981:205).

Here, Barth develops four paragraphs.

Under the first paragraph, "revolt against disorder," he argues that the genuineness of human zeal for God and accordingly of the passion with which human beings pray the first petition has to be tested (Barth 1981: 205-212). This testing brings human beings within the sphere of ethical discussion, in particular within the ethical struggle for human righteousness. According to Barth, zeal for God's honour can be good, obedient, and full of promise only when it is directly accompanied by the struggle for righteousness (Barth 1981:206). The struggle, which is about revolt, conflict and warfare, however, is not against people, but against dangerous situation. Hence, Barth distinguishes struggle for righteousness from all kinds of other struggles because it is not directed toward the wicked on account of their wickedness and oppression or on account of what Christians have to suffer at their hands in coarser and more refined forms. Instead, the Christians' struggle is for the betterment of all people (Barth 1981:210-211). Ultimately, all people together are suffering from a common plight – which is a real enemy – a disorder, which controls and penetrates and poisons, inwardly and outwardly, and disrupts all human relations and interconnections (Barth 1981:211). Thus, Christians call and cry "thy kingdom come," as a revolt demanded from them against this disorder and human plight.

In the second paragraph Barth has the petition, "thy kingdom come." Here, Barth discusses "the lordless powers" that he calls "ethical implications of this petition." He discusses closely the enemy, the great disorder, the plight, the forms of human unrighteousness that contradicts and opposes God's law. For him, the enemy comprises human rebellion against God, and the many rebellions unleashed by the rebellion against God (Barth 1981:215). Among these enemies are the demonism of politics, the very mobile demon called Mammon, the intellectual constructs called ideologies and –isms, and from what he calls "chronic" forces, from the physical spheres of the created cosmos, including technology, fashion, sport, pleasure, and transport. These, John Calvin says, disrupt life and rob people of freedom. These do oppress people by afflicting and harassing them, and hence, under their lordship, people become "people of disorder," estranged from God, from themselves and from others. But Karl Barth says that these tear apart the individual, as much as they tear society also apart.

In the third paragraph Barth has "thy kingdom come." Here, Barth discusses the kingdom of the divine order. According to the New Testament, "this coming kingdom" has already taken place in the person of Jesus Christ, because in him human beings have received knowledge of this kingdom (Barth 1981:247). Therefore, the coming of the kingdom is manifested in the story about Jesus, his words, deeds, suffering, death, resurrection and the gift of the Holy Spirit, as narrated in the New Testament (Barth 1981:248).

In the fourth paragraph Barth has the following Latin legal phrase: *"fiat iustitia ruat cælum,"* meaning "Let justice be done though the heavens fall" (https://en.wikipedia.org/wiki/Fiat_justitia_ruat_caelum) The maxim signifies the belief that justice must be realized regardless of consequences. Here, Barth discusses about people that are professing about God's kingdom to come that they are capable of hearing the command to lift up their heads and call upon God to come. Indeed, their humble but rigorous use of the freedom to call upon God in this way is their true and essential revolt against the unrighteousness and disorder (Barth 1981:260-261). Therefore, the heart of the Christian ethos is that people obediently use their freedom to live with a view to the coming kingdom (Smit 2007: 313). Christians are called to witness what God is and does for human beings – they may and can and should reflect and practice God's being and acting for humanity (Smit 2007: 314); Christians' total definitive decision is always for human beings, and hence, will never let themselves be addressed as prisoners of their own decisions (Smit 2007: 315); and Christians should see people as human beings, as objects of the eternal covenantal love of the Triune God, and therefore, God calls Christians to see other human beings in their suffering and need hope (Smit 2007: 315).

THE RESEARCH PROBLEM

Against the background above, and given the brief overview of recent documents and studies from a Reformed perspective on human rights, the specific research problem of the present project can be described in more detail.

The right to being human or the dignity of being human indeed justifies and supports a general picture of human dignity in a very broad way. The problem arises from the popular uses of the major aspects of the classic Reformed view of the atonement. The following are the major aspects of the classic Reformed view of the atonement: Centred on God's glory alone, Based on God's Word alone, and Justification by Faith Alone, Saved by Jesus Christ Alone and Structured by the Covenant. These major aspects of the classic Reformed view of the atonement tend to create misunderstandings, and therefore, make the task to develop a human rights language and culture in Malawi more difficult. Faith Alone, Saved by Jesus Christ Alone and Structured by the Covenant. These major aspects of the classic Reformed view of the atonement seem to contradict the very idea of human rights. Although they may therefore affirm the broad idea of human dignity, but at the same time they may seem to contradict the very idea of human "rights," as if sinful human beings can claim rights before the face of the sovereign God or over against their fellow human beings. The Reformed faith, one could claim, indeed supports and justifies a view of human beings which affirms everyone's dignity and importance and which therefore claims respect and love for others. But does this affirmation also specifically support and justify the practice of human rights, in the modern sense of human rights?

How should these tensions be understood and dealt with? Are these suspicions, amongst Reformed believers in Malawi, that the atonement contradicts and even resists a commitment to human rights in the modern sense of the word, justified, or ill-founded in the Reformed faith itself? The following are Reformed theology's natures of major aspects of the classic Reformed view of the atonement.

Reformed theology is centred on God and affirms the glorification of God by humanity. Glorifying God or seeking the glory of God is indeed a very central concept in the Christian faith (The Westminster Shorter Catechism affirms, Question 1; 1 Corinthians 10:31; Psalm 73:25), and hence, Reformed theology affirms the sovereignty of God over every aspect of the believer's life. All of life is to be lived to the glory of God. Therefore, human beings should allow God to sanctify all of their activities unto his glory, and hence, they should refrain from sanctifying their own works into their own glory. Here, human good works are not for human glory, but good works must be targeted toward God's glory.

Also, Reformed theology teaches that to God alone is glory (*Soli Deo Gloria*) because 'He chose us' rather than 'we chose God'. That is why, when human beings sinned, God chose to save them graciously through his Son Jesus, sinful as they are. Here, human beings are without deservedness but glory and praise goes to God. God saved human beings in order that he puts his supreme greatness on display and vividly. Certainly, God pardons sinners in Jesus Christ so that human beings may praise him.

Furthermore, Reformed theology is based on God's Word alone (Bible-based) and stresses the Bible's inspiration, authority and sufficiency. It understands the sufficiency of Scripture to mean that human beings need not supplement the Bible by new or ongoing special revelation. The Bible is seen as an entirely sufficient guide for what human beings ought to believe unto salvation and how human beings are to live as Christians [*The Westminster Confession of Faith* 1 (vi); *The Belgic Confession of Faith V*]. Therefore, Reformed theology affirms that the Bible is sufficient in all matters of faith and practice. Any writings of people, however holy these people may have been cannot be of equal value with those of divine Scriptures (*The Belgic Confession of Faith VII*). The Bible is the only infallible rule of what human beings are to believe and how human beings are to live. The Word of God in the Bible is most necessary because through it alone comes the knowledge of God and his will, which are necessary unto salvation [*The Westminster Confession of Faith* 1 (i)], and not necessarily human good works. Apart from God's saving activity, as revealed in the Bible, each human being would want to do it their own way, rather than God's way. But in his Word, God has his regenerating work that makes human beings capable of loving his holy law and doing good works.

As such, according to many, the Reformed view of the atonement seems to imply that the life of Jesus Christ and his everyday discipleship as narrated in the Gospels do not necessarily play a meaningful role in human beings' lives. And therefore, the Gospels in particular do not provide any base for grounding human rights in the light of the classic Reformed view of the atonement. In fact, the Reformed tradition and churches do understand the doctrine of atonement primarily in the context of Christ's death and resurrection (The Reformed Ecumenical Synod 1983:44). Such is characteristic of the New Testament images of the death and resurrection of Jesus Christ.

In the New Testament, atonement meant Jesus' death on the cross and his resurrection from the dead on the third day of his burial. The New Testament distinguishes four main images of the atonement by Jesus' first followers, which often overlap with each other (Guthrie 1994:252). There is the Financial Imagery that describes Jesus as paying the price for our redemption. The New Testament has several texts that support this imagery, like Jesus giving ransom for many (Mark 10:45), being bought at a price (1 Corinthians 6:20; 7:23), being redeemed from sinfulness (1 Peter 1:18; Titus 2:14; Romans 3:24) and redeemed from the curse of the Law (Galatians 3:13). There is the Military Imagery that describes God and the devil as being at war. To the triumph of God against the devil, Jesus rises up from the dead on Easter morning. In the New Testament this triumph by God is described as God rescuing us from the dominion of darkness and bringing us into the kingdom of his Son Jesus (Colossians 1:13), disarming the powers and authorities and triumphing over them by the cross of Jesus (Colossians 2:15), and Christ putting all his enemies under his feet (1 Corinthians 15:24-28). There is the Sacrificial Imagery that describes Jesus Christ as our High Priest who offers himself by death as atoning shedding of blood. Hence, in the Last Supper with his disciples, Jesus talks about his blood of the covenant which is poured out for many (Mark 14:22-24), whilst Paul mentions God who presents his Son Jesus as a sacrifice of atonement (Romans 3:25), John the Baptist points at Jesus as the sacrificial Lamb of God who takes away the sin of the world (John 1:29), and the Apostle Paul refers to Jesus as Passover lamb that has been sacrificed (1 Corinthians 5:7). There is the Legal Imagery that describes humankind as being found guilty in a court of law. Jesus Christ, a righteous man who has obeyed the law perfectly takes the sentence, declared on humankind, upon himself – and hence, sets free the accused humankind. In this direction, the Apostle Paul in Romans 5:6-11 refers to Jesus as a righteous man who took up our sentence for our sinfulness and died in our place. In 2 Corinthians 5:16-21 Paul speaks of God who made Jesus carry human sinfulness, though himself righteous so that human beings, through faith, might take the righteousness of Jesus on to themselves.

For Reformed faith, faith alone in Jesus Christ is the substance or matter, of what sinful human beings must do in order to be saved. Here, faith is the receiving of and resting on Jesus and his righteousness [*The Westminster Confession of Faith* 8 (viii)]. It is the only instrument of human justification, and not human good works. However, all other saving graces ever accompany true faith. That is why Reformed faith has it that human beings are saved and made righteous before God through faith in Jesus alone. Reformed faith affirms salvation by Jesus Christ alone; it affirms Jesus as the sole Mediator between God and humanity.

As human beings' Mediator, Jesus died on the cross, and took the punishment for their sin upon him and bore the judgment due to them as sinners. With his blood that he shed on the cross, Jesus expiated the sins that made human beings enemies of God and thereby satisfied God's justice. Hence, believers are delivered from the penalty and power of their sin. This deliverance was accomplished by the sin bearing of Jesus Christ, and not necessarily by human beings' good works. Therefore, human beings look to Jesus alone for divine favour and fatherly love. Reformed theology affirms that salvation is found exclusively in Jesus Christ of the Gospel, most especially, through his death on the cross, and his resurrection from the dead. It is through Jesus' death on the cross, and his resurrection from the dead that human beings experience God's covenantal faithfulness to his people.

Reformed theology certainly affirms God's covenantal faithfulness to his people through the covenant of works and the covenant of grace. In the covenant of works, God promised life to Adam and Eve, and in them to all of their descendants, upon the condition of perfect and personal obedience. Unfortunately, Adam, Eve, and all their descendants sinned and fell by breaking God's command – the moral law. According to John Calvin, the moral law required that Adam and Eve be dependent upon the will of God and stand firm in that alone which is pleasing to him (Calvin, *Institutes* 2.8.2). God by his right as the Father and Lord of human beings, wants them to be and remain righteous and upright in what they are and in whatever they do as his people. Until God intervened through the death and resurrection of Jesus, every human being was dead in sin after Adam and Eve's sin. Everyone was condemned and destined for everlasting punishment. However, in the covenant of grace God intervened.

Corrupt and imperfect as human beings are, they are never able to fulfil the works of the law. Jesus Christ accomplishes the law for human beings by way of his justice and satisfaction [*The Westminster Confession of Faith* 15 (i), (ii)]. Since real love is costly, God in Jesus genuinely sympathises with the guilty party (human beings), as, himself, the injured party, and sets a plan to share the pain (Guthrie 1994:260) – and hence, the atonement took place. That is, God saved human beings in Jesus Christ, out of his grace (his free will and love), when they were still sinners. The Reformed tradition and churches emphasize that it is the grace of God, through Jesus, that saved sinful human beings from their sin. Hence the Reformed faith argues that an emphasis on merit and good works would undermine human beings' salvation through Jesus Christ by the grace of God.

Indeed, the study recognizes that the Reformed tradition is only interested in what God does. The argument, however, is that it has never been the intention of this tradition to emphasize God's work at the expense of human participation and works. A case is made that the Reformed tradition in fact includes the human response to participate in God's work. In practice, however, the widespread understanding and the popular spirituality in Reformed circles often ignored this emphasis on human response and participation. This is also true in Malawi. Reformed teaching, as reflected in the works of Calvin and Barth and also the Westminster Confession, seems to view human action and good works as essential parts of God's work of justification. However, in reality, many Reformed churches tend to emphasize the grace of God to such an extent that they do not give adequate attention to the ethical implications of the life of Jesus. The result is that many Reformed churches and believers seem to doubt whether their own tradition and faith really support a human rights culture. The thesis investigates the question of whether this doubt – also present in church circles in Malawi – is truly justified, or perhaps it is a misunderstanding of the very heart of the Reformed faith.

HYPOTHESIS

It may therefore be concluded, in a first and provisional conclusion, that although the classic Reformed view of atonement and a broad notion of human dignity may be related, the very classic doctrine view of atonement itself poses as hindrance to the building of a human rights culture in contemporary Malawi. The very identity of the Reformed tradition, as expressed in several fundamental convictions, tends to be problematic to the building of a human rights culture in contemporary Malawi.

The Reformed tradition's very identity seems to pose a hindrance when it restricts itself to the New Testament images on atonement, which the first followers of Jesus Christ used to interpret the meaning of Jesus' death and resurrection. For the first followers of Jesus, the meaning of Jesus' death was their atonement from which they drew four main images in relation to God. It is around those four main images that the Reformed theology, being Bible-based, understands and develops its meaning of the atonement.

Unfortunately, the atonement images by Jesus' first followers, and therefore according to many Reformed believers and even preachers, do not give adequate attention to the life of Jesus, especially the everyday life of Jesus that greatly transformed the society around Jesus. For many Reformed Christian theologians, atonement is something that includes less than can be appreciated of the life of Jesus. In fact, these Reformed Christian scholars show in their views of the atonement inadequate understanding of the ministry, words and deeds of Jesus, depicted in the Gospel narratives.

It should be understood that the earliest Christians viewed the atonement story in a background and context of their time, which is very different from our world today. In his *A Handbook of Theological Terms*, Van A. Harvey describes the symbols used in the images by these earliest Christians as having been naturally rooted in Hebraic religious practice of those old days, especially sacrifice – and hence, strange to our world today (Harvey 1964:33-34). The earliest Christians believed that God ordained the sacrificial ritual so that the believers might participate in and realize the forgiveness of Yahweh. According to their religious and cultic roots, sinners seeking reconciliation laid a hand upon the head of the sacrificial animal, signifying their own identification with it. In the shedding of the blood, the sinners symbolized the giving up of their own life. The blood was taken into the Holy of Holies, the offering burned and the meat eaten, once again signifying identification with the sacrificial victim.

However, sacrificial imageries about Jesus no longer convey the same strong and meaningful message to the contemporary church as they did in the biblical times. Therefore, whilst remaining faithful to the lordship of Jesus Christ and the church's historical tradition, the church needs to move forward into the contemporary world and imagery in order to meet the needs of its members today. It must be able to explain the Bible in pictures that are relevant to and understood by people in this world. The Reformed church today should not undermine its sense of being Reformed. The church reformed is always reforming[6] – *Ecclesia Reformata Semper Reformanda* (CCAP. Constitution 2002:12). We, as disciples of Jesus today, need to have our own background and context through which we may be able to understand Jesus Christ and his salvation work for us.

---

[6] The Church of Central Africa Presbyterian in Malawi understands reforming as a means of faithfulness as God breaks forth yet more light from his Word. This is of course also the understanding of confessional documents that was characteristic of the Reformed churches from the very beginning, in distinction from other views regarding confessions and their authority, in Protestantism.

The four main imageries of the atonement, even though they are "objective," biblically right and suited to the identity of our Reformed heritage, do easily and often contribute towards a misunderstanding of the deepest intention of the new life in Jesus Christ for believers. Here, the "objective view of the atonement" insists that God himself is the chief actor in the drama, and that the reconciliation does not take place from the human side. The objective view lies in the fact that it represents the work of atonement as from first to last the continuous work of God himself (Aulen 1970:5). Here, over-objectivity about the atonement may easily develop into a hindrance that may result into inadequate treatment of the everyday works Christ did as a human being, and hence, regard them as of minor importance. Moreover, the Gospels make it clear from the beginning to the end that Jesus was one of us, who identified with us, and took part in our life as a human being (Schmiechen 2005: 348). Here, it was God himself actually participating in the joy and goodness of human life. John H. Leith affirms that believers can understand and explain well what Jesus does for them only from the picture of who Jesus really is in his life as human being, besides his life as divine (Leith 1993: 151-154). Also, human beings should avoid the temptation to limit Jesus Christ to being more human, and deny his deity, or pushing him further away from humanity towards divinity. Doing that would result into overlooking much of his human good works that caused tremendous transformation of the society he lived in.

    The hypothesis of this study is therefore that a broader and more faithful understanding of the atonement amongst Reformed churches and believers could help these churches and believers to see clearly the importance of a culture of human rights for the faithful practice of their own Reformed faith and piety. The hypothesis involves the relevance of the life and ministry of Jesus Christ towards a more positive view of human rights. Such relevance of the life and ministry of Jesus Christ towards a more positive view of human rights may help to correct many of the misunderstandings created so often and easily in the light of

Reformed convictions. What then is a fuller and more faithful understanding of the atonement? Here, a fuller and more faithful understanding of the atonement that concerns the restoration of the broken relationship between God and human beings, must comprise of everything about believers' justification and their connectedness with society.

The restoration of the broken relationship between God and human beings is made possible through Jesus Christ, immediately human beings become justified in God's sight (Bizer 1978: 543-544). Justification is a forensic act of God in which he, as the supreme magistrate, shows grace to the guilty and relaxes the vigour of the Law. Therefore, in justification God implants sinful human beings in Jesus Christ and regards them as owning all that Christ has done and has suffered for them.

Human beings, here, are convicted of sin and liable to eternal death. But yet they are elect from eternity and called in time on account of the pledge of "Christ's death on the cross" and of Christ's obedience in suffering and righteousness. Christ's obedience in suffering and righteousness is given freely and imputed to sinful human beings and apprehended and applied solely by human beings "faith" in Jesus. Those who are called, drawn and led to Jesus are thus joined and "united" to him in order that they have communion with him (1 Corinthians 1:19). God thus commended his own love toward us, in that while we were yet sinners, Christ died for us (Romans 5:8-9).

In justification also, God enters into the relationship of God the Father with the sinner, and hence, the sinner is assured of eternal life as "an adopted son or daughter" (Bizer 1978: 552). Thus, those justified by faith and reconciled to God through and on account of Christ are also assumed as sons and heirs, and co-heirs with Jesus Christ. Again, those who are in Christ are said to have been made unto them righteousness and sanctification (1 Corinthians 1:30; Bizer 1978: 543).

Sanctification is the gratuitous act of God by which he renews believers after his own image in order that they may be rendered fit to glorify him by good works (Bizer 1978: 565). Subjectively considered and as gratuitous act of God towards believers, sanctification is about believers being guided by the Holy Spirit of God dwelling in them to live their daily life with good works. This is called the Christian life and new life of participation with Christ, who himself lived a life of good works and never sinned the whole of his life.

As evident above, God sought in Jesus Christ to save and justify people who live in a society of self-respect or self-praise, and hence, we must not lose the connection between theology and the principles of human society (Kang 2006: 279). Otherwise, we will lose the ground needed for believers' participation in Jesus' practical life on earth (Paas 2004: 137-138). Indeed, a fuller and more faithful understanding of the classic doctrine of atonement one hand includes God's covenantal faithfulness to his people, God's incarnation in Jesus his Son; death of the Son of God Jesus. On the other hand, the classic doctrine of atonement includes the resurrection of Jesus from the dead, human beings' union with Jesus, election of human beings by God in Jesus his Son, repentance by human beings, the calling of human beings by God in Jesus, faith in human beings, human justification by God, adoption of human beings in Jesus as God's children, sanctified human life in community, human beings created in the image of God and the gathering of human beings by the Holy Spirit in the Church.

The hypothesis states that a fuller appreciation of the life and ministry of Jesus as integral to his work of atonement could contribute to a positive view of human rights. The fuller appreciation of the life and ministry of Jesus would help to correct many of the misunderstandings created so often and easily on Reformed soil and in light of Reformed convictions.

The good works by Jesus Christ during his earthly ministry play a meaningful role in believers' lives for their participation in their renewed life, and this fact has its basis in the New Testament teaching (Leith 1993:152, 154). Jesus' admirable life as seen in the parables gives believers an insight, and illumination that enables them to know their own lives and the meaning of the world in which they live. Also, Jesus' admirable life as seen in the parables, gives believers a transformative power which evokes their participation with Jesus. In this direction, Paul ChulHong Kang – in his doctoral work dealing with the imputation of Christ's righteousness - speaks about the brutal Japanese Imperialism and the Korean War in the twentieth century that gave Koreans a desperate desire to restore their safe world. He affirms that it was the Gospel of our Lord Jesus that gave these Koreans hope in their hopeless world (Kang 2006: 278). For many believing Koreans, it was the transformative power of the Gospel that moved them and liberated them from a hopeless world and restored hope in them. Certainly, God through Jesus Christ means to encourage believers that their daily works (good works) are of the ways in which they live as Christians out of their Christian faith, and are not something done in addition to being Christians or in spite of their being Christians. The idea that the transformative power of Jesus in the Gospels enables believers to move from a hopeless world and restored hope will indeed contribute to a culture of human rights.

However, despite human beings' good works as believing Christians, all glory must go to God because the cause of their good works is not from their own free will. In the same way, a life of practising human rights should be seen by Reformed churches and believers as an integral part of giving the glory to God.

The claim of the analysis of the Reformed doctrine of atonement, by the study, accordingly demonstrates that human rights do not stand in tension with the classic Reformed doctrine of atonement. Instead, it plays a central role at the very heart of the doctrine, as understood by authoritative and representative voices from the Reformed tradition at work in Malawi today.

STRUCTURE OF THE ARGUMENT

Chapter 1 has introduced the problem by showing how the Reformed faith supports a strong respect for human dignity. The chapter has also shown how, at the same time, central convictions of the Reformed faith are often and easily seen by Reformed churches and believers as contradicting the actual practice of human rights. The chapter therefore explains why the grounding of human rights in the Reformed view of the atonement tends to meet differing Christian responses within the Reformed tradition and churches. The chapter also explains why it is important for the research to limit itself to the atonement views by Anselm, John Calvin, Karl Barth and the Westminster Confession of Faith, in affirming the classic Reformed view of the atonement. Again, Chapter 1 discusses why throughout history there has not been a single authoritative theological position regarding the theories and practices of social, economic and legal justice; it highlights the limitation that major aspects of the classical Reformed view of the atonement cause to the research, and the questions that the study is addressing. Chapter 1 also reviews recent works relating to the classic Reformed view of the atonement and human dignity, and suggest that these recent works fall short of grounding human rights in the classic Reformed view of the atonement. Hence, it briefly shows how the recent works fall short of grounding the human rights in light of the classic view of the atonement. It thus points out some of the serious implications of the major aspects of the Reformed view of the atonement for the grounding of human rights in light of the classic Reformed view of the atonement, particularly in the life of Jesus and discipleship. A hypothesis to guide the research is formulated at the end of the chapter, arguing provisionally that a more comprehensive understanding of the atonement could help to overcome these difficulties and challenges.

Chapter 2 is the longest of all the chapters because it is a key to an understanding of the classic Reformed doctrine of atonement, which had to be dealt with comprehensively. Also, this chapter does not say anything about human rights because it is solely meant to explain the classic Reformed doctrine of atonement, and not intended to investigate about human rights. The notion of human rights is a modern development; therefore, Anselm, John Calvin or the Westminster Confession of Faith cited in the chapter could not have commented anything on it in their times. Chapter 2, therefore, argues for a more faithful understanding of the Reformed view of the atonement, particularly in the central and innovative notion of Jesus Christ's active obedience in this tradition. The more faithful understanding of the Reformed view of the atonement will always lead to consideration about the relevance of Jesus' ethical examples and their transformative effect for believers' renewed life. Anselm of Canterbury, John Calvin, the Westminster Confession of Faith, and Karl Barth have been used to seek and explain such an understanding of the Reformed doctrine of atonement. Therefore, in the section preceding the conclusion, Chapter 2 lays down some concluding affirmations on Jesus' active obedience to God and his ethical examples, and describes their transformative effect for believers' renewed life, in the light of an understanding of the Reformed view of the atonement.

Chapter 3 provides the necessary background against which to see the history of the Church of Central Africa Presbyterian in Malawi and its involvement in political change as well as its response to the introduction of human rights and freedom in Malawi. In addition, using the affirmation of the classic Reformed view of the atonement in Chapter 2 as a measurement, Chapter 3 investigates whether and how the Church of Central Africa Presbyterian in Malawi received or did not receive the Reformed view of the atonement. It also examines whether or not The CCAP received or did not receive the broader view of the atonement. Particular interest is in the Reformed understanding of Jesus' active obedience and Jesus' transformative power for believers' renewed life as an integral part of this Reformed account of the atonement. Furthermore, Chapter 3 discusses how the Reformed Christians in Malawi seem to or not seem to affirm Jesus' ethical examples. These are ethical examples from Jesus' life, sayings, and parables.

Chapter 4 then discusses human rights in Malawi, and assesses the potential implications of Jesus' transformative power, in the Gospels, for believers' renewed life. This chapter therefore discusses human rights in Malawi, in light of the broader view of the Reformed view of the atonement.

The last chapter will, first, give the introductions, and then draw some implications and points toward possible additional research. This will be followed by a summary and conclusions with regard to the process of ascertaining the classic Reformed view about Jesus' active obedience. Jesus' active obedience constitutes his transformative power toward believers' renewed life in him. The conclusions of the chapter will discuss the reception of this Reformed view by the Church of Central Africa Presbyterian in Malawi – leading to the effect of Jesus' transformative power, in the Gospels, onto the Reformed Christians in Malawi. Then there will be made a summary about the application of the findings in Chapter 2 and Chapter 3 onto Chapter 4, which is meant to show the impact and difference the Reformed view of the atonement and Jesus' transformative power in the Gospels for the renewed life can make in the lives of the Reformed Christians in Malawi – in their reception of human dignity and human rights. Finally, the chapter will give a summary of new contributions made by the study.

CHAPTER 2

THE CLASSIC REFORMED VIEW OF THE ATONEMENT

INTRODUCTION

This chapter discusses the classic Reformed view of the doctrine of atonement. In the course of the discussion, the chapter gives special attention to the Reformed tradition's view about Jesus Christ's active obedience to God his Father. In addition, the chapter discusses the impression that Jesus' ethical example impresses on the Christian believers in their renewed life. Also, the chapter explains the Reformed view of the atonement with reference to the views of Anselm of Canterbury, John Calvin, the Westminster Confession of Faith and Karl Barth.

Even though Anselm lived some centuries before the Reformation took place, his theology has been and is still very influential in the Reformed tradition. As for Calvin and Barth, they are both very prominent persons in the Reformed tradition and theology. The Westminster Confession of Faith is a confession of the Church of Central Africa Presbyterian in Malawi, the focus of this research.

For John Calvin's view of the atonement, the research primarily uses Calvin's *Institutes of the Christian Religion* Book 3, and authoritative secondary interpretations, such as *Basic Christian Doctrine* by John Leith, *The Cambridge Companion to John Calvin*, edited by Donald K. McKim, and *Grace and Gratitude* by B.A. Gerrish. For Karl Barth's view of the atonement the primary source is his *Church Dogmatics* Volume IV/1 and IV/2, with additional studies such as *The Cambridge Companion to Karl Barth* edited by John Webster, and *Basic Christian Doctrine* by John Leith. For the Westminster Confession of Faith's view of the atonement, the study uses the *Westminster Confession of Faith*, the *Westminster Larger Catechism*, and the *Westminster Shorter Catechism*, and *Reformed Confessions* by Jan Rohls.

This chapter is organized according to the following sections. The first section explains the basic meaning of the doctrine of atonement and its components. The second, third, fourth, and fifth sections discuss respectively Anselm's view of the doctrine of atonement, John Calvin's view of the atonement, the Westminster Confession of Faith's view of atonement, and Karl Barth's view of the atonement. The sixth section summarises the fundamental affirmations on the Reformed view of the atonement. The seventh section then focuses specifically on the Reformed tradition's view about Jesus' active and passive obedience. Jesus' active and passive obedience are very important notions in this tradition for understanding the atonement, which play a central role in the argument of this thesis. The eighth section lays down Jesus' ethical examples for human beings' renewed life, in light of the classic Reformed view of the atonement, and specifically in the light of the crucial role of Jesus' obedience. The ninth section is the summary and evaluation of the classic Reformed view of the doctrine of atonement.

ATONEMENT

The concept of atonement, in Christian theology, belongs to soteriology. As Soteriology, the doctrine of atonement is concerned with God's salvation of human beings from sin. It is about the restoration of the broken relationship between God and human beings that was accomplished in the life, death and resurrection of Jesus Christ, the Son of God. The relation between God and human beings had been broken by sin on the human side. The doctrine of the atonement covers a whole range of soteriological themes such as covenant, incarnation, death of Jesus, resurrection of Jesus, union with Jesus, election, repentance, calling, faith, justification, adoption, sanctification, human community, regeneration, created in the image of God and the gathering of human beings by the Holy Spirit (in Church). Here, human response of faith, gratitude and renewal will, in this study, prove of crucial importance for a proper understanding of the Reformed church's views regarding a human rights culture.

In the Reformed tradition, "covenant" is a key biblical notion around which much of the Bible's teaching on God's love for his creation is gathered. Here, God is the one who covenants. Covenant means God's up-keeping work in the world and in human history, despite human sinfulness. In the covenantal faithfulness of God to his creation, we see God's justice, love and mercy for his people, vowing to care for them, in spite of who they are in their sinfulness. In turn, God's care to his creation constitutes a basis for Christian love, mercy and care for others in society, in spite of who they are. Certainly, the covenantal faithfulness of God is evident in human salvation, particularly in his Son Jesus Christ. Equally important, human history, here, is marked by certain (or ultimate) goals. That is, God is somewhere in the historical context, pushing the world he created towards redemption, towards where human beings ought to be. Jeremiah 7:23; 11:4; 31:33 are some of the many parts of scripture where this notion of "covenant" is found: *"I will be your God, and you will be my people"*. Jeremiah 7:23 says, "...but I gave them this command: Obey me, and I will be your God and you will be my people. Walk in the ways I command you, that it may go well with you." Jeremiah 11:4 says, "..the terms I commanded your forefathers when I brought them out of Egypt, out of the iron-smelting furnace, 'I said, 'Obey me and do everything I command you, and you will be my people, and I will be your God." And Jeremiah 31;33 says, "This is the command I will make with the house of Israel after that time," declares the Lord. "I will put my law in their minds and write it on their hearts. I will be their God, and they will be my people."

Here, *"I will be your God"* precisely means *"God is the Creator"*. And, *"You will be my people"* precisely means *"God is the Redeemer"*. The really critical point in the Christian doctrine of creation is the character of the creator, not merely that the world is created (Leith 1993: 70). *"God Creator"* and *God Redeemer"* are not just names for God, but are a dynamic way of speaking about the act of God as Creator and the act of God as Redeemer. The action of God is the act of Creator who is moving towards redemption – a process that goes through reconciliation because of human beings' sin. Hence, the act of creation and the act of reconciliation are both acts of the covenant. God is really the same God right from creation, and throughout to redemption. We might as well say, God is at stake in the realm, and he takes certain risks in creating, and reconciling. It is reconciliation that prompted the incarnation in God.

The "incarnation" is the "becoming flesh" of the divine *Logos* in Jesus Christ. It is also the story of the taking on of human nature by the divine *Logos*. Jesus Christ was fully divine and fully human. How these two realities combine in the one authentic person, Jesus Christ, is a mystery. Also, with reference to *"extra-calvinisticum"* (the controversy between the Reformed Calvinists and the Lutherans), it is argued and discussed whether the *Logos* in Jesus Christ was completely consumed in the human. Hence, the question, "What happened to the divine *Logos* when Jesus died on the cross?" However, Jesus was born human in the incarnation just like human beings, and stands in solidarity with human beings before God the Father. Here, the Father looks through Jesus and sees human beings as if they are as perfect as Jesus. In turn, human beings in Jesus must see other human beings as perfect through being in solidarity with the vulnerable, the poor and suffering in our world.

Jesus died on the cross for human salvation. "Death on the cross" (crucifixion) was the form of capital punishment that Romans in Jesus' time used for notorious criminals. In the Old Testament, too, there is declaration for capital punishment for those guilty for sin (Deuteronomy 21:23). Jesus was no ordinary human being, and hence, his death on the cross was unique. It was unique in the sense that Jesus is God, who, in his justice, mercy and love for human beings, became human himself in order that he satisfies the demands of his own justice on behalf of all human beings. Therefore, Jesus' death on the cross demonstrates and affirms the compassion of a merciful and loving God who himself dies and pays the penalty of sin of the whole world. Likewise, Christians ought to suffer and be persecuted for the sake of justice for all in human society.

Jesus' death on the cross would have been meaningless without his resurrection from the dead and hope for those who believe in him. Hence, without Jesus' resurrection from the dead and hope there would be nothing worth believing and trusting in Jesus Christ and God. The resurrection of Jesus Christ is the very heart of Christianity. The resurrection of Jesus from the dead, therefore, constitutes a basis for Christians to be of hope for a better future and a better world. In 1 Corinthians 15 Paul reasoned,

> "If Christ has not been raised, our preaching is useless and so is our faith. "We are then found to be false witnesses about God, for we have testified about God that he raised Christ from the dead."

In that same chapter Paul says,

> "If Christ has not been raised, your faith is futile; you are still in your sins. Then those also who have fallen sleep in Christ are lost. If only for this life we have hope in Christ, we are to be pitied more than all men. "But then Paul triumphantly declares, "But Christ has indeed been raised from the dead, the first fruits of those who have fallen asleep" (1 Corinthians 15:14-20).

To believe in Jesus Christ and his death and resurrection means relating to him and uniting with him to make a bond. It is because of relating to Jesus and uniting with him that the relational bond between Jesus Christ and those who believe in him is called "union with Christ". Here, union with Christ is historical, ethical and personal in the sense that Jesus Christ took on human beings' nature and filled it with his virtue. The taking on of human beings' nature by Jesus and filling, it with his virtue, therefore, constitutes a basis for Christians to be in solidarity with others for social justice in society. Here, the Holy Spirit is the bond by which Jesus Christ effectively unites believers onto himself. The principal elements of human beings' union with Jesus Christ are thus election, calling, regeneration, repentance, faith, justification and adoption.

In election of human beings, God eternally decrees to choose from sinners deserving condemnation those whom he will save, and therefore, provides salvation through his Son Jesus Christ. The presupposition of God's eternal decree of election is that all human beings are fallen, and therefore, election involves God's gracious rescue plan. Here, the source of election is in God alone, and that is why Jesus in John 6:37 explains that only those that his Father gives him he will save. The Apostle Paul also says that God chooses those that he saves in Jesus, even before the foundation of the world, to be holy and blameless in his sight (Ephesians 1:4). The cause of election is God's compassionate mercy and his own glory, and is not based on human works or God's foreknowledge of works (Rom. 9:11). God's compassionate mercy in election, therefore, constitutes a basis for human beings to treat others with dignity without consideration of who they are. Here, the objects of election are individual sinful human beings. God, thus, chooses human beings to be holy and blameless in his sight through Jesus his Son, despite their sinfulness, and hence, human beings are adopted as God's children.

"Calling", as one of the principal elements of human beings' union with Jesus Christ, is that work of God by his Spirit in which, by his grace, he summons men and women to come to him and receive his love and mercy in Jesus Christ (Rohls 1977: 172; Milne 1986: 85). This summoning by God to come to him for love and mercy, therefore, constitutes the basis for Christians to relate favourably to other human beings. This act by God that he summons human beings to come to him for love and mercy mirrors God's eternal being and character. The particularity of effective calling to grace, and thus of salvation, follows from the particularity of election.

"Faith" in Christian theology is the trust involving a Christian's active personal commitment to God in Jesus Christ, and not simply an awareness of God's reality. Equally important, faith is a gift God, by his Spirit, gives his elect because he is saving them. It is God's grace, not their faith, which saves them. In his mercy, God saves his elect, by giving them faith, and hence, justifies them through his Son Jesus Christ.

Daniel Migliore refers to "justification" as God's saving act, when God restores human beings' broken relationship with him by his act of free grace and forgiveness (Migliore 1991:175). Such manifestation of God's act of free grace and forgiveness was accomplished in his Son Jesus Christ. "Justification" is a term from the judicial sphere and means "acquitting" or "making right". Therefore, by way of Jesus Christ's sacrifice on the cross sinners are acquitted of their sin. Sinners no longer have their guilt reckoned against them. And by accepting that pardon by faith, the sinners receive in themselves the imputation of Christ's righteousness. According to David Steinmetz, the now believing sinners can stand confidently before God as children of God, not because they have actually been transformed by grace into real saints, but because they have been reckoned on the grounds of the righteousness of Jesus Christ.[7] Here, God means to adopt human beings as his children in his Son Jesus and his righteousness, in spite of who they are in their sinfulness.

"Adoption" is used in Christian theology to illustrate the believers' new relationship with God. In the Roman law, adopted children were guaranteed all legal rights to their fathers' property, even if they were formerly slaves. They were not second-class sons and daughters, but were equal to all other sons and daughters, biological or adopted, in their fathers' families. The adopted children, hence, lost all rights in their old family and gained all

---

[7] Steinmetz, David C. *The Council Of Trent* in David Bagchi & David C. Steinmetz. Eds. *Cambridge Companion to Reformed Theology*. Cambridge, United Kingdom: Cambridge University Press. 2004.

rights of legitimate children in their new families. Therefore, adopted children had the same rights and privileges as biological children, and became full heirs to their new fathers' estates. Likewise, when human beings become Christians, they gain all the privileges and responsibilities of children in God's family. Adoption, therefore, is that work of God's grace by which he receives sinful human beings as his own children through Christ and in union with him. God adopts sinful human beings as his own children through his beloved Son Jesus Christ, and brings them into his family and makes them heirs along with this beloved Son of his. This attitude by God that he receives sinful human beings as his own children, therefore, constitutes a basis for Christians to accept and include other human beings in their life, and to share public benefits with them in society. As adopted children of God, Christians share with the Son of God Jesus all rights to God's resources. As God's heirs, adopted children of God can claim what God has provided for his beloved children – a full identity as his children. And, because God himself is holy, so must his children be. Hence, after being justified and adopted into children of God, the believing Christians undergo sanctification.

The term "sanctification", based on the Latin word *sanctus*, means "holy". Many have used this term traditionally in Christian theology to describe the continual renewal of the inward person of the Christian believer. It comprises the release of the Christian believer from the compulsive power of sin and guilt towards love God and service to the neighbour. In other words, "sanctification" is the change God makes in a believer's life as the Christian believer grows in faith, after being justified. Hence, for some people like John Calvin there is no sharp line between "sanctification" and "justification". Calvin tends to interpret the new life in being sanctified as an aspect of "justification". Here, soon after justification (declared not guilty of sin by faith in Jesus Christ) a Christian believer faces a continued struggle with sin. The fact that a believer is declared not guilty of sin does not make sin less serious. God's Son Jesus Christ's death for sin shows the dreadful seriousness of sin. Jesus Christ paid with his life so that a sinner could be forgiven of sin. Also, the availability of God's mercy, grace, and forgiveness of sin is no excuse for careless living and moral laxness. As such, there is need for the believer to have victory over sin in Jesus Christ. Atonement, therefore, includes the claim that God does not only declare a sinner not guilty of sin, but also offers the Christian believer freedom from sin. The Christian believer is empowered to do God's will by the power of the Holy Spirit. God. This constitutes a basis for Christians to live a life of justice in society. Here, the Holy Spirit is called the Spirit of life because he empowers the believer to live the Christian life through regeneration.

"Regeneration" means literally "rebirth", and it is a term used to signify the actual renewing of the self, which, according to Christian theology, occurs with the reception of God's grace through faith in Jesus Christ and enabled by the Holy Spirit. How this takes place has been the subject of much discussion in the history of Christian thought. Moreover, regeneration has something to do with human beings conforming to their creation in the image of God in Jesus Christ. Human beings conforming to their creation in the image of God in Jesus Christ constitutes a basis for Christians' moral transformation in society.

God created human beings in his own image (Genesis 1:26-27). Creation of humankind in the "image of God" distinguishes it from all other life forms. What then is the "image of God"? We cannot understand the image of God (*imago Dei*) in human beings well without our knowledge of Godself (God's character and behaviour). God is a Trinity existing in a communion of the Father, Son and the Holy Spirit – a relation to one another of mutual love and respect. In this direction, when God created human beings in the divine image God did not create them as isolated individuals. He created human beings in the divine image with an intention that they relate to one another with mutual respect and love. Therefore, human beings exist in relation with other persons, with God, with the world, and with themselves. According to this conception, human beings are not isolated individuals but essentially relational beings that reflect their sense of relation to others from God's character and behaviour. The fundamentally relational character of the image of God (*imago Dei*) itself in human beings constitutes a basis for its exercise of freedom and responsibility found in God himself that he is capable of caring and dignifying human beings. – freedom to exist as individuals, but at the same In the same manner, human beings should practice respect for the dignity of other human beings and God.

Indeed, God deals with human beings directly as individuals. That is, every individual Christian is summoned to repent from sin at a cost so as to attain the highest standards of holiness. Nevertheless, each follower of Christ is a member of God's family of faith, the body of Jesus Christ. The Holy Spirit calls every human being into Christ's body, which is the Church. It is in the Church, therefore, that each believer is dignified. In the Church of Jesus Christ, a Christian member is loved, fed, protected and equipped for faithful living and witness.

The early church in the New Testament is a practical example of the Church of Jesus Christ whose members not only identified themselves as individual Christians, but identified themselves as a loving and caring community in spite of their differences as individual members. Despite their individual weakness, character defects, or personality problems, the early church, thus, complemented, supported, healed, and compensated one another as members of same body of Jesus Christ.

Against this broad and general background, it is possible to focus explicitly on the typical Reformed understanding of the atonement and on some of the most important contributors to the theological understanding of atonement in this tradition. In order to do that, the study begins with Anselm of Canterbury, who lived centuries before the Reformation itself.

ANSELM'S VIEW OF THE ATONEMENT

Background

Archbishop Anselm is a widely influential philosopher and theologian of the middle ages. He held the office of Archbishop of Canterbury from 1093 to 1109. His constant endeavour was to render the contents of the Christian consciousness clear to reason, and to develop the intelligible truths interwoven with the Christian belief. Anselm's greatest work is the *Cur Deus Homo* ("Why did God become Human?") in which he undertook to make plain the rational necessity of the Christian mystery of the atonement.

In his *Cur Deus Homo*, Anselm taught what is called objective view atonement. Objective view of atonement has it that Christ suffered and died for the sake of bringing back honour to God, which had been lost when human beings sinned. In so doing, satisfaction was made towards God's justice (Milne 1986: 165; Loonstra 1990: 382). Here, Anselm meant to replace the older and more "physical" idea of salvation with the moral idea of salvation - that of deliverance from guilt of sin. Indeed, it is from Anselm of Canterbury that the Reformed tradition draws alternative terms of punishment or satisfaction towards view of atonement. The Reformed tradition was able to do this through John Calvin. Therefore, the Reformed tradition views sin as a contravention of the moral law, which is correlative with the eternal character of God. Equally important, the Reformed tradition finds its strong characteristics in Anselm's "objective atonement", according to which God is the object of Christ's atoning work, and is reconciled through the satisfaction made to his justice (Aulen 1970: 2).

Specifically, Anselm formulated a moral understanding of the justice of God. He understands God as having originally established the created order (Schmiechem 2005: 328). The created order was originally moral in nature and essence, and therefore, the created order reflects the divine will and the divine nature. Anselm has it that the moral ordering of the creation extends to the relationship between human beings and God, and between human beings amongst themselves. Here, the relationship extends towards human relationship with God in Jesus Christ, particularly as Jesus' "active obedience" to God in the atonement.

Anselm's view of the atonement

Covenantal faithfulness of God

Anselm argues that it was God's eternal will and intention to create human beings whom he would later redeem by completely satisfying the penalty of their sin through his Son Jesus Christ (Anselm *Cur Deus Homo* 2:4: 148). In the first place, God created these human beings in order that they rejoice in God through their honour and obedience to God, which Anselm refers to as "God's creation order". Unfortunately, human beings became selfish, and hence, they dishonoured and disobeyed God. Human beings, thus, sinned and were incapable of satisfying God's justice for their sin against God.

According to Anselm, God was bound by his faithfulness to his covenant with human beings and he felt that it would be incongruous for him to let human beings perish in sin altogether. God thus went forward to redeem human beings. In his Son Jesus Christ, God satisfied his own justice. God did this in Christ through Christ's honour and obedience towards God his Father, as a genuine human being, up to his death on the cross. As much as Christ's work was primarily for the satisfaction of God's justice through honour and obedience, secondarily, Jesus found himself being a representative of these helpless human beings, in God's bid to redeem his people. Jesus thus teaches us that as much as we have our everyday life to ourselves as Christians, at the same time, we have other people who come into our lives for our support and love.

Incarnation

Anselm says that God was capable of making a complete satisfaction for human beings' sin when he stooped to lowly things and became a human being in his Son Jesus Christ, in the incarnation (Anselm *Cur Deus Homo* 1:8, 1:10, 2:7, 2:13, 2:16, 2:18: 110-111, 118, 151, 162, 166, and 176). Anselm describes Jesus as a true God and a true man - one person in two natures and two natures in one person. When God became a human being in Jesus, he bore humiliation or human weakness. In so doing, God identified with his own creatures - human beings - humiliated or weak in sin as they were.

In the incarnation, therefore, God stooped low to become a human being, and demonstrated his affection for his children, human beings. Malawians would understand Anselm in the same sense as their popular saying, "What has affected a child, affects also the parent." It does not matter that the parent is not part of the child's problem, but by virtue of being a parent the parent shares the child's problem since the child is like the parent in terms of genealogy.

Hence, God's Son Jesus Christ, though divine, did bear humiliation and weakness of the human body, and identified with sinful humanity, satisfying what humans owed God. It is inspiring and encouraging to believers that Jesus, as God's representative stands by human beings' problems as what ba parent would do for his or her children. Every day Christian believers find themselves in situations where they should mirror Jesus as God's representatives who should relate favourably with other people in society, even though they are neither their own children nor their close relations. What affects other members in society, should also affect all human beings by virtue of their being of the same membership of the society.

Death of Jesus

Anselm describes Jesus as having endured injuries, insults and death on the cross for the sins of human beings (Anselm *Cur Deus Homo* 2:18: 177). Jesus endured all these for his obedience towards God his Father. Also, Jesus endured all these in order to satisfy God's justice on behalf of humanity. No matter how dangerous the process would turn out to be, and even though he himself did not owe God any justice, Jesus was not able to resist doing satisfaction of God's justice.

God's justice is what human beings had violated and required a death penalty - without which there could not have been a satisfaction. Jesus, therefore, was a representative for human beings by his being a human being. Jesus was also a representative for human beings when he went ahead to give up his precious life and dying on the cross for human sin as a penalty for human sin. It took so much courage, endurance and love toward human beings for Jesus to die such a terrible death on the cross. Moreover, he did not violate God's justice himself, but human beings did.

It is sad that many people, in the world today, tend to turn away from doing justice toward fellow members of society, especially those members of society who have violated the law. For example, in Malawi a mob would beat a thief to death, instead of doing justice by taking the thief to police and court. However, as followers of Jesus, Christian members should work towards justice for all in society, even if it means dying for it, because everyone in our society is equally human as everyone else.

Union with Jesus

Anselm speaks of Jesus Christ's union with human beings in terms of his being mortal and a sharer in the misfortunes of the human beings, in his divine and human unity of being (Anselm *Cur Deus Homo* 2:12: 161-163). According to Anselm, Jesus existed full of God and full of humanity. As full of God, Jesus was full of God's power, might and wisdom. Therefore, human beings' union with Jesus Christ presupposes human redemption in Jesus and sharing of God's power, might and wisdom, as much as Jesus shares in human sin and its consequences.

Until one puts oneself in someone's shoes, one cannot understand or feel the pain being experienced by someone. Anselm speaks about human beings' union with Jesus Christ, in his divine and human unity as an opportunity that enables Jesus to understand what human beings are passing through in terms of worldly life. Jesus Christ, therefore, is able to share human beings' misfortunes, in his divine and human unity, and hence he was capable of upholding God's justice on behalf of all humanity, which humanity had violated.

Jesus took onto himself human sinfulness and punishment by God and shared the pain therein, which he persevered unto death on the cross in anticipation of the benefit of being exalted by God. Here, Anselm means that as much as Jesus shares in human sin and misfortunes, human beings also share in Jesus' stand for God's justice, and benefits from God, which include exaltation. Here, as followers of Christ, Christian believers ought to suffer with the oppressed and suffering in society. Also, Christian believers ought to suffer with the oppressed and suffering in society in a bid to uphold justice in that society. and to uplift the lives of the oppressed and suffering people so that they can fully enjoy the privileges that they (Christian believers) enjoy.

Justification

Anselm describes justification of human beings as God's declaration of human beings sinfulness through the representative punishment that Jesus Christ went through in order that he restores God's justice (Anselm *Proslogion* 9-10: 79-81). Here, human beings need to be justified because they are in a serious position before God. Human beings have violated God's justice when they sinned. Therefore, they need to be justified because they are incapable of rescuing ourselves. Salvation is only possible if it comes from God.

Anselm has it that human beings' salvation through justification comprises God's punishment of and God's forbearance. That is, in his justice, God spares the wicked and makes good people out of bad people. Here, as much as God is willing to punish the wicked, in his mercy, he resorts to saving them through his Son Jesus Christ. Indeed, it is just for God to punish the wicked in accordance with their wickedness. In Jesus Christ we see a transformative effect of compassion and mercy according to the nature of human beings. God thus spares the wicked human beings in his compassion and mercy, who in justice he might destroy. Here, Anselm portrays human beings as so much liable to sinfulness that they need Jesus' intervention in terms of salvation. In the same manner, Christian believers as followers of Christ ought to exercise forgiveness. They should spare other human beings in society from condemnation resulting for the wrongs they have done. In justice these wrongful human beings would be sued and taken to court for judgment and sentencing.

Conclusion

Therefore, according to Anselm, in the incarnation God stooped to lowly things – the human beings - by becoming a human being in Jesus Christ because no one but God could make satisfaction of his own justice. The debt was so great that, while human beings alone owed it, only God could pay it.

In making the satisfaction, Jesus died on the cross and paid for sinful human beings what he did not owe for himself in order that he satisfies God's justice. As followers of Jesus Christian believers should work towards upholding God's justice and justice for all in society, even if it means dying for it, because everyone in society is equally human as everyone else.

In dying on the cross, therefore, Jesus Christ affirmed his unity with human beings. And in his union with human beings, therefore, Jesus Christ proves that he is mortal and a sharer in human misfortunes. He, thus, took onto himself human beings' sinfulness and punishment by God in order that he restores God's justice. In so doing, Jesus was so compassionate in accordance with the nature of human beings. Jesus, thus, justified human beings, saving them, who in justice might be destroyed. As followers of Jesus, Christian believers, too, ought to be compassionate in accordance with the condition of fellow human beings in society. Their compassion in accordance with the condition of fellow human beings should result into their being in solidarity with the poor, suffering and vulnerable in society, in a bid to uphold justice in society.

JOHN CALVIN'S VIEW OF THE ATONEMENT

Background

John Calvin was born in 1509, and died in 1564. He was born in Noyon, Picardy, France. Therefore, he was a Frenchman, although he spent the major part of his career working in Geneva, Switzerland, serving in a congregation of a majority of exiles. The humanistic learning that Calvin attended, naturally influenced him. Humanism rejects religion in favour of a belief in the advancement of humanity by its own efforts. However, at some points between 1528 and 1533, Calvin experienced a "sudden conversion to Christianity" and became part of a new movement that would become to be known as Protestantism.

In the course of his Christian life, Calvin developed a love for scholarship and literature. In 1536 the first edition of his *Institutes of the Christian Religion* was published in Basle. It was revised on a number of occasions and the final edition was published in 1559. This book was a clear explanation of his religious beliefs. The later versions expanded especially on how the church should be organised.

John Calvin is very important for his contributions to the Reformed tradition. He and other reformers like John Knox are regarded highly by believers in the Reformed tradition as having made specific contributions to Reformed theology. The Reformed tradition owes John Calvin on the key element of piety and the notion of thankfulness to the grace of God which God extends toward human beings (Tamburello 2004). Calvin defines God as the fountainhead of all goodness which God gives in his justice and by his grace. Therefore, the only proper response to God's gifts of creation and redemption is a life filled with gratitude, thanksgiving and praise to God. This point is echoed in the *Institutes'* definition of piety as "that reverence joined with love of God which the knowledge of [God's] benefits induces" (Calvin, *Institutes* 1.2.1).

Again, the Reformed tradition owes Calvin for his teaching about the centrality of Christ, the sacraments and pneumatology (Tamburello 2004). For the notion of the centrality of Christ, Calvin describes faith as the engrafting of human beings into Christ. "Christ, when he illumines us into faith by the power of his Spirit, at the same time so engrafts us into his body that we become partakers of every good" (Calvin, *Institutes* 3.2.25). One of the foundations for this Christological accent in Reformed theology is Calvin's teaching on the twofold grace of Christ – righteousness and sanctification, "the one never without the other." Calvin lays out this teaching with particular clarity:

"Do you wish . . . to attain righteousness in Christ? You must first possess Christ; but you cannot possess him without being made partaker in his sanctification, because he cannot be divided into pieces. Since, therefore, it is solely by expending himself that the Lord gives us these benefits to enjoy, he bestows both of them at the same time, the one never without the other. Thus it is clear how true it is that we are justified not without works yet not through works, since in our sharing in Christ, which justifies us, sanctification is just as much included as righteousness" (Calvin, *Institutes* 3.16.1).

The discussion on the work of grace by God in human beings is one of Calvin's most significant contributions to Reformed theology (Tamburello 2004). Here, Calvin's notion of grace makes a distinctive contribution to contemporary dialogue on justification and sanctification. He probably discussed the relationship between "justification" and "sanctification" more carefully than any other theologian (Leith 1993: 187, 192; Calvin, *Institutes* 3.6.3). Here, Calvin's theology set the direction of future Reformed theology in emphasizing that progress must be made in the Christian life – in nothing less than following the "pattern" of Christ as an "example" for Christian believers' own life. Hence, one could claim that "Christ, through whom we return into favour with God, has been set before us as an example, whose pattern we ought to express in our life" (Calvin, *Institutes* 3.6.3). Calvin, thus, affirmed that human beings' "justification" will have real effects in their lives leading to them to regeneration. That is, faith available in them will point toward doing good works. For Calvin, faith and works are not Christian believers' own – otherwise human beings would be in a position to boast about it – but rather they are, equally, gifts of God. Also, Calvin affirmed "sanctification" as not primarily about good works, but about "union with Christ." Therefore, Calvin stresses that human beings do not attain sinless perfection, but that ".with a wonderful communion, day by day, Jesus Christ grows more and more into one body with them, until he becomes completely one with them' (Calvin, *Institutes* 3.2.24).

In his teaching on the sacraments, Calvin rejected the doctrine of transubstantiation, believing that it was a wrongheaded way of understanding the Eucharist. In his mind, it made no sense to speak of Christ becoming attached to the elements of bread and wine. Rather, he believed that in receiving the Eucharist, the believer was drawn up into the life of Christ by the power of the Holy Spirit (Calvin, *Institutes* 4.17.16; 4.17.33). Calvin insisted that this communion was both spiritual and real. He goes on to say in his *Institutes* that the Lord's Table should have been spread at least once a week for the assembly of Christians, and the promises declared in it should feed us spiritually (Calvin, *Institutes* 4.17.46).

Again, in his teaching on pneumatology, Calvin was always aware of the role of the Holy Spirit that pervaded every aspect of his thought. He defined faith, for example, as "a firm and certain knowledge of God's benevolence toward us, founded upon the truth of the freely given promise in Christ, both revealed to our minds and sealed upon our hearts by the Holy Spirit" (Calvin, *institutes* 3.2.7). Similarly, Calvin spoke of the Holy Spirit as taking human beings through faith to union with Christ (Calvin, *institutes* 3.1.3), He also spoke of the Holy Spirit as affecting the bond Christian believers experience with Christ in the Lord's Supper (Calvin, *Institutes* 4.17.33).

John Calvin's view of the atonement

Covenantal faithfulness of God

John Calvin discusses "covenantal faithfulness of God" to his creation in his second book of the *Institutes of the Christian Religion* (*Institutes* 2.11-2.12). He tends to balance the scale towards the consistency of God's gracious character. Actually, his discussion on the covenantal faithfulness of God comes after his discussion and exposition on the Old Testament Law, especially the Ten Commandments. Calvin goes through the similarities between the Old and New Testaments (*Institutes* 2.10) and the differences between the Old and New Testaments (*Institutes* 2.11).

For Calvin, the Old Testament and the New Testament form a Covenant of Grace, inasmuch as the Law is a guide for people already redeemed by God:

"The law was added about four hundred years after the death of Abraham [cf. Galatians 3:17]. From that continuing succession of witnesses which we have received it may be gathered that this was not done to lead the chosen people away from Christ; but rather to hold their minds in readiness until his coming; even to kindle desire for him, and to strengthen their expectation, in order that they might not grow faint by too long delay" (Calvin, *Institutes* 2.7.1).

Calvin speaks of one people of God, one salvation history, and one covenant (Loonstra 1990: 382). Nevertheless, Calvin is quick to point out that the Old Testament and the New Testament are representing two different administrations with one covenant[8]. That is the reason why these two testaments do tempt some biblical scholars to define them as "the Covenant of Law", and "the Covenant of Grace" respectively. Here, these biblical scholars would portray the Covenant of Law (the Old Testament) as being restrictive and enslaving and which has to be observed by human

---

[8] In this contract-like covenant, God the Father stipulates that, as a surety, his Son Jesus accepts both the demand of obedience, expressed in the covenant of works, and the penalty for Adam's breaking of it, in order to redeem humanity.

beings even out of unwillingness. They would portray the opposite for the Covenant of Grace (the New Testament).

For Calvin, however, God did not give his people the Law in the Old Testament was as bondage. Rather, God gave his people the Law in the Old Testament as a means by which they might know his will. And, knowing God's will, the people will act it out, and as such, live out their calling. Hence, it is true freedom in the sense that the people are living out the Law subject to their rightful Lord, God.

In the same manner, as human communities develop they require laws to protect both individuals and groups. Since every community has been penetrated by violence, crime and sin, human beings need laws to protect both individuals and groups. The earliest law to be found in the Bible is the "covenant," the agreement God made with Israel after their rescue from Egypt. The making of the covenant was a recognition that if a society is to work, it requires a common structure of law to give a framework for living. Even though the covenant had two administrations, according to Calvin, it crystallized the duty of God's people to "serve God only and honour others in the community." The covenant, therefore, was produced to give a pattern for life. It is as if God is saying, "You belong to me; this is how I want you to live" - "Pattern your life on mine" – "You belong to me, and I want you to live like Jesus my Son."

Incarnation

Calvin's discussion of the "incarnation" in the *Institutes of the Christian Religion* 2.12 comes after his description of the calling of the gentiles by God as a notable mark of the excellence of the New Testament over the Old Testament. He begins his discussion of the incarnation with acknowledgement of Jesus as Mediator between God and human beings in *Institutes* 2.12.1. In the incarnation, God who had been before far distant from human beings, he now draws near human beings in Jesus Christ. Here, John Webster

(2003: 116-117) speaks of the birth of Jesus Christ on earth as the drawing near of God to human beings.

For Calvin, Christ did not surrender anything proper to himself as God, but he allowed his divinity to be hidden by the veil of flesh. Calvin was intent on affirming the fullness of Christ's divinity and the genuineness of Christ's humanity in the incarnation (Hesselink 2004: 81; Princeton, vol. 1 Number 2, 1993: 7). He understands Jesus Christ as having always existed with God from eternity, besides his being God's Word in flesh. Hence, in the incarnation Jesus, the pre-existence Son of God, voluntarily assumed a human body and human nature. Jesus is, thus, the Son of God, who is the Word of God, and is equal to God because he is God.

Certainly, Jesus Christ as the Word of God had to relinquish his high place with God his Father (self-emptying), without ceasing to be God, to become a human being. Calvin understands Jesus' self-emptying in the incarnation as consisting in the addition of human nature. Here, Jesus did not just have the appearance of being human, but he actually became a true human being. It means that in the incarnation God voluntarily became the wholly human person in Jesus of Nazareth. As a wholly human person, Jesus was subject to place, time and other human limitations And hence, as human beings "our common nature with Christ is the pledge of our fellowship with the Son of God" (Calvin, *Institutes* 2.12.3). As human beings our fellowship with Jesus Christ "makes us sharers with him in the gifts with which he has been endowed' (Calvin, *Institutes* 3.11.10).

Calvin stresses that it was crucial for Jesus not to remain above humanity, up in heaven, because he had a very important task to do. For him, Jesus bears a relation to the whole human race through his incarnation (Thomas 1988: 27). The life of Jesus is, thus, redemptive from the time he took on the form of a servant and when he began to pay the price of liberation in order to redeem humanity[9] (Calvin, *Institutes* 2.16.5). Neither as God alone

---

[9] Princeton, vol. 1 Number 2, 1993: 22.

could Jesus feel death, nor as man alone could he overcome it. Here, Calvin has in mind the picture of well-to-do people in society coming down to the level of the needy and poor in order that they understand them well. Although God loved human beings from eternity, their restoration, expiation and the cessation of separation from God were actually accomplished only after the incarnation in Jesus (Thomas 1988: 28). Christian believers, too, ought to stoop down towards others in society, especially the underprivileged. Christian believers must be willing to do that in order to uplift the lives of these underprivileged because they (the Christian believers) are in a better position to do that. Jesus Christ himself was privileged and better placed than all human beings, and hence, he was capable of uplifting them onto God. Jesus was privileged in the sense that he was God and an original human being as Adam and Eve were before their fall into sin. At the same time, Jesus was sinful human being in the sense that he represented sinful human being. Christian believers, too, are better placed in their union with Jesus and his benefits. In so doing they already have the measurement, through their life experience, of what it means to be privileged.

Jesus' death

Calvin discusses "Jesus' death" in *Institutes of the Christian Religion* 2.16. Calvin does that after his discussion of Jesus as Mediator between God and human beings and Jesus' fullness of his divinity and the genuineness of his humanity (*Institutes* 2.12-2:14). Also, he discusses Jesus' death after describing Jesus' offices as Prophet, King and Priest (*Institutes* 2.15) and human beings' alienation by sin from God (and hence, God's wrath) and Jesus as Redeemer in the work of atonement, leading to his death, and deriving from God's love and mercy (*Institutes* 2.16.1-4).

Calvin understands Jesus' death on the cross as being similar to the animal sacrifices in the Old Testament. He describes human beings as owing God both obedience to God and punishment for sin, and that Jesus Christ born on earth in order that he suffers the penalty of death on the cross that was meant for human beings because of their sinfulness (Calvin, *Institutes* 2.12.3; Thomas 1988: 26). Here, Jesus Christ was as innocent as an animal that would be sacrificed in place of a guilty person making an offering. In the Old Testament times, animal sacrifices (sin offering) were continually offered at the temple. The sacrifices showed the Israelites the seriousness of their sin. Animal blood had to be shed, in place of the Israelites, before sins could be pardoned (Leviticus 17:11). The blood of the innocent animal would be shed, representing a life infected by sin of the person making the offering. At the same time, the blood represented the innocence of the animal being sacrificed on behalf of the guilty person. Therefore, God would grant forgiveness to the sinner through the death of the animal which fulfilled the penalty of death on behalf of the sinner.

Likewise, Jesus Christ as Mediator between God and human beings shed his blood on the cross, representing humanity's life infected with sin and headed for death at the cross. At the same time, the blood represented the innocence of Jesus who was being sacrificed in sinful human beings' place. Jesus Christ as "the Son of God, utterly clean of all fault, nevertheless took upon himself the shame and reproach of our iniquities, and in return clothed us with his purity" (Calvin, *Institutes* 2.16.6). Human beings as sinners cannot reconcile, but a Mediator – Christ - must atone for their sin (Bizer 1978: 373). Here, Calvin conceives of obedience as the thread that joined the life of Jesus to his death, and this obedience reached its apex in Jesus' voluntary submission to death on the cross (Andrew 22-36).

Again, in connection with Romans 8:3, Calvin understands the cross as condemnation of sin in innocent Jesus' flesh on behalf of sinful human beings. Hence, the curse that was meant for human beings was transferred onto innocent Jesus. Indeed, God allowed his Son Jesus Christ to die on the cross, innocent as he was, taking upon himself the shame and blame of humanity's sin and clothing humanity with his innocence:

> "The Father destroyed the force of sin when the curse of sin was transferred to Christ's flesh. Here, then, is the meaning of this saying: Christ was offered to the Father in death as an expiatory sacrifice that when he discharged all satisfaction through his sacrifice, we might cease to be afraid of God's wrath" (Calvin, *Institutes* 2.16.6).

In 2 Corinthians 5:21, we read that God made Jesus, who knew no sin, to be sin on our behalf. For Calvin, "sin" in this passage refers not to a sinful nature but guilt. To be "made sin," for Calvin, means that the guilt that held human beings liable for punishment has been transferred to Jesus Christ[10] (Calvin, *Institutes* 2.16.5). As much as God will not let sin go unpunished, God is also so merciful that he cannot stand the erosion of the dignity of his people. Here, Calvin conceives of God's wrath and mercy as being very close together. Even though God, in his justice, had wrath against sinful human beings, at the same time his grace and mercy were so great that he saved the human beings by Jesus' death on the cross. God, therefore, gave human beings room for their rehabilitation in Jesus. Here, Calvin was convinced that the grace and mercy of God are the effective ground of the atonement[11] (Calvin, *Institutes* 2.16.3).

Human beings are living in a world full of violence, crime, and injustice. At the same time the world has lots of people who seem never to mind or even act upon what is happening around them. These people tend to leave all the work of dealing with the violence, crime or injustice in the hands of the government. Of course, human beings themselves can feel the pain resulting from the evils happening in the society they live, but most do not do anything about them.

Again, with such violence, crime and injustice going on in society, there are also some people who will do something about it, but with total wrath and hatred towards perpetrators of

---

[10] Princeton, vol. 1 Number 2, 1993: 19, 26
[11] Princeton, vol. 1 Number 2, 1993: 27

violence, crime and injustice. They would love harsh punishment of the perpetrators of such violence.

However, Christian believers as followers of Jesus may be concerned about the violence, crime or injustice that affects other members of society, but at the same time they would let the law take its course. Moreover all human beings in society deserve humane treatment, even though some may be criminals or perpetrators of violence. That is the reason why societies also need to have laws that will give room for rehabilitation of the criminals and evildoers in society. Yes, prisons should be places for punishing criminals, but at the same time prisons should be places where criminals are given a second chance to reform. Prisoners have dignity just as all other human beings have and need to be treated in a humane way. God treated all human beings in a humane way when they were still sinners.

The Resurrection of Jesus

Calvin discusses "Jesus' resurrection from the dead" in *Institutes of the Christian Religion* 2.16.13, soon after his discussion on Jesus' death, burial and descent into Hell. He affirms that without the resurrection of Jesus Christ, "only weakness appears in the cross, death and burial of Christ" (Calvin, *Institutes* 2.16.13). However, Jesus was resurrected so that the Christian believers' faith must leap over death and burial to something hopeful that will enable their faith to attain full strength.[12] Therefore:

> "...we are said to 'have been born new to a living hope' not through his death but 'through his resurrection' [1 Peter 1:3 p.]. For as he, in rising again came forth victor over death, so the victory of our faith over death lies in his resurrection alone...We are not only invited through the example of the risen Christ to strive after

---

[12] Haas, Guenther. *Calvin's Ethics*. in McKim, Donald K. ed. *The Cambridge Companion to John Calvin*. Cambridge, United Kingdom. 2004. p.95.

newness of life; but we are taught that we are reborn into righteousness through his power" (Calvin, *Institutes* 2.16.13).

Our world, too has a lot of weaknesses in terms of the violence, injustice and crime that are going on, and many times it just makes one believe that there is nothing one can do anything about it, or that the world will never ever be a better place to live at all. But Calvin finds a transformative power beyond Jesus' death and in the resurrection of Jesus, which leads Christian believers toward being born anew to a living hope.

Hence, in the world today Christian believers cannot have hope for a better world if they are always negative about what is happening around them in the world. Christian believers cannot have hope for a better world if their eyes remain fixed on the evils, crime or violence. Rather, they should let their eyes move on beyond and visualize a world without violence, crime or injustice. Christian believers should even go further to even treat troublemakers in our world today with dignity as part of the process of making this world a better place for all.

Union with Jesus

Calvin discusses human beings' "union with Jesus" in his *Institutes of the Christian Religion* 3.2.24, where he affirms the indestructible certainty of human beings' faith as resting upon Jesus' oneness with human beings. This discussion comes after his discussion on the definition of faith in human beings. For Calvin, the Holy Spirit is the bond by which Christ unites believers with himself. This union is the foundation of Christian faith and Christian life, and it is an indivisible bond of fellowship in the union between Jesus and believers by which Jesus holds on to believers. By this union, Jesus makes Christian believers share with him in the gifts with which he has received from God the Father (Opocenskey & Reamonn 1999: 118; Beeke 2004: 128; Husbands & Treier. Eds 2004: 102). One of the gifts that Jesus Christ shares with Christian believers is his righteousness which he imputes into the Christian believers through faith. In stressing that it is the Holy Spirit who is the bond by which Jesus unites us to himself, Calvin seeks to maintain the distinction between Jesus' divine being and human being.'[13] With such a wonderful communion, and in his active obedience to God his Father, Jesus Christ grows together with believers:

> "...we await salvation from him not because he appears to us afar off, but because he makes us, engrafted into his body, participants not only in all his benefits but also in himself...Not only does he cleave to us by an indivisible bond of fellowship, but with a wonderful communion, day by day, he grows more and more into one body with us, until he becomes completely one with us" (Calvin, *Institutes* 3.2.24).

What do we mean by Jesus' active obedience to God his Father? Calvin explains that:

> "...man, who by his disobedience had become lost, should by way of remedy counter it with obedience, satisfy God's judgment, and pay the penalties for sin. Accordingly, our Lord came forth as true man and took the person and the name of Adam in order to take Adam's place in obeying the Father, to present our flesh as the price of satisfaction to God's righteous judgment, and, in the flesh, to pay the penalty that we had deserved" (Calvin, *Institutes* 2.12.3).

It should be kept in mind that, in this section about human beings' union with Jesus, there is discussion about Jesus' active obedience to God his Father in his union with human beings today, after his resurrection and ascension has already taken place. Jesus' active obedience toward God his Father today, in our Christian life, is by way of what Calvin calls "a mystical union":

> "Therefore, the joining together of Head and members, that indwelling of Christ in our hearts – in short, that mystical union - are accorded by us the highest degree of importance, so that

---

[13] Princeton, vol. 1 Number 2, 1993: 23.

Christ, having been made ours, makes us sharers with him in the gifts with which he has been endowed" (Calvin, *Institutes* 3.11.10).

Thus, in Christian believers' union with him, Jesus grows into one body with Christian believers as participants of his benefits and himself. For Calvin, "justification" and "sanctification" are a double grace of our union with Jesus. They are two benefits that cannot be confused without error and yet cannot exist apart from one another.[14] The basis for both is the righteousness of Jesus, which Jesus acquired through his perfect obedience to the will of the Father. There is a transformative power from Jesus that affects Christian believers here, that in their union with him, he grows into one body with them as much as they appreciate and share in his benefits, so that in turn they come to appreciate and share their benefits with others in society.

The late former President of Malawi, Dr. Hastings Banda used to believe in "contact and dialogue." His philosophy was that if one has an enemy, one must not isolate that enemy if one is hoping to become friends again with the enemy. As much as possible, one needs to create an environment for contact and dialogue. For Dr. Banda, the more the distance is between oneself and an enemy, the more difficult it is to reconcile and become friends again. In contact and dialogue there are chances for talking and appreciation of each other.

At one time Dr. Banda had to invite one of the South African apartheid Presidents to Malawi. In his defence against his critics, Dr. Banda argued that he had invited a white South African apartheid President to come to Malawi so that the white South African apartheid President could come closer to a black Malawian President and to the black people in Malawi, the apartheid President would at one point begin to appreciate the black people in Malawi. In turn, therefore, the apartheid President would come to love and appreciate the black people of South Africa.

---

[14] Princeton, vol. 1 Number 2, 1993: 23-24

Election

John Calvin discusses "election" deeper into his presentation, and ends the discussion in his third book of the *Institutes of the Christian Religion*. The third book deals with the Holy Spirit and how God makes salvation effectual in believers' lives. Calvin discusses election and predestination at the end of the whole discussion and description of the Christian life (Calvin, *Institutes* 3.6-10).

For Calvin, election is God's choice among human beings, and the chosen have legal union with Jesus Christ as an immediate outcome of their justification by faith alone (Kang 2006: 74). Calvin is ambiguous on whether election occurs before creation or after the fall. But he speaks about a double predestination:

> "...that salvation is freely offered to some while others are barred from access to it... God's eternal decree, by which he compacted with himself what he willed to become of each man. For all are not created in equal condition; rather, eternal life is foreordained for some, eternal damnation for others" (Calvin, *Institutes* 3.21.2, 5).

Calvin believes that the world is full of damnation, and that most people are not redeemed – hence, not elect. The elect, here, is a small number of people, but those not saved are in God's purpose and plan. What use, then, is the Gospel proclamation if God predetermines all salvation and damnation by way of election, one may ask? For John Calvin, election was merely the explanation of conversion (Thomas 1988: 21). Positive responses to the Gospel, according to Calvin, are not due to the good will of human beings. If human beings were to be left to themselves, they would all reject the gospel because of the corruption of their human nature. That is why Calvin tries to link the meaning of election of human beings squarely to who God is in Jesus Christ. He affirms that God elects human beings as his covenant partners in a free act of the overflowing of his love in his Son Jesus Christ. As a human being, Jesus Christ himself was always giving God his Father the honour and obedience God deserved and he did it on human beings' behalf, in spite of their sinfulness. It is because of this that Jesus lived a righteous life. Calvin, then, goes on to say that:

> "Christ, then, is the mirror wherein we must, and without self-deception may, contemplate our own election. For since it is into his body the Father has destined those to be engrafted whom he has willed from eternity to be his own" (Calvin, *Institutes* 3.24.5).

Therefore, as much as Jesus lived a life acceptable to God his Father, he did it for human beings' election and human beings' redemption from all unrighteousness by application of his righteousness onto them. In turn, Christian believers ought to mirror the life of Jesus into their lives. They ought to live a life acceptable in society for the sake of others, because they themselves would love others to live a life acceptable in that same society for their sake.

Whatever Christian believers do in society will indeed affect others in the society. That is why "covenantal faithfulness" (mentioned above) is required in a society to give framework for living. Therefore, when a member of a society lives according to the law of that society that member is indeed living a life acceptable in that society. That member is, indeed, living in accordance with the well-being and security of the other members of the same society. Any break of the law of a society by a member will definitely affect other members of the society.

Calling

Calvin discusses "calling" (*Institutes* 3.10.1-6) toward the end of his descriptions of the Christian life (*Institutes* 3.6-10). The discussion on "calling" comes after his meditation on the future life (*Institutes* 3.9). He speaks about "calling" when he refers to the specific calling or vocation that each human being receives from God:

> "...he has appointed duties for every man in his particular way of life. And that no one may thoughtlessly transgress his limits, he has

named these various kinds of living 'callings'. Therefore each individual has his own kind of living assigned to him by the Lord as a sort of sentry post so that he may not heedlessly wander about throughout life" (Calvin, *Institutes* 3.10.6).

That is, God grants grace and gifts appropriate to the diversity of callings in life so that each one can carry out his or her appointed duties. Such gifts are to be exercised in faithful service to Jesus Christ so that the restoration of his kingdom is promoted. Therefore, Calvin urges everyone to:

"Let this be our principle: that the use of God's gifts is not wrongly directed when it is referred to that end to which the Author himself created and destined them for us, since he created them for our good, not our ruin" (Calvin, *Institutes* 3.10.2).

In this direction, Calvin cautions that there must be moderation in the use of gifts received in human beings' calling by God.

Moderation serves to guide Christian believers in the proper use of creational gifts with a humble spirit, and, hence makes them capable of loving their neighbours from the heart. God freely gives creational gifts that Christian believers may discover to possess. Christian believers tend to feel full of esteem as frequent use of such gifts grows in them. There may also be a growing number of admirers that have very often led many Christian believers to pride and even being pompous about themselves. It is not wrong to feel great about such gifts. But are they not for edification of the whole society that Christian believers live in? Jesus as a human being had gifts that he used in his life to care for others around him. To avoid being pompous about these gifts, and whenever Jesus healed anyone, he would say, "Do not tell anyone about it." Or he would tell someone to tell others about what great things God has done in his life. Hence, by the Spirit of Jesus Christians are capable of living a life of moderation with gifts, resulting into Christians' care for others in society.

Justification

Calvin discusses "justification" in his third book of the *Institutes*, after his discussion on the Christian life (*Institutes* 3.6-10), and soon after his discussion on "human beings' call by God". His lengthy treatment of "justification" shows that the doctrine is of great importance. That is why he calls it the "main hinge on which religion turns" (*Institutes* 3.11.1; Calhoun 2005 a.: 1).

In a key section of the *Institutes*, Calvin develops his understanding of justification in conjunction with John 3:16, pressing justification back to its origin in the being and actions of the triune God as the triune God addresses the fundamental challenge of the world's fall into sin (Rusch 2003: 65). For Calvin, without "justification" a Christian believer has neither a foundation on which to establish one's salvation, nor a foundation to build piety toward God in terms of one's good works. Here, good works come forth in a justified believer as the fruit of faith, the struggle against temptation, doubt and sin – the real transformation of the believer (Opocenskey & Reamonn 1999: 117). To 'justify,' here, means to acquit the guilt of him or her who was accused.. Here, acquittal differs from clemency in that the latter does not expunge a conviction of wrongdoing from the record of the accused (Husbands & Treier. Eds. 2004: 97). Clemency merely means that an individual has been granted some sort of release from the debt he or she owed to society as a consequence of his guilt. Therefore, Calvin understands justification by faith as God's calling of the unrighteous, the outcasts and downcasts in order that he forgive their sins and clothe them in the righteousness of Jesus (Calvin, *Institutes* 3.11.21; Husbands & Treier. eds. 2004: 97). For Calvin, the righteousness in which the outcasts' and down-casts' are clothed is the acquired righteousness of Christ. This is the righteousness that Jesus as God-man acquired through his acts of obedience performed throughout his life in his divine-human unity (Calvin, *Institutes* 3.2.23; Husbands & Treier. eds. 2004: 97). Here, Calvin affirms that "justification" begins with faith in Jesus. Thus, Christ unites human beings - under-dignified, as they are - onto him in a spiritual union in such a way that all that Christ is becomes theirs, as believers (McGrath 1990: 166; Billings 2007: 158-161). Hence, by Jesus' Spirit Christian believers will accommodate others in society. This is because Christian believers themselves do need accommodation into other peoples' lives by virtue of their being members of the same community.

Adoption

Calvin discusses human beings' "adoption" by God in the *Institutes of the Christian Religion* 3.18.2, where he argues for human beings' adoption by God as God's sons and daughters through mercy alone, and not through good works. Also, human beings are adopted by God through being justified by faith in his Son Jesus Christ (Calvin, *Institutes* 3.17).

On justification of human beings, on one hand, God adopts them as his children. Here, Calvin conceives of human adoption by God in terms of Adam and Eve as first parents of all humanity (Donald 2004: 117; Gerrish 1993: 88, 89, 100). In the Garden of Eden and before the fall of Adam and Eve into sin, all humanity is presupposed to have been of the original status as children of God.

> "This will become clearer if we call to mind that what the Mediator was to accomplish was no common thing. His task was so to restore us to God's grace as to make of the children of men, children of God; of heirs of Gehenna, heirs of the Heavenly Kingdom" (Calvin, *Institutes* 2.12.2).

Therefore, when Adam and Eve sinned against God, all humanity lost that status of being children of God together with them. The result was that all human beings became children of humanity. In spite of that, all human beings needed to come back to the status of God's children, but they could not do so without God himself intervening. Certainly, at a point in time God did intervene in his Son Jesus Christ, and hence, adopted human beings as his children once again.

"...the Kingdom of Heaven is not servants' wages but sons' inheritance [Eph. 1:18], which only they who have been adopted as sons by the Lord shall enjoy [cf. Galatians 4:7], and that for no other reason than this adoption [cf. Ephesians 1:5-6]" (Calvin *Institutes* 3.18.2).

On the other hand, Jesus Christ, in his graces that stem from his humanity, death and resurrection, redeems human beings from being outsiders to God's family. He thus redeems human beings that are on the edge of the society and are undignified, and makes them children of God his Father by adoption. In the same way, Christian believers live in a society with lots of people on the edge of the society and are undignified. While others would tend to press down on such people in order that those people remain below and undignified, Christian believers in their adopted life in Jesus will always work towards uplifting the lives of such people.

Sanctification

Calvin discusses "sanctification" of believers in his book 3 of the *Institutes* (3.3.10-15), where he argues for the Christian freedom that comes as a result of regeneration from the bondage of sin. This argument is a continuation of Calvin's discussion on human beings' regeneration by faith and repentance, through the power of the Holy Spirit and rebirth in Christ. Moreover, book 3 of the *Institutes* deals with the Holy Spirit and how God makes salvation effectual in human beings' lives. For Calvin, "sanctification", "regeneration", "repentance", and "conversion" are synonyms (Calhoun 2005 b.: 1). That is, he uses sanctification to equal regeneration, repentance and conversion.

God puts believers through "sanctification" as his adopted children by "justification". For Calvin, Christ justifies no one whom he does not at the same time sanctify (Calvin, *Institutes* 3.16.1). "Sanctification" is a process of continual renewal of believers by the work of the Spirit, whilst "justification" is a one–time activity and guarantees believers a total state of holiness (Kamiruka 2007: 106). The two are closely related to each other because of the role of the Holy Spirit in each. While "justification" is imputed on account of faith, yet faith is the work of the Holy Spirit, and the product, which comes forth from the process of "sanctification" (Kamiruka 2007: 105). All in all, justification and sanctification are both direct consequences of the believers' incorporation into Christ. That is, in their union with Christ Christian believers are at one and the same time made acceptable in the sight of God (justification). At the same time, Christian believers are launched on the path to ethical improvement (sanctification) [McGrath 1990: 166]. Therefore, Calvin conceives of "justification of believers" as flowing immediately into "sanctification of believers", and hence, inseparable. As such, Calvin speaks about believers receiving a double grace, through their reconciliation with God in Christ and through sanctification by Christ's Spirit, in their partaking of Christ (Leith 1993: 188-189):

> "Christ was given to us by God's generosity, to be grasped and possessed by us in faith. By partaking of him, we principally receive a double grace: namely, that being reconciled to God through Christ's blamelessness, we may have in heaven instead of a Judge a gracious Father; and secondly, that sanctified by Christ's Spirit we may cultivate blamelessness and purity of life (Calvin, *Institutes* 3.11.1).

For Calvin "justification by grace through faith in Jesus Christ" tends to create a living context, out of which the Christian believer is sanctified. Thereafter the Christian believer lives and grows into blamelessness, purity and a life of righteousness. A life of righteousness seeks to live in accordance with God's expectations and mirrors the character of God as practically lived. It is not a life that is merely based on human thoughts of ideologies but a life that entails action (Kamiruka 2007: 95). In their union with Jesus Christ and in their life of righteousness, Christian believers are free of evil desires, bondage in sin; their love of sin dies with Jesus (Christ McKim 2004: 94). Calvin says:

> "But since Christ has been so imparted to you with all his benefits that all things are made yours, that you are made a member of him, indeed one with him, his righteousness overwhelms your sins; his salvation wipes out your condemnation; with his worthiness he intercedes that your unworthiness may not come before God's sight" (Calvin, *Institutes* 3.2.24).

Now that Christian believers are united with Jesus by faith (in Jesus' resurrection life), they have unbroken fellowship with God and freedom from sin's hold on them. Thus, the risen Jesus Christ redeems believers from their unrighteousness. He enables radical transformation of their sinful heart to understand and embrace God's moral order for their life - as powered by the regenerating work of the Holy Spirit. The work of the Holy Spirit is made available to believers by grace in faith by Jesus, which both equips and calls to good works (Rusch 2003: 69). Here, since believers have been engrafted into Jesus Christ's body, Jesus himself communicates his life to them. Therefore, Christ dwells in them so that they are progressively able to live the life that is pleasing to God, such as promotion of moral order and justice in society.

Regeneration

Calvin discusses "regeneration" in *Institutes* 3.3.9, where he argues for believers' "rebirth in Christ". This argument comes after Calvin's argument for mortification and vivification component parts of repentance. The argument interprets "repentance", newness of life (*Institutes* 3.3.1), as "regeneration". Indeed, Jesus Christ died and rose from the dead, applying salvation onto believers not only for their sanctification, but also for their regeneration.

> "Both things happen to us by participation in Christ. For if we truly partake in his death, 'our old man is crucified by his power, and the body of sin perishes' [Romans 6:6 p.] that the corruption of original nature may no longer thrive. If we share in his resurrection, through it we are raised up into newness of life to correspond with

the righteousness of God. Therefore, in a word, I interpret repentance as regeneration, whose sole end is to restore us the image of God that had been disfigured and all but obliterated through Adam's transgressions" (Calvin, *Institutes* 3.3.9).

Believers are thus engrafted into the body of Christ and into the regenerating work of the Holy Spirit (McKim 2004:94, 128, 129, 177).

"For we await salvation from him not because he appears to us afar off, but because he makes us, ingrafted into his body, participants not only in all his benefits but also in himself" (Calvin, *Institutes* 3.2.24). Christ makes us his body not by faith only but by the very thing itself'" (Calvin, *Institutes* 4.17.6). "He therefore sits on high, transfusing us with his power, that he may quicken us to spiritual life, sanctify us by his Spirit...." (Calvin, *Institutes* 2.16.16).

Here, the sinner should treat himself or herself as unworthy before God, since the actual source of regeneration is God himself. The Spirit of God, whom Calvin also calls "the Spirit of Christ", works in a sinner what has already been accomplished in Jesus Christ. In regeneration, therefore, the Holy Spirit brings Jesus Christ into the hearts and lives of the elect on earth to grow up together with him into one body. In so doing, Jesus shares his Holy Spirit with the elect on earth. Therefore, Calvin describes Christ as one through whom believers return into favour with God, and has been set before believers as an example, whose pattern they ought to express in their life (Calvin, *Institutes* 3.6.3).

We are created to conform to the image of God

Calvin discusses "human creation to conform to the image of God" in *Institutes* 1.15. This discussion comes after his discussion on human contemplation of God's goodness in his creation. Under contemplation of God's goodness, Calvin says that when human beings contemplate of the God's goodness in his creation it leads them to human thankfulness and trust of God (*Institutes* 1.14.22).

Although Calvin did not totally reject the interpretation of the image of God as physical, he affirmed the "soul" or heart and mind of a human being as being "the proper seat" of the image of God (McKim 2004: 93; Gerrish 1993: 42-44; Migliore 1991: 122; Leith 1993: 194).

> "Also, a reliable proof of this matter may be gathered from the fact that man was created in God's image [Genesis 1:27]. For although God's glory shines forth in the outer man, yet there is no doubt that the proper seat of the image is in the soul' (Calvin, *Institutes* 1.15.3).

The image of God as physical as "soul" or heart and mind of a human being goes well with the Hebrew word *"nephesh"* for human beings as "living souls". In the New Testament *"pseuche"* is the name for "soul". According to Calvin, the image of God prescribes human beings' relation to God, to their fellow human beings and to the rest of creation. He is of the notion that the true nature of the image of God is derived from what the Scripture says of its renewal through Christ:

> "Consequently, the beginning of our recovery of salvation is that restoration which we obtain through Christ, who also is called the Second Adam for the reason that he restores us to true and complete integrity.... Therefore elsewhere he (Paul) teaches that "the new man is renewed...according to the image of his Creator" [1 Corinthians 15:45], commends the richer measure of grace in regeneration, yet he does not remove that other principal point, that the end of regeneration is that Christ should reform us to God's image...From this (Paul's writings) we infer that, to begin with, God's image was visible in the light of the mind, in the uprightness of the heart, and in the soundness of all parts" (Calvin, *Institutes* 1.15.4).

Again, for Calvin the image of God (*imago Dei*) includes an activity (*action*) because it is a mode of personal existence rather than simply human nature as such. It is a relationship rather than simply a natural endowment (Gerrish 1993: 42-44):

> "Hence, whatever excellence was engraved upon Adam, derived from the fact that he approached the glory of his Creator through the only-begotten Son. 'So man was created in the image of God' [Genesis 1:27 p.]; in him the Creator himself willed that his own glory be seen as a mirror (Calvin, *Institutes* 2.12.6).

Therefore, human beings were created to contemplate God's wisdom, justice, goodness and power in a conscious response of thankfulness. Here, Calvin practically equates the image of God in human beings with the action of gratitude. He states expressly that the image of God embraces the knowledge of the highest good – God. This means that human beings, all the way from creation, are directed to relate to God and amongst themselves by the image of God in them. Moreover, God brought into existence not only all creatures (human beings included), but he also brought into existence "the very order of things". Hence, God directs all creation and all creatures in their diversity, to obey him by submitting to his "order of nature" that he has destined for them. For human beings, the order of nature in them is the image of God that directs them in all their endeavours, whilst they remain obedient to God.

However, Calvin says that the image of God in human beings is affected when the human beings distort the order of creation and cast off reverence for God through their disobedience. Thus human beings have a broken relation with God whenever they distort the order of creation and cast off reverence for God.

> "Therefore, after the heavenly image was obliterated in him...there came forth the most filthy plagues, blindness, impotence, impurity, vanity, and injustice..." (Calvin, *Institutes* 2.1.5). "There is no doubt that Adam, when he fell from his state, was by this defection alienated from God" (Calvin, *Institutes* 1.15.3).

When human beings distort the order of creation and cast off reverence for God. the reflection of God in human beings disappears, and human beings tend to enjoy God's gifts without gratitude, and human beings set up idols of own fancy, and so suppress tokens of divinity (McKim 2004: 93, 95). The whole human nature and its faculties are corrupt. It is sin that corrupts the mind, the will, and the affections with the result that human beings cannot know moral truth, are not drawn to it and do not choose to practice it. But is the image of God in human beings totally erased as a result of sin? Calvin affirms that the image of God is not wholly erased in human beings as a result of sin, but it is distorted and defaced. Nevertheless, at this stage, human beings are helpless, and need renewal and God's intervention if they have to regain the former glory.

Hence, the renewal of the image of God in human beings is accomplished through the redemptive work of Jesus Christ, the Second Adam, and it is the goal of the Christian life (McKim 2004: 93).

> "Consequently, the beginning of our recovery of salvation is in that restoration which we obtain through Christ, who also is called the Second Adam for the reason that he restores us to true and complete integrity" (Calvin, *Institutes* 1.15.4).

As the goal of the Christian life is to conform to the pattern of human life in Jesus Christ, therefore,

> "...Christ, through whom we return into favour with God, has been set before us as an example, whose pattern we ought to express in our life" (Calvin, *Institutes* 3.6.3).

Here, Jesus Christ is the true image of God to which Christians are called to conform, particularly as regards to Christ's humility. Christians ought to imitate the pattern of Christ's own life of humility: death and resurrection in their union with Christ. Only then, will Christians die to sin and the sinful nature and be capable of rising up with Christ to a new life of the Spirit in fellowship with God (McKim 2004: 95). Here, Calvin sees the pattern of believers' imitation of Christ's death as both an inward and an outward aspect.

In the inward aspect, there is self-denial,

> "Here then, is the beginning of this plan: the duty of believers is "to present their bodies to God as a living sacrifice, holy and acceptable to him," and in this consists the lawful worship of him [Rom. 12:1]. From this is derived the basis of the exhortation that "they be not conformed to the fashion of this world, but be transformed by the renewal of their minds, so that they may prove what is the will of God" [Rom. 12:2]. Now the great thing is this: we are consecrated and dedicated to God in order that we may thereafter think, speak, meditate, and do, nothing except to his glory" (Calvin, *Institutes* 3.7.1)

Thus, self-denial comprises of believers' acceptance that they are not their own, but that they belong completely to God. Hence, it gives them the right attitude toward their fellow human beings and makes them love their neighbours:

> "Now in these words we perceive that denial of self has regard partly to men, partly, and chiefly to God. For when Scripture bids us to act toward men so as to esteem them above ourselves [Phil. 2:3], and in good faith to apply ourselves wholly to doing them good [cf. Rom. 12:10]..." (Calvin, *Institutes* 3.7.4).

Love of neighbour is not dependent upon believers' manners but looks to God who created all human beings equally in his own image. In this direction, Calvin says:

> "The Lord commands all men without exception "to do good" [Hebrews 13:16]. Yet a great part of them are most unworthy if they be judged by their own merit. But here Scripture helps in the

> best way when it teaches that we are not to consider that men merit of themselves but to look upon the image of God in all men, to which we owe all honour and love" (Calvin, *Institutes* 3.7.6). "Humanity is both the image of God and our flesh. Wherefore, if we would not violate the image of God, we must hold the human person sacred – if we would not divest ourselves of humanity, we must cherish our own flesh...The Lord has been pleased to draw our attention...to watch over our neighbour's preservation - that is to revere the divine image impressed upon them, and embrace our own flesh (Calvin, *Institutes* 2.8.40)

Neighbours are human like all other human beings, and human beings are all equally created in the image of God. According to the Book of Genesis, all human beings were equally formed out of the ground, and hence, all are of the same flesh.. Everyone with a sound mind would not dare wilfully to cause injury to one's own body, but rather cares for one's own flesh or body and protects one's body from any possible danger. Likewise, our neighbours, as other human beings, deserve our respect and protection from any harm or danger. Again, our neighbours, as other human beings, have dignity and are sacred, both because they are the image of God and because they are also human, like we are.

In the outward aspect, there is the imitation of the death of Jesus Christ in bearing the cross that involves accepting the hardships and difficulties that God allows in our lives. The hardships and difficulties that God allows in our lives, are both the afflictions we share with all human beings and those undergone for the sake of the gospel and the cause of righteousness (Calvin, *Institutes* 3.8.1-11; McKim 2004: 95).

Solidarity through the Spirit (in the church)

John Calvin presents "solidarity through the Spirit in the church" in his fourth book of *Institutes of the Christian Religion*. The fourth book of the *Institutes* discusses "the external means by which God invites us into the Society of Jesus Christ." The book starts, in

Institutes 4.1.1, with Calvin's argument for the necessity of the church.

John Calvin affirms that God's Church, which he refers to as a "mother", plays a very important role in the lives of believers, towards forgiveness of sins or salvation by God (McKim 2004: 131).

> "For there is no other way to enter into life unless this mother conceive us in her womb, give us birth, nourish us at her breast, and lastly, unless she keep us under her care and guidance until, putting off mortal flesh, we become like angels [Matthew 22:30]" (Calvin, *Institutes,* 4.1.4). "But let us proceed to set forth what pertains to this topic. Paul writes that Christ, "that he might fill all things," appointed some to be "apostles, some prophets, some evangelists, some pastors and teachers, for the equipment of the saints, for the work of the ministry, for the building up of the body of Christ…" (Calvin, *Institutes* 4.1.5).

That is, the church is capable of fostering solidarity among individual members. The church does that by gathering, educating, or nourishing its members by the Holy Spirit of God. Here, the Holy Spirit is not a private spirit. Therefore, the Church as that which the Holy Spirit gathers presupposes the community, and the community presupposes individuals. Of course, there cannot be one without the other.

Again, Calvin affirms the gathering of Christ's church through the Baptism and the Lord's Supper. On Baptism, believers are immersed in water, or water poured or sprinkled upon them, individually, in the triune name of God, and therefore, they are united to Christ. On this, Calvin adds to say that in believers' baptism Christ makes them sharers of his blessings, and hence, they are capable of the firmest bond of union and fellowship as children of God:

> "…our faith receives from baptism the advantage of its sure testimony to us that we are not only engrafted into the death and life of Christ, but so united to Christ himself that we become

> sharers in all his blessings. For he dedicated and sanctified baptism in his own body [Matt. 3:13] in order that he might have it in common with us as the firmest bond of the union and fellowship which he has deigned to form us. Hence, Paul proves that we are children of God from the fact that we put on Christ in baptism [Gal. 3:26-27]" {Calvin, *Institutes* 4.15.6).

Thus, in Baptism believers are united with Christ as the covenant community, and hence, they are united with each other and with the people of God in every time and in every place (Migliore 1991: 223-224). Because in Baptism believers are united with Christ as a covenant community, therefore, it constitutes a basis for Christians not to discriminate against others in society.

In the Lord's Supper, there are elements of bread and wine, which represent for believers (what John Calvin calls) "the invisible food" that they receive from the flesh and blood of Christ. Such, therefore, affirms believers' growth into the one body of Christ as heirs in the Kingdom of Heaven.

> "Godly souls can gather great assurance and delight from this sacrament; in it they have a witness of our growth into one body with Christ such that whatever is his may be called ours. As a consequence, we may dare assure ourselves that eternal life, of which he is a heir, is ours; and that the Kingdom of Heaven, into which he has already entered, can no more be cut off from us than from him; again...(Calvin, *Institutes* 4.17.2).

The Lord's Supper is inseparable from Jesus' practice of table fellowship with sinners and the poor throughout his ministry (Mark 2:15; Luke 15:1-2). Jesus' practice of table fellowship discloses what human life by God's grace is intended to be. Human life should be a life together in mutual sharing and love with other people in society. Our lack of love may contradict our participation in the Lord's Supper. Hence, Jesus' practice of table fellowship encourages Christian believers to anticipate, in the midst of present suffering, God's promise of a new, liberated, and reconciled humanity in a new heaven and a new earth.

Summary

Calvin, just like Anselm of Canterbury, expresses basically the same idea about the atonement, namely that we own a debt to God and that Christ alone can pay this debt. Therefore, Jesus Christ made a proper, real, and full satisfaction of his Father's justice on our behalf when he died on the cross as a sin offering. However, Calvin takes it further to discuss the double grace that believers receive from God in Jesus. This double grace is about being reconciled to God through Christ's blamelessness and being empowered by Christ's Spirit to be capable of cultivating blamelessness and purity of life. And hence, double grace leads to a new life, which is characteristic of the Reformed tradition.

In our calling and in our justified, sanctified and regenerated life as Christian believers, therefore, God sets forth a godly and righteous rule of living within his covenantal faithfulness to us, his people, through his Ten Commandments or "moral law," according to Calvin. A Christian believer's justified, sanctified and regenerated life, therefore, constitutes a basis for all social institutions in human society to come under the criticism of the Word of God.

In the incarnation, God's Son Jesus Christ, though divine, shares human common nature and fellowship with believers. Christian believers are thus well placed in their common nature and fellowship with Jesus and his benefits. In their common nature and fellowship with Jesus and his benefits, therefore, Christian believers are capable of sharing with others in society.

Jesus rose from the dead on the third day of his burial. Jesus' rising up from the dead symbolises his transformative power that strives towards newness of life. Christian believers, therefore, have not only been invited through the transformative power of the risen Christ to strive after newness of life. They are also taught that they have been reborn into Jesus' righteousness through his power of the Spirit. Christians are, thus, reborn into the righteousness by the Spirit of Jesus.

Jesus' death and resurrection are among Jesus' benefits that believers participate in as a result of their being united to him. In their union with Jesus, he grows into one body with Christian believers as participants of his benefits and himself. Christian believers, therefore, are God's elect in their union with Jesus Christ. In gratitude they become transformed in their relationship with God and others in society.

God has elected Christian believers through Jesus who has lived a life acceptable to God his Father for their redemption from all unrighteousness by his application of his righteousness onto them so that they live a life acceptable to God for others.

God has, thus, called Christian believers through Jesus Christ, who is full of humble spirit and love from the heart, such that he suffered and died on the cross for their justification, in order that they live according to God's will through caring for others in society. Therefore, there has to be good works in Christian believers, which God will do through them after their justification in Jesus Christ. That may, indeed, be considered as signs of their salvation.

Nevertheless, we are not justified by good works, but we are made, unconditionally and without merit, accepted by God the Father of Jesus and his heavenly kingdom, in spite of who we are and our alienation from God. Jesus Christ rendered his life as a sacrifice for the satisfaction of God's justice and for our justification - and hence, Jesus made us capable of rendering our lives as a sacrifice acceptable and meaningful to God and neighbours, in spite of who they are.

Justified as Christian believers are in Jesus Christ, they are now children of God in his kingdom of heaven, adopted sons and daughters of God, brothers and sisters of Jesus Christ, and therefore, they have the assurance of God's up-keeping and protection. Such is an encouragement for Christian believers to willingly, and with gratitude, care and protect others in society for God.

And, since Christian believers have been engrafted into Jesus Christ's body, as children of God, Jesus himself communicates his life to them by his Spirit. Therefore, Christ dwells in them so that they are progressively able to live the life that is pleasing to God through Christ's communication of his life onto them, since they have been engrafted into his body. Christ, through whom they return into favour with God, has, thus, been set before them as an example, whose pattern they ought to express in their life (Calvin, *Institutes* 3.6.3). Here, the image of God in Christian believers as human beings goes along with their actions of gratitude.

Therefore, Christian believers are not to consider that people have merit of themselves, but they have to look upon the image of God in all human beings, as Scripture teaches, to which they owe all honour and love. The Scripture bids them to act toward all others so as to esteem them above themselves, and in good faith to apply themselves wholly to doing them good. The Lord has been pleased to draw their attention to watch over their neighbour's preservation. Christian believers must revere the divine image impressed upon them, and embrace their own flesh in them. They must always be willing to treat other human beings with dignity and as sacred, both because they are the image of God and because Christian believers are also human, like they are. Moreover they are equal members of God's Church, which is God's family. Jesus Christ is the genuine image of God who treated sinful humanity with dignity. All human beings, despite any differences, must treat each other with dignity because they all belong to God for each other in society.

Here, God's Church is Christian believers' "mother", and hence, it plays a very important role in their lives as Christians, towards their gathering and the forgiveness of their sins or salvation by God, by the power of the Holy Spirit. The Holy Spirit, here, is not a private spirit, and therefore, the Holy Spirit gathers the Church. Hence, the Church presupposes the community, and the community presupposes individuals. Of course, there cannot be one without the other. That is why Jesus has dedicated and sanctified baptism in his own body, the church, in order that he might have it in common with Christian believers as the firmest bond of the union and fellowship, which he has deigned to form Christian believers. Also, the Lord's Supper produces a life together in Christian believers' mutual sharing and love. And hence, the Lord's Supper makes Christian believers anticipate, in the midst of present suffering, God's promise of a new, liberated, and reconciled humanity in a new heaven - a new earth and a new community.

THE WESTMINSTER CONFESSION OF FAITH'S VIEW OF THE ATONEMENT

Background

The *Westminster Confession of Faith* is a Reformed confession of faith, in Calvinistic theological tradition.[15] It is largely of the Church of England, drawn up by the 1646 Westminster Assembly. By 1647 the *Westminster Confession of Faith,* and the *Shorter* and *Larger Catechisms* were completed (van Wyk 2004: 80-81). It became, and remains the "subordinate standard" of doctrine in the Church of Scotland, a church that sent missionaries to Malawi in 1875 and 1876[16] to establish what used to be known as the Presbytery of Livingstonia and the Presbytery of Blantyre. Eventually, the Presbyteries of Livingstonia and Blantyre merged to become

---

[15] Authority of Scripture, absolute predestination, total depravity, limited atonement, justification by faith, irresistible grace and final perseverance are assumed as foundational for Calvinistic tradition (Ross 1988: 9); McEwen, James S. *How the Confession Came to be Written.* In Heron, Alasdair I.C. *The Westminster Confession in the Church Today.* Edinburgh, United Kingdom: The Saint Andrew Press. 1986. p.11-13, 16.

[16] Authority of Scripture, absolute predestination, total depravity, limited atonement, justification by faith, irresistible grace and final perseverance are assumed as foundational for Calvinistic tradition (Ross 1988: 9).

synods of the Church of Central Africa Presbyterian in Malawi in 1925. Later in 1926, Nkhoma Presbytery of the Dutch Reformed Church (in the central region of Malawi) merged with the Church of Central Africa Presbyterian to become one big church, unifying all the three regions of Malawi. Because of such historical connections with the Church of Scotland, the Church of Central Africa Presbyterian, up to this day, adheres to the *Westminster Confession of Faith*, the *Westminster Larger Catechism*, and the *Westminster Shorter Catechism* as its subordinate standard of doctrine. Various churches around the world, too, have adopted the Westminster Confession of Faith and its Catechisms as their standard of doctrine, subordinate to the Bible.

The history of the *Westminster Confession of Faith* goes back to 1643, when the English Parliament called upon "learned, godly, and judicious Divines", to meet at Westminster Abbey, in order to provide advice on issues of worship, doctrine, government and discipline of the Church of England. The meetings were held over a period of five years, and produced the *Confession of Faith*, as well as a *Larger Catechism* and a *Shorter Catechism*.

The Westminster Confession of Faith's view of the atonement

Covenantal Faithfulness of God

The *Westminster Confession of Faith* affirms God's covenantal faithfulness to his people in its discussion of the Old and the New Testaments. It says that the two testaments are one, but presenting two administrations with a single covenant of grace (Heron 1986: 31-32; Rohls 1977: 88-90).

> "There are not, therefore, two covenants of grace differing in substance, but one and the same under various dispensations" [*The Westminster Confession*, 7 (vi); *The Westminster Confession*, Question 33]

Here, the *Westminster Confession* defines the covenant as God's revelation in Jesus Christ, in order that his human beings would be capable of benefiting from him in terms of blessedness and reward.

> "The distance between God and the creature is so great, that although reasonable creatures do owe obedience unto him, yet they could never have any fruition of him as their blessedness and reward, but by some voluntary condescension on God's part, which he hath been pleased to express by way of covenant" [*The Westminster Confession*, 7(i)].

The *Westminster Confession*, here, mentions "the distance between God and the creature," which is analogous to the gaps in relations that human beings sometimes create in human society between people or groups, in terms of enmity or isolation. Also, human beings often talk about people who tend to distance themselves from what may be happening in their society around them, and may be cut off from any benefits the society is able to realise for its members.

However, God closed up the distance between himself and his people in his Son Jesus, the Mediator. Jesus Christ thus bridged human beings to God, and hence, they are now capable of enjoying fruits of blessedness and reward that emanate from God. Jesus Christ by his Spirit thus calls Christian believers to always work toward bridging gaps in relations, which have been created by those people who hate each other or will not work together. Hating each other and unwillingness to work together tears society apart and possibly depriving other people of the benefits they should have been able to receive from the society.

The *Westminster Confession* goes on to explain that while there is an identity of substance of the covenant of grace in both the Old and New Testaments of the Bible, there is a difference in the covenants' administration. In the Old Testament, the administration of the covenant occurred through such ordinances as promises, prophecies, sacrifice, circumcision or Passover lamb. In the Old Testament God dealt with Adam as representative of all his descendants. The promise of the covenant was life, and the condition was perfect and personal obedience [*The Westminster Confession* 7 (ii); Hodge 1978: 120, 122-124]. The promises, sacrifice, circumcision or Passover lamb, above, pointed towards Jesus Christ - the incarnate of God - as the Mediator.

> "...under the law it was administered by promises, prophecies, sacrifices, circumcision, the paschal lamb, and other types and ordinances delivered to the people of the Jews, all fore-signifying Christ to come..." [*The Westminster Confession*, 7 (v); *The Westminster Larger Catechism*, Question 34; Hodge 1978: 129-130].

Adam and Eve's fall into sin made all human beings incapable of life by the covenant. God was, therefore, pleased to institute the New Testament's covenant administration, which is carried out through the proclamation of the Word and the distribution of the sacraments of Baptism and the Lord's Supper.

> "Under the Gospel, when Christ the substance was exhibited, the ordinances in which this covenant is dispensed are the preaching of the Word and the administration of the sacraments of Baptism and the Lord's Supper..." [*The Westminster Confession* 7 (iv); *The Westminster Larger Catechism*, Question 35; Hodge 1978: 124-126].

In the New Testament, therefore, God freely offered sinful human beings life and salvation by Jesus Christ, which requires faith in them that they may be saved. God also promised to give all those that are ordained unto life, his Holy Spirit who would make them willing and able to believe. Because of this understanding, the *Westminster Confession* rejects the use of two separate covenants (Hodge 1978: 126). The rejection is intended to avoid the impression that God had not been consistent in his free fatherly grace, and that persons who lived before Christ's historical appearance are excluded from the covenant of grace, and thus are not beneficiaries of the promise of Christ. Moreover, Jesus Christ's work was aimed at redeeming all humanity, even though in the Old Testament the incarnation under Jesus Christ had not yet taken place (Williams 1964: 82; Cf. Thomas 1988: 28).

Incarnation

The *Westminster Confession* affirms the "incarnation" under Jesus Christ as Mediator.

> "It pleased God, in his eternal purpose, to choose and ordain the Lord Jesus, his only begotten Son, to be the Mediator between God and men…" [*The Westminster Confession*, 8 (i)].

It describes Jesus as Mediator between God and humanity, besides his being the second Person in the Trinity, the very being of God, and of one and same nature with God. The Westminster Confession of Faith says that it was the intention of God to be born a human being in Jesus Christ. Here, Jesus was born human in order that he becomes Mediator to offer reconciliation between God and human beings. Therefore, it prompted Jesus, even though he was divine, to take upon himself human nature in the true sense of human being, with all its physical weakness or frailty, yet was without sin.

> "The Son of God, the second Person in the Trinity, being the very and eternal God, of one substance, and equal with the Father, did, when the fullness of time was to come, take upon him man's nature, with all the essential properties and common infirmities thereof; yet without sin…the only Mediator between God and man" [*The Westminster Confession*, 8 (ii)].

The *Westminster Confession* thus affirms that Jesus Christ's divinity and humanity were two whole, perfect and distinct natures of Godhead and manhood. Jesus' divinity and humanity were inseparably joined together in one person. Here, Christ is God, and that he is also man, having supernaturally entered into human nature without sin, and that he is yet one person, Christ the only

Mediator between God and humanity (Williams 1964: 73-77). The bond between Jesus' divinity and humanity is without conversion, composition, or confusion, which were qualifications worth of a Mediator between God and man. Here, the *Westminster Confession* has a picture in mind of mediators in human society. Mediators in human societies are people who must win the favour of all the different parties they are trying to reconcile. In Malawi, we have had instances whereby some people have been denied to mediate in a conflict just because they tended to be biased toward one or more of the parties involved.

Certainly, as a qualified Mediator, Jesus won favour from both parties that he facilitated reconciliation. On one hand, Jesus was the second person in the Trinity and the very being of God, and on the other hand, Jesus took upon himself human nature with all its physical weaknesses, except sin. Also, Jesus Christ was born human so that he might be made under Law of God (of which he perfectly fulfilled) and that he might sacrifice himself.

> "This office the Lord Jesus did most willingly undertake, which, that he might discharge, he was made under the law, and did perfectly fulfil it..." [*The Westminster Confession*, 8 (iv)].

Indeed, Jesus Christ was capable of perfectly satisfying the justice of God his Father by his perfect obedience and sacrifice of himself. Because Jesus was capable of perfectly satisfying the justice of God, he therefore purchased reconciliation and everlasting inheritance in the kingdom of heaven for human beings [*The Westminster Confession*, 8 (v)]. By his Spirit, Jesus thus calls Christian believers to imitate him and take every opportunity of mediation in human conflict, aimed at human beings' need for lasting peace and joy.

iii. Death of Jesus Christ

The *Westminster Confession of Faith* conceives of Jesus Christ's death on the cross as a curse and as an offering for sin.

> "Christ humbled himself in his death...he laid down his life an offering for sin, enduring the pain, shameful, and cursed death of the cross" [*The Westminster Larger Catechism Question,* 49].

In the Old Testament, everyone who did not do according to the Book of the Law was cursed (Deuteronomy 27:26). It meant that everyone who broke even one commandment stood under condemnation. And because everyone has broken the commandments of God, everyone stands condemned – a state the Law itself cannot reverse. Because everyone stands condemned, everyone needs to make a proper, real and full satisfaction for breaking God's commandments. But no one is incapable of doing such a need.

Therefore, in the love and mercy of God, Jesus died on the cross as a sin offering, making a proper, real and full satisfaction for breaking God's commandments on behalf of human beings (Heron 1986: 32). Christ, thus, made full satisfaction for breaking God's commandments, on behalf of human beings. He, therefore, made a complete redemption for these human beings (Williams 1964: 79-81). In the making of full satisfaction for breaking God's commandments by Jesus Christ, there is the element of the Old Testament's animal sacrifice for sin.. While animal sacrifices were repeatedly offered to God for the remission of sins of the Israelites in the Old Testament, but sin offering by Jesus Christ was done once. Hence, it offers total and permanent forgiveness from God. When Jesus hung on the cross on behalf of human beings, he took the curse of the law upon himself. He, thus, made a proper, real and full satisfaction of his Father's justice on behalf of human beings. Therefore, human beings will not have to bear their own punishment for the restoration of God's justice.

> "Christ, by his obedience and death, did fully discharge the debt of all those that are thus justified, and did make a proper, real, and full satisfaction of his Father's justice in their behalf" [*The Westminster Confession,* 11 (iii)].

In so doing, Jesus Christ fully paid the debt for all those that are thus justified, so that they would not have to face eternal death.

The *Westminster Confession* means to interpret the death of Jesus as a consequence of sin by humanity. It is of the view that God does not condone sin, and will not just let it go unpunished. However, there is a dilemma for God here: God does not want his people to suffer for their sin. Therefore, God takes the suffering and death for sin onto his Son Jesus Christ.

Jesus Christ suffered and died on the cross. He made a proper, real and full satisfaction of his Father's justice on behalf of humanity. Here, Jesus made a proper, real and full satisfaction of his Father's justice to show his determination of up-keeping his Father's justice. Here, Jesus means to influence Christian believers and empowers them to assist in the up-keeping of justice among fellow human beings in society. Human beings need justice for the well-being of their society. Therefore, Christian believers must be willing to assist in seeing that all people adhere to the laws of society. The tendency of letting others in society be above the law does undermine the security and justice system of a society or a nation. Those who break the law must be ready to face the consequences of their behaviour. In cases where there is an amnesty, still there must be acceptance of guilt by the persons involved.

iv. The resurrection of Jesus Christ

The *Westminster Confession of Faith* conceives of Jesus' resurrection as one of the four components of Jesus Christ's exaltation: his rising again from the dead on the third day, his ascending up into heaven, and in sitting at the right hand of God the Father:

> "Christ's exaltation consisteth in his rising again from the dead on the third day, in ascending up into heaven, in sitting at the right hand of God the Father, and in coming to judge the world at the

last day" (*The Westminster Shorter Catechism*, Question 28; *The Westminster Larger Catechism*, Question 5).

Again, the *Westminster Confession* affirms that Jesus (prior to his exaltation) subjected himself to a life of humiliation such as undergoing miseries because of the Law, which he perfectly fulfilled, and to the indignities of the world, which he persevered.

> "Christ's humiliation consisted in his being born, and that in a low condition, made under the law, undergoing the miseries of life, the wrath of God, and the cursed death of the cross, in the being buried, and continuing under power of death for a time" (*The Westminster Shorter Catechism*, Question 27; *The Westminster Larger Catechism*, Questions 49).

Because Jesus Christ underwent miseries and humiliation so successfully for the sake of satisfying God's Law, God exalted him. God exalted Jesus from being a servant to being Lord of all, which he did as a public person, and the head of the Church. By his resurrection from the dead, therefore, Jesus redeems human beings from death. He raised human beings' sinful and dead bodies to become conformable to his own risen and glorious body of honour.

The *Westminster Confession,* here, is of the view that perseverance is a process, and being a process it requires humbling oneself, staying low, and waiting upon with the hope that someday things will be fine. Here, the *Westminster Confession* equates this understanding of perseverance with Christ's obedience to the Law, his suffering and death on the cross. By perseverance Jesus looked forward to the rising up from the dead, without which it becomes very difficult or even impossible to persevere.

All the same, Jesus underwent humiliation in his perseverance in suffering and death on the cross, which he did so successfully. God thus made him rise up from the dead (in his exaltation) to give human beings new life and to become the head of his church. Jesus thus, by his Spirit, calls Christian believers to persevere the many hardships that come into their lives as they struggle daily for a better world for everyone.

Union with Jesus Christ

The *Westminster Confession of Faith* affirms Jesus Christ's union with believers in the unity of his divine nature and human nature. Such is a qualification worthy of a Mediator and as Surety between God and human beings.

> "The Lord Jesus in his human nature thus united to the divine, was sanctified and anointed with the Holy Spirit above measure...to end that being holy...he might be thoroughly furnished to execute the office of a Mediator and Surety" [*The Westminster Confession*, 8 (iii)].

With such endowments worthy of a Mediator, Jesus Christ was capable of satisfying the justice of God by his perfect obedience and sacrifice of his body in his death on the cross. Therefore, by virtue of his union with believers and by the power of the Holy Spirit, Jesus is capable of effectually applying and communicating his graces onto believers.

> "To all those for whom Christ hath purchased redemption, he doth certainly and effectually apply and communicate the same; making intercession for them, and revealing unto them, in and by the Word, the mysteries of salvation; effectually persuading them by his Spirit to believe and obey..." [*The Westminster Confession*, 8 (viii)].

The *Westminster Confession,* here, has in mind a picture of unions that human beings form in the modern world, which may aim at strengthening an economic or a political or social base of the parties involved in a union. In such unions, it is expected that the parties involved will communicate and share what each has onto each other for the betterment of them all as a single group or entity.

In the same manner and by virtue of Jesus' union with Christian believers, he was capable of effectually applying and communicating his graces onto believers (while believers themselves are capable of communicating faith onto Jesus). Because of their union with Jesus, therefore, Christian believers are made to enjoy the benefits that Jesus offers them. In turn and by the power of Jesus' Spirit, believers are made into people who are willing to unite with others in society in order that they support each other and share in the benefits or gifts that their society may offer. Indeed, the benefits in a society equally belong to all members. In the same way, because of their union with Jesus Christ, Christian believers can claim that what belongs to Jesus belongs to them also.

Faith

The *Westminster Confession of Faith* affirms "faith" as a gift from God that enables human beings (as the elect of God) to believe in God's salvation for all human beings in Jesus Christ.

> "The grace of faith, whereby the elect are enabled to believe the saving of their souls, is the work of the Spirit of Christ in their hearts." [Opocensky & Reamonn 1999: 120; *The Westminster Confession*, 14 (i)]. "By faith, a Christian believeth to be true whatsoever is revealed in the Word, for the authority of God himself speaking therein..." [*The Westminster Confession*, 14 (ii)]

The Confession of Faith adds on to say that faith is the work of the Holy Spirit in the hearts of the elect of God, through Jesus Christ.

> "Christ...persuading them by his Spirit to believe and obey; and governing their hearts by his Word and Spirit..." [*The Westminster Confession*, 8 (viii)].

As such "faith" enables the Christian to accept the authority of God as he speaks and reveals himself in his Word. A Christian believer's life is, thus, transformed by believing in God's Word, by which the

Christian believer is capable of yielding obedience to God and embracing God's promises for this life and that which is to come. Here, the *Westminster Confession* affirms that the Christian believer's transformation is possible in as much as Jesus Christ is the Mediator between God and man.

As Mediator, Jesus Christ is both the author and finisher of a Christian believer's faith in terms of growing up and victory in faith. Here, the *Westminster Confession* conceives of the Christian believer's growing up and victory in faith, in as much as Jesus Christ's applies of his righteousness on to believers for their resting in him.

> "This faith is different in degrees, weak or strong; may be often and in many ways assailed and weakened, but gets the victory; growing up in many to the attainment of a full assurance through Christ, who is both the author and finisher of faith" [*The Westminster Confession*, 14 (iii)].

The *Westminster Confession,* here, is of the view that "faith" is a process just like a programme in society would have a process. Starting a programme may be all that easy, but sustainability needs to be there. That is why the *Westminster Confession* affirms, here, that Jesus Christ is both the author and finisher of a Christian believer's faith in terms of growing up and victory in faith. By his Spirit, Jesus thus calls Christian believers to continuously support (the whole of their life) people in society who are vulnerable, needy or disadvantaged.

Election

On human beings' election by God, the *Westminster Confession of Faith* speaks not of double predestination, as John Calvin does, but of a double decree. [10 (i)-(iv); *The Westminster Larger Catechism*, Question 12, 38, 39, 40; Rohls 1977: 152-153]. That is, the triune God, in eternity, did predestine some into life and reprobated some into death.

"God, by an eternal and immutable decree, out of his mere love, for the praise of his glorious grace, to be manifested in due time, has elected some angels to glory; and in Christ has chosen some men to eternal life, and the means thereof; and also, according to his sovereign power...has passed by and foreordained the rest to dishonour and wrath..." (The Westminster Larger Catechism, Question 13)

Here, the *Westminster Confession* tends to portray a positive act of God's will and makes a fundamental difference between predestination and reprobation. With regard to those sinners whom God does reprobate, the *Westminster Confession of Faith* does not say that God rejects them (a view that would portray a negative act of God's will), but rather "God does not elect them", or "God passes over them."

The *Westminster Confession of Faith* describes the election of some sinners into life as God's free grace and love, which God does without consideration of faith, good works or perseverance in the life of the sinner [The Westminster Confession, 16 (v)]. Therefore, God by his grace, Word and Holy Spirit, does elect human beings by renewing their wills and by effectually drawing them to Jesus his Son. As such, human beings resort to coming freely and willingly to unite with Jesus and God. Here, Jesus Christ is very important for human election in terms of his being Mediator between God his Father and human beings. Jesus Christ, as Mediator, was both God and man in one person, which are the natures that enabled him to elect human beings for reconciliation with God. This Jesus did through proper works of each nature that might be accepted of God for man. The divine nature in Christ sustained and kept the human nature from the power of sin and death.

The *Westminster Confession,* here, has in mind the picture of opposing forces that need reconciliation, which if improperly handled may result into chaos. Hence, Jesus by his Spirit thus encourages and empowers Christians toward treating fairly and accordingly those parties involved in a conflict. Christian believers must be mindful that there has to be proper relationship with the parties involved, in a bid to pave way for reconciliation to take place. There is always need for whoever is involved in mediation talks to handle each party properly and with care, which requires listening carefully to the concerns and suggestions by each party.

Calling

As elected people of God, human beings are called to come to Jesus Christ. Here, the *Westminster Confession of Faith* speaks about God's effectual calling of human beings (Rohls 1977: 159).

> "All those whom God hath predestined unto life, and those only, he is pleased, in his appointment and accepted time, effectually to call, by his Word and Spirit…This effectual call is of God's free and special grace alone…" [*The Westminster Confession*, 10 (i) and (ii); Opocensky & Reamonn 1999: 120].

The *Westminster Confession of Faith* affirms God as effectually calling sinners, inviting them to freely will that which is good by coming to Jesus Christ.

> "Effectual calling is the work of God's almighty power and grace, whereby (out of his free and special love to his elect, and from nothing in them moving him thereunto) he does, in his accepted time, invite and draw them to Jesus Christ, by his Word and Spirit…All elect, and they only, are effectually called…" (*The Westminster Larger Catechism,* questions 67 and 68; *The Westminster Shorter Catechism,* 31 and 32).

The life of sin, here, is seen as a life of slavery in sin. Hence, by the Holy Spirit Jesus Christ redeems the sinner from slavery in sin by God's free and special grace. However, the reprobate wilfully neglect God's calling and are, therefore, contempt of God's grace offered to them, and do never truly come to Jesus Christ. But the elect, despite their sinfulness, are effectually called through faith in Jesus Christ to partake justification, adoption, and sanctification in this life.

The *Westminster Confession,* here, has in mind the unexpected favours or gifts that are freely given and that are freely received in human society. The giver, here, means to freely rescue the receiver from an ailment, and it is up to the receiver to accept the offer or not. With this understanding, therefore, Jesus Christ by God's free and special grace and by the Holy Spirit, calls sinners to freely will that which is good by coming to him. Here, we see that God treats his people with dignity, and he lets them will or not will to accept his call for salvation. God in Jesus Christ thus calls on Christian believers to invite others, especially the needy and disadvantaged, into willing to receive the Christian believer's genuine favours or assistance given them freely.. Again Christian believers should never treat the needy and disadvantaged members of society (with indignity) as damping grounds for useless stuff. Some world governments in our world today would treat poor nations around the world as damping ground for their products, which are not worthy for human use or consumption.

Adoption

The *Westminster Confession of Faith* conceives of adoption as an act of God's free grace in Jesus Christ, whereby human beings are received into the God's family and have a right to all the privileges of the children of God.

> "Adoption is an act of God's free grace, whereby we are received into number, and have a right to all the privileges of the sons of God." (*The Westminster Shorter Catechism*, Question 34; The *Westminster Confession of Faith,* 12; Opocensky & Reamonn, eds. 1999: 120).

This is made possible by Jesus Christ, who redeems human beings from being outsiders in God's family. God thus makes them partakers of his grace of adoption in Jesus Christ. As adopted children of God in Jesus Christ, therefore, Christian believers are entitled to enjoy the liberties and privileges of the children of God. The liberties and privileges comprise of: their putting on of God's name as God's children, their receiving the Spirit of adoption, their having access to the throne of grace with boldness, their being pitied, protected, provided for, and chastened by God as a good father, and their inheriting God's promises as heirs of everlasting salvation (*The Westminster Confession,* 12).

Here, the *Westminster Confession's* "adoption into children of God" is analogous to adoption of children into families in our human society. The *Westminster Confession* has in mind children who are needy and helpless and those who are in need of parental support and guidance. When such children are adopted, they will enjoy the privileges as the children born in the family. Hence, in human beings' adoption into children of God, by his Spirit Jesus makes them into those who are willing to adopt the needy and orphaned children. And when adopted into families, such children should never be ill-treated, but should be given the liberties and privileges of children born in those families.

Justification

The *Westminster Confession of Faith* affirms that God in his grace justifies human beings by forgiving their sins, declaring them not guilty, and all charges for sin are, thus, removed from their record.

> "Those whom God effectually called, he also freely justifieth; not by infusing righteousness into them, but by pardoning their sins, and by accounting and accepting their persons as righteous...God did, from all eternity, decree to justify the elect; and Christ did, in the fullness of time, die for their sins and rise again for their justification..." (*The Westminster Confession,* 11 (i) and (iv); Opocensky & Reamonn, eds. 1999: 120)

Human beings, now, are free of slavery of sin, a state that had restricted them from freely willing and doing that which is good and pleasing to God. Nevertheless, human beings may will to do that which is evil because of some remnants of corruption in them. That is why the *Westminster Confession* adds on to say that God justifies sinful human beings through faith alone in Jesus Christ [*The Westminster Confession*, 11 (ii)].

Why does God save by faith alone? The Westminster Confession sees human beings as unable to keep the law of God or measure up to God's standards. Therefore, the only thing human beings should do is to look up to God himself, in their faith that he will save them. Here, the Westminster Confession sees faith as based upon human beings' relationship with God in Jesus Christ - and not human beings' performance for God aimed at righteousness. Here, Jesus Christ took human beings' place under the just judgment of God and accepted all the implications of human beings' guilt (Heron 1986: 32). Hence, the Westminster Confession affirms:

> "Faith, thus receiving and resting on Christ and his righteousness, is the only instrument of justification; yet is it not alone in the person justified, but is ever accompanied with all other saving graces..." [*The Westminster Confession*, 11 (ii)].

After justification, human beings now can rest in Jesus Christ because he has completely satisfied God's demands and standards for them. Here, the *Westminster Confession* does not mean to say that human beings are justified without their good works, even though human beings are not justified based on their good works (McGrath 1988: 119). Definitely, works are not the ground for human beings' justification. However, the *Westminster Confession* stresses that there must be fruits and evidences of a true and lively faith in human beings through their good works done in obedience to God's commandments.

> "These good works, done in obedience to God's commandments, are the fruits and evidences of a true and lively faith; and by them believers manifest their thankfulness, strengthen their assurance, edify their brethren..." [*The Westminster Confession*, 16 (ii)].

Here, the good works of the justified Christian believers are accepted in Jesus Christ, not as though they were life wholly without blame or without fault in God's sight. Rather, God accepts only the good works of the justified Christian believers, through the good works of his Son Jesus, and which he did in his satisfaction of God's Law. God looks upon the good works of the justified Christian believers, in his Son Jesus Chris, and is pleased to accept and reward that which is sincere in the good works, although accompanied with many weaknesses. This means that works produced by unjustified sinners (by unbelievers) can never be good works in the required sense. They may be things that God commands, and of good use both to themselves and others. Yet, they are not good works in the strict sense, since they proceed not from a heart purified by faith in Jesus Christ.

Indeed, in the fullness of time, Jesus Christ died for human sin and rose again for human justification. Here, the Malawian people would understand the *Westminster Confession's* death by Jesus for the justification of humanity in the sense of freedom fighters that led their people in the struggle for liberation from oppression. These freedom fighters would lead their people in liberation struggle even to the point of giving up their lives in death. Hence Jesus' death for human sin, here, encourages and empowers Christians to be determined in the struggle toward the liberation of their neighbours that are under oppression.

Sanctification

The Westminster Confession of Faith treats "sanctification by the Holy Spirit" and "justification" processes as inseparable because they build on one another in a process (Rohls 1977: 133). Sanctification by the Holy Spirit conceives of justified sinners as having been effectually called by the grace of God in Jesus, and then made capable of producing the intended results in life, good works. For this reason, after sanctification follows regeneration of the sinners, by which sinners have a new heart and new spirit created in them. It is at this stage that the justified sinner can then be further sanctified.

> "They, who are effectually called and regenerated, having a new heart and a new spirit created in them, are further sanctified, really and personally, through the virtue of Christ's death and resurrection, by his Word and Spirit dwelling in them..." (*The Westminster Confession*, 18 (i); Opocensky & Reamonn, eds. 1999: 120-121).

For the *Westminster Confession,* sanctification is the renewal of the whole human being, towards the holy image of God in Jesus Christ.

> "...the dominion of the whole body of sin destroyed, and the several lusts thereof are more and more weakened and mortified, and they more and more quickened and strengthened, in all saving graces, to the practice of true holiness, without which no man shall see the Lord" [*The Westminster Confession*, 18 (i)]. "Sanctification is the work of God's free grace, whereby we are renewed in the whole man after the image of God, and are enabled more and more to die unto sin, and live unto righteousness" (*The Westminster Shorter Catechism*, Question 35).

Here, Jesus Christ is the true image of God and a transformative power that enables the now justified sinner to more and more die unto sin and to practice true holiness in this life.

Regeneration

The Westminster Confession of Faith conceives of those believers that have been genuinely (effectually) called and regenerated as having a new heart and new spirit created in them.

> "They who are effectually called and regenerated, having a new heart and a new spirit created in them..." [*The Westminster Confession,* 13 (i)].

It is for this reason that the Holy Spirit of God goes further to sanctify them. Sanctification, here, means their whole body of sin and several lusts thereafter are more and more weakened and mortified. At the same time, they are more and more quickened and strengthened to practice true holiness.

> "...are further sanctified, really and personally, through the virtue of Christ's death and resurrection, by his Word and Spirit dwelling in them; the dominion of the whole body of sin is destroyed, and the several lusts thereof are more and more weakened and mortified..." [*The Westminster Confession,* 13 (i)].

On being sanctified and regenerated, the Christian believer's old way of life is completely pushed in the past. The Christian believer puts the old way of life behind like old clothes thrown away. Putting the old way of life in the past is both a once-for-all decision when a sinner decides to accept Christ's gift of salvation, and it is also a daily conscious commitment. Here, the Christian believer puts on a new role, and heads in a new direction with a new way of thinking that the Holy Spirit gives.

What role does Jesus Christ play in the life of believer going through regeneration? Here, the Westminster Confession describes the believer's regeneration process in terms of the death and burial of the old way of life in the death and burial of Jesus Christ, and the rising up from the dead old life into new life in the resurrection of Jesus Christ from the dead.

> through the virtue of Christ's death and resurrection...the dominion of the whole body of sin is destroyed "... and several lusts thereof are more and more weakened and mortified, and they more and more quickened and strengthened ...to the practice of true holiness" [*The Westminster Confession,* 13 (i)].

That is, if the believer is to think of the old life as dead and buried in Jesus, he or she has a powerful motive to resist. Now the believer can consciously choose to treat the desires and temptations of the old human nature as if they were dead and buried with Jesus. Only then, can the believer continue to enjoy wonderful new life with the resurrected Jesus Christ.

Created to conform to the image of God

The Book of Genesis affirms that, in Adam and Eve, all human beings were created in the image of God. Here, the *Westminster Confession of Faith* affirms of God's creation of human beings in his own image as the enduing with knowledge, righteousness, and true holiness in human beings by God. Human beings thus had originally the power to will and to do that which is good and well-pleasing to God in society. This means that human beings were originally righteous and in communion with God.

> "After God had made all other creatures, he created man, male and female, with reasonable and immortal souls, endued with knowledge, righteousness, and true holiness after his own image, having the law of God written in their hearts, and power to fulfil it...Man, in his state of innocence, had freedom and power to will and to do that which is good and well-pleasing to God" [*The Westminster Confession* 4 (ii), 9 (ii)].

At the fall of Adam and Eve, therefore, all human beings fell from their original righteousness and communion with God. Human beings became dead in sin. As such, human beings wholly lost all ability of free will to do the will of God, and hence, human beings lost their communion with God.

> "Man, by his fall into state of sin, hath wholly lost all ability of will to any spiritual good accompanying salvation; so as a natural man, being altogether averse from that good, and dead in sin, is not able, by his own strength, to convert himself, or to prepare himself thereunto" [*The Westminster Confession*, 9 (iii)].

It pleased God, therefore, in his eternal purpose to choose and ordain Jesus Christ his Son to be Mediator between himself and human beings. As Mediator, Jesus was obedient to God unto his death on the cross, and satisfied God's Law and justice. In so doing, Jesus redeemed sinful human beings from unrighteousness by making all those effectually called by God to rest in him and his righteousness. Jesus by his Spirit thus invites Christians to open up their lives in order that they accommodate the poor and needy in society, into their life of righteousness in the family of God.

Jesus' righteousness on which redeemed sinners rest symbolizes the true image of God himself, which was lost in the fall of humanity into sin through Adam and Eve. And the true image, here, would symbolise those few people in a society whom we might say are dignified in the sense that they have fair amount of essentials in life - whilst around them there are lots of underprivileged people, whom we might say are under-dignified. It is up to these few privileged people to make up the difference between them and the underprivileged friends.

Solidarity through the Spirit (in the church)

The Westminster Confession of Faith discusses the gathering of the church by the Holy Spirit under the theme, "Communion of the Saints."(*The Westminster Confession,* 24). It describes those united with Jesus as saints who have been gathered by the Holy Spirit through their fellowship with Jesus in his graces and in their being united to one another in love.

> "All saints that are united to Jesus Christ their head, by his Spirit and by faith, have fellowship with him in his graces, sufferings, death, resurrection, and glory: and, being united to one another in love, they have communion in each other's gifts and grace, and are obliged to the performance of such duties, public and private, as to conduce to their mutual good, both in the inward and outward man" [*The Westminster Confession,* 26 (i)]

Here, those united with Christ gather together to form the "Communion of Saints." As Communion of Saints, therefore, they are capable of uniting to one another in love, having communion in each other's gifts and grace and being in solidarity in times of suffering and need.

"Saints by profession, are bound to maintain an holy fellowship and communion in the worship of God, and ...also in relieving each other in outward things, according to their several abilities and necessities..." [*The Westminster Confession,* 26 (ii)].

Summary

Christian believers have regard for other human beings, as part of their justified and sanctified life. They are justified and sanctified through their being united with Christ, their faith in Christ, their effectual calling by Jesus, their life of regeneration, their conformity to the image of God in Jesus and in their being gathered by the Spirit of Jesus (in the Church).

By virtue of his union with believers and by the power of the Holy Spirit, Jesus Christ is capable of effectually applying and communicating his graces onto believers. Here, besides Christ's graces in his death and resurrection, is Christ's power to will and to do that which is good and well-pleasing to God, which he did as a human being. Moreover, Jesus Christ is the true image of God to which all human beings should conform, if they are to return to their original state of innocence. Here, Jesus plays a role of Mediator between God and human beings.

As Mediator, Jesus Christ is both the author and finisher of a Christian believer's faith in terms of growing up and victory in faith in this life. Christian believers grow up and have victory in faith in as much as Jesus Christ's application of his righteousness on to them for their resting in him. As Christians rest in Christ, therefore, they are no longer under power of sin, but under Christ in whom they have faith and his righteousness. Therefore, there must be fruits and evidences of a true and lively faith in them through their good works done in obedience to God's commandments, in the society they live.

For their faith in Christ, human beings are called "the elect" because they have been effectually called through in Jesus Christ to partake justification, adoption, and sanctification in this life, despite their sinfulness. Despite human beings not being saved by their good works, however, there must be fruits and evidences of a true and lively faith in them. The true and lively faith should be evidenced through their good works done in obedience to God's commandments and in relation to fellow human beings.

"Sanctification" and "justification" are inseparable because they build on one another in a process. In sanctification, Jesus Christ is the true image of God that enables the now justified sinner to more and more die unto sin, not only for the preparation of the life to come, but also for the practice of true holiness in life the sinner lives. In so doing, a sinner is regenerated in terms of the death and burial of the old way of life in the death and burial of Jesus Christ, and the rising up from the dead into new life in the resurrection of Jesus Christ from the dead. Here, as much as there is the death and burial of the old way of life of a sinner, but there is the sinner's rising up into new life in society. Moreover God created human beings to conform to his own image, enduing them with knowledge, righteousness, and true holiness. Therefore, human beings have the power to will and to do that, which is good and well pleasing to God and in relation with other human beings in society. Even now, sinful as they are, human beings unite with Christ as "Communion of Saints" by the power of the Holy Spirit, resulting into their uniting to one another in love in society.

KARL BARTH'S VIEW OF THE ATONEMENT

Background

Karl Barth was born in Basel on 10th May 1886, and was reared in Bern where his father taught. His father was Fritz Barth, who was a Swiss Reformed minister and New Testament scholar. Karl Barth himself was an influential Swiss Reformed Christian theologian, a pastor, and one of the leading thinkers, not only in the Reformed world during the 20th century, but also in the ecumenical church in general.

From 1904 to 1909, Karl Barth studied theology at the universities of Berlin, Tubingen and Marburg. He served as a Reformed pastor in the village of Safenwil in Canton Aargau from

1911 to 1921. Later, he was professor of theology in Gottingen (1921-1925), Munster (1925-1930), and Bonn (1930-1931). He had to leave Germany in 1935 after he refused to swear allegiance to Adolf Hitler. He went back to Switzerland and became professor in Basel (1935-1962).

Originally, Karl Barth trained in German Protestant Liberalism, under such teachers as Wilhelm Herrmann. However, he reacted against this theology at the time of the First World War. He did not like the support most of his liberal teachers had for the German war aims. For example, the 1914 "Manifesto of the Ninety-Three German intellectuals to the Civilized World" carried the signature of his former teacher Adolf von Harnack. Barth believed that his teachers had been misled by the prevailing liberal theology and social order, and that liberal theology had accommodated Christianity to modern culture. He stressed the discontinuity between the Christian message and the world, and rejected the typical liberal points of contact between God and humanity in feeling or consciousness or rationality.

In his commentary on *The Epistle to the Romans* (1919), Karl Barth argued that God who is revealed in the cross of Jesus challenges and overthrows any attempt to ally God with human cultures, achievements or possessions. Again, in his study of Anselm of Canterbury, he found a catalyst leading to what he called "a breakthrough". He discovered in Anselm's "faith seeking understanding" that theology did not have to justify itself by some outside criterion, as it has its own rationality and internal coherence in the form of witness to the event of Jesus Christ. Subsequently, in his study of the gospel, he began his *Church Dogmatics* after confirming that theology was a fully rational procedure. Hence, Barth's theology found its most sustained and compelling expression through his thirteen-volume *Church Dogmatics*. Eventually, the *Church Dogmatics* has come to be widely regarded as one of the most important theological works of all time, representing the pinnacle of Barth's achievement as a theologian.

Some consider Karl Barth as the greatest Protestant theologian of the twentieth century and possibly the greatest since the Reformation. In history, Barth is very well remembered for his reaction against German protestant liberalism and his rejection of the typical liberal points of contact between God and humanity in feeling or consciousness or rationality. With reference to the Reformed view of the doctrine of atonement, Barth has put it more forcefully and positively than any other, that creation is already the work of the free, fatherly grace and mercy of God (Leith 1993: 70, 189). Also, he reaffirms the Reformed tradition, in his discussion of "justification" and "sanctification", but interestingly carries it forward to explain how justification may be superior to sanctification, and sanctification superior to justification.

Karl Barth's view of the atonement

Covenantal faithfulness of God

Karl Barth discusses the covenantal faithfulness of God in his *Church Dogmatics* Volume IV/1, chapter XIII, in a more detailed manner than elsewhere, under the sub-themes of "The work of God the Reconciler" and "The doctrine of Reconciliation". He conceives of God's "covenant" as the internal basis of God's "creation", and God's "creation" as the external basis of God's "covenant", in the sense that God structured his creation in order that it becomes suitable for the accomplishment of his covenant (CD III/1, pp.94ff). It is because of this that Barth describes the covenant as the free act of the faithfulness of God in Jesus in which he takes the lost cause of human beings, who ruined him as Creator (CD IV/1, pp.3, 67). In ruining him as Creator, they also ruined themselves as God's creation. It is by the covenant that God purposes to bring human beings into reconciled relation with himself (Wester 2000: 144). That is why Barth describes the "covenant" as presupposing "reconciliation", consisting in the fact that God realises his eternal will with humanity by making "covenant" true and actual within human history.

> "The history of man from the very first – and the same is true of the history of every individual man – consisted, not in the keeping but the breaking of the covenant...The man to whom it comes fails to receive it" (CD IV/1, pp.67, 68)

For Barth, it is in the eternal will that God originally created human beings' non-deity so that their differentiation can be real partners, capable of action and responsibility in relation to God (CD III/1, pp.184-85), and hence, it forms the core of God's covenant with his people. Unfortunately, human beings broke the covenant along the way. But, blessed are human beings because Jesus fulfilled and restored the broken covenant on their behalf:

> "But since man has broken the covenant, that can mean only in the light of the covenant fulfilled and restored in Jesus Christ and therefore in the light of the atonement made in him" (CD IV/1, p.141).

It is because Jesus fulfilled and restored the broken covenant on human beings' behalf that there is a similarity between human Jesus in whom God elected all human beings, and human Jesus in whom the true human existence originally intended by God is reflected (CD II/2: p.219).

Therefore, Barth conceives of the "covenant" as God's eternal decision to elect and save in his Son Jesus:

> "The fellowship which originally existed between God and man, which was then disturbed and jeopardised, the purpose of which is now fulfilled in Jesus Christ and in the work of reconciliation, we describe as covenant" (CD IV/1, p.22). "In Jesus Christ God has demonstrated that he loved the world that he did not will to be God without it, without all men, without each individual man in particular...The love of God in Jesus Christ is decisively, fundamentally and comprehensively his coming together with all men and their coming together with him" (CD IV/1, p.103).

Here, the covenant originated in the infinite, where the triune God himself has always existed and still exists in the relation of love and partnership as Father, Son, and Holy Spirit. The relation of God and Jesus Christ corresponds to God's own inner self-relation of covenant.

> "He (God) is the Father of Jesus Christ. He is ...the Father of the eternal Son..." (CD II/2, p.8). "He executes, maintains and directs this covenant, in his decision "in Jesus Christ...This act demonstrates his mercy and righteousness, his constancy and omnipotence" (CD II/2, p.9).

To maintain and direct the covenant, God sent Jesus to redeem human beings from their sin. That is why Barth conceives of creation, reconciliation and redemption as the acting out of the covenant by God, in Jesus Christ, which is aimed at bringing God and human beings together, despite human beings' sinfulness and corruptness. Therefore, Jesus, by his virtue as eternal partner in the eternal Holy Trinity, willingly and lovingly, became human in the incarnation in order that he relates to human beings. In so doing, Jesus made human beings capable of relating to the eternal Holy Trinity itself – and hence, human beings relate to the eternal Holy Trinity as covenant partners.

Barth also affirms of God as eternally existing in a relation of Father, Son and Spirit, which extends to human beings as an external expression of the fact that this triune God himself exists in the relation of love (CD II/2, pp.220f.). Hence, Jesus Christ fulfils the covenant, which originally existed between God and humanity, and which was then disturbed and jeopardised. Jesus fulfilled the covenant in the light of the atonement made in him. Here, Barth seems to have a picture in mind of two parties that are in disagreements. There is God on one side that does not will to be God without humanity, and on the other side there is humanity that is failing to receive the covenant with God. Therefore, Jesus comes in and addresses the situation with the love from God in him. With the love from God he comes to be with humanity, therefore, humanity comes to be with Jesus and with each other. Such an equation of God's love, if taken by Human beings, would end the many disagreements that rise up in human society.

Christian believers would be capable of swallowing up the anger and pain that is experienced by disagreeing parties in any society, if they were to apply this love from God. Such would be an appealing behaviour and influence, which Christian believers would expose onto society. Barth would regard Jesus as appealing and influential both to God and humanity such that the covenant was not difficult to restore. Indeed, with love from God in Jesus, the pain that was experienced on both sides (of God and human beings) was swallowed up in Jesus. In our world, we have had people like Nelson Mandela of South Africa, who was a very appealing and influential figure that mediated a number of disagreeing parties world-wide.

Incarnation

For Barth, the incarnation was a concrete historical event: (Webste 2000: 135; Gorringe 1999: 233).

> "But the divine Yes which sin negates and by which it is negated is the Yes of God's covenant with man which is the mystery of creation the covenant of grace concluded in Jesus Christ from all eternity and fulfilled and revealed in time" (CD IV/1, p.140).

He affirms the incarnation as occurring in Jesus Christ's identity of his truly human action with his truly divine action. That is, at the incarnation Jesus acted as God when he acted as a human being; he acted as a human being when he acted as God. Certainly, the incarnation is the meeting of the two natures of divine and human in Jesus Christ.

> "...he is very God and very man, i.e., the Lord who became a servant and the servant who became Lord, the reconciling God and the reconciled man" (CD IV/1, p.136).

Furthermore, Barth has two ways of looking at the incarnation as a whole. He sees the incarnation as the humiliation of Jesus as much as it is the exaltation of Jesus. For Barth, humiliation and exaltation occupy together simultaneously in the course of their enactment. Humiliation and exaltation are two ways of looking at the incarnation as a whole, and not as two different stages in sequence. The humiliation of God in Jesus Christ took place in and with the exaltation of human beings. God humiliated himself in his Son Jesus Christ by coming down in human form to die on the cross for sinful human beings. At the same time, human beings were exalted based on that same self-humiliation by God, despite their sinfulness.

> "In and with his humiliation (as the Son of God) there took place also his exaltation (as the Son of Man). This exaltation is the type and dynamic basis for what will take place and is to be known as the exaltation of man in his reconciliation with God. In his fellowship with him, this One, there is achieved our fellowship with God, the movement of man from below to above, from himself to God" (CD IV/2, p.19).

Barth affirms Jesus as having assumed human essence in the incarnation. He, thus, united his human essence with his divine essence in order that he addresses the two, one to the other, especially the divine to the human.

> "It is the history of God in his mode of existence as the Son, in whom he humbles himself and becomes also the Son of Man Jesus of Nazareth, thus assuming human essence, uniting this with his divine essence, addressing the two one to the other, especially the divine to the human, and in this way accomplishing its exaltation" (CD IV/2, p.106).

Indeed, at the incarnation Jesus acted fully God when he acted fully human being. He was the very God and the very human being in order that he addresses the two, one to the other. Christian believers, too, should address the poor and needy in society with the benefits from their union with Jesus through sharing what they have with the poor and needy, and therefore, uplift the lives of the poor and needy. Indeed, the poor and needy, as human beings, equally deserve what every other human being deserves.

Moreover, Jesus was humble himself in order that he becomes capable of exalting humanity (an expense on the part of Jesus). Jesus thus empowers Christians to live a life that aims at exalting other human beings. Barth, here, seems to have a picture in human life where there are two different levels – one fairly positioned and the other unfairly positioned. For the unfairly positioned to be uplifted to become fairly positioned, there is need to first compare it against the fairly positioned level, in such a way that the fairly positioned will act like a measurement to uplift the unfairly positioned.

In our world, we have the affluent people on one level, whom we might put as fairly positioned, and on another level we have the poor, whom we might put as unfairly positioned. If we are to uplift the status of the poor people, their levels of poverty needs to compared against the level of the affluent, and therefore, at the expense of the affluent do something about it in favour of the poor.

Jesus' death on the cross

Barth speaks about the death of Christ on the cross as the judgment of death that was fulfilled by the Representative of all other people, Jesus (Gorringe 1999: 228). He understands Jesus' death on the cross from two angles. One, the cross was a place where God, in Jesus Christ, rejected human sin. In other words, the death of Jesus on the cross was a substitutionary bearing by God in Christ of God's rejection of human sin (Webster 2000: 145). Jesus bears our rejection, so that we may be elect, by which is meant brought into reconciled relation with God.

For Barth, the righteous judgment of God expresses itself in the event of the cross as wrath and condemnation (Princeton 1993:

30). It was on the cross that Jesus willingly humbled himself and endured God's rejection of human beings' sin in order that he satisfies (Princeton 1993: 31) God's justice by accepting the responsibility for human beings' sin. Jesus thus took human sin upon himself by placing himself under divine judgment (Princeton 1993: 32) and by making himself liable for human guilt and consequences. Human beings had sinned, and had brought upon themselves the wrath and rejection of God. Therefore, human beings must die. That is, human beings, as sinful as they were, deserved suffering, pain and death on the cross because they had disobeyed and dishonoured God. Instead, God in his justice, love and mercy (Princeton 1993: 29) rejected human sin through his Son Jesus, who took human beings' sin by his death on the cross.

> "But it is true only as it derives from the decisive thing that in the suffering and death of Jesus Christ it has come to pass that in his own person he has made an end of us as sinners and therefore of sin itself by going to death as the one who took our place" (CD IV/1, p.253).

Two, the cross was a place for sinful human beings to be exalted.

> "It is only then – not before – that there did and does take place the realization of the final depth of humiliation, the descent into hell of Jesus Christ the Son of God, but also His supreme exaltation, the triumphant coronation of Jesus Christ the Son of Man (CD IV/2, p.141).

Overall, on dying on the cross, Jesus Christ suffered humiliation and God's judgment in human beings' place, but also, at the cross, did take place Jesus' supreme exaltation.

> "The passion of Jesus Christ is the judgment of God in which the Judge himself was judged. And as such it is at its heart and centre the victory which has been won for us, in our place, in the battle against sin" (CD IV/1, p.254).

Karl Barth affirms Jesus Christ's death on the cross as the fulfilment of Jesus' humiliation as much as it was the fulfilment of his exaltation. That is, Jesus' death on the cross was a moment of supreme simultaneity of humiliation and exaltation. It was the final depth of humiliation, but also its supreme exaltation. In other words, on the cross, Jesus deeply humbled himself by suffering human beings' punishment of sin and died on the cross. Jesus thus redeemed human beings of their sin, once for all. Jesus struggled for God's justice in his suffering and dying on the cross. He thus did suffer God's judgment – humiliation – in humanity's place, but also at the cross he did receive exaltation together with humanity. It is the humiliation of the Son of God, as such, which is the exaltation of the Son of Man and in him of human essence (Gorringe 1999: 227). Here, the humiliation of God on the other hand reveals not the powerlessness of God, but rather the nature of God's power, which is love in humility, the seeking, and recreation of relation.

Thus in his suffering God's judgment, Jesus thus influences and empowers Christian believers not to turn away from struggle for justice for all in society on account of any humiliation, suffering, trials or even death they may experience. Christian believers and others, as community, must all stand together in relation as human beings. In our world, we have witnessed torture, deaths or humiliation of many of our people who have struggled for the uplifting of the lives or dignity of their fellow human beings. Before the introduction of democracy in Malawi in 1994, many people that tried to voice out for change from one-party system of government to multi-party system of government were tortured, beaten or even killed. Nevertheless, many more struggled on until the dictatorial regime gave in.

The resurrection of Jesus

Karl Barth conceives of the resurrection from the dead by Jesus in terms of a historical event (Webster 2000: 136).

> "But when we speak of this history, we mean the history which took place once and for all in the birth and life and death of Jesus Christ and was revealed for the first time in his resurrection. To that extent it unquestionably belongs to a definite time. It has happened. But in so far as it has not ceased to be history and therefore to happen" (CD lv/2, p.107).

That is why Barth affirms of Jesus Christ as having physically died, and that God had to physically raise him up from the dead. All this came to pass in order that Jesus reconciles human beings to God.

> "As his revelation, his resurrection and ascension were simply a lifting of the veil. They were a step out of the hiddenness of his perfect being as Son of God and Son of Man, as Mediator and Reconciler into publicity of the world" (CD IV/2, p.133).

Here, the resurrection of Jesus Christ is the great verdict of God, the fulfilment and proclamation of God's decision concerning the event of the cross. The resurrection is its acceptance as the act of Jesus' obedience, which judges the world, but judges it with the aim of saving it (CD IV/1, p.309; Webster 2000:146). Here, Barth affirms that Jesus accomplished reconciliation in his rising up from the dead, after his death on the cross, and hence such enjoys eternal reality and significance (Jesus' and human beings' exaltation).

> "...in his resurrection there is a sovereign operative power of revelation, and therefore of the transition from him to us, of his communication with us, a power by whose working there is revealed and made known to us our own election as it has taken place in him, his humiliation as the Son of God as it has occurred for us, and therefore, the deliverance and establishment of our own being, so that our existence receives a new determination" (CD IV/2, p.318).

Here, Barth seems to say that Jesus' death and resurrection are closely knit together in the sense of hope. If there should have been death of Jesus alone, then we should have not been talking about hope or new form of existence of human beings in the resurrection of Jesus. Again, Barth insists that God's grace is valid and effective so that it is only in light of the "yes" God says to us in Christ's resurrection from the dead that we can grasp the true meaning of sin, and that the kingly Man is the bringer of the messianic kingdom of freedom (Husbands & Treier. eds. 1999: 238). The resurrection, here, is thus not only the exaltation of Jesus, but is also the exaltation of human beings. The resurrection is the new creation of human beings' or the new form of existence in Jesus Christ that enables believers look beyond every struggle for justice in human society, with a hope for a new and better world or society for all. By looking beyond life struggles, it makes a vision or a goal real, and hence, it is very encouraging.

Union with Jesus

Karl Barth speaks about "union with Jesus Christ" in terms of believer's participation in the eternal love and fellowship of the Triune God (Webster 2000: 190). He affirms that the Triune God exists in love and fellowship of which Jesus Christ is a sharer. Therefore, it is through Jesus Christ and in union with him that believers are capable of participating in the eternal Triune fellowship.

> "On the basis of the grace of the incarnation, on the basis of the acceptance and assumption of man into unity of being with God as it has taken place in Jesus Christ, all this has become truth in this man, in the humanity of Jesus Christ" (CD II/1, p.252).

Here, Barth conceives of believers as participating in the Triune fellowship in order that they become human subjects of the knowledge of God, with Jesus Christ himself as the first and proper human subject of the knowledge of God.

> "It means that we let the place of our knowledge of God be that in which God's temptation and God's comfort have come to pass for us and from which the temptation and comfort of faith come to us.

> And this is simply Jesus Christ. For it is because he is this place, but only because he is, that we too become and are this place...This does not leave only the general meaning that we must know him in order to know God. It has the particular meaning that we must know him as the first and proper Subject of the knowledge of God" (CD II/1, p.252).

In believers' union with Jesus and his graces, Jesus incorporates them into God's kingdom and takes them into fellowship and love with himself and that of the rest of the Trinity.

> "God is good in the fact that he is Father, Son and Holy Spirit, that as such he is our Creator, Mediator and Redeemer, and that as such he takes us up into his fellowship, i.e. the fellowship which he has and is in himself, and beyond which as such there is no greater blessing which has still to be communicated to us through his fellowship with us" (CD II/1, p.276).

Barth affirms that God in Jesus Christ is concerned with a seeking and creation of love and fellowship with believers.

> "God's loving is concerned with a seeking and creation of fellowship for its own sake. It is the fellowship of the one who loves with the loved himself, and therefore that which the One who loves has to impart to the loved and the loved has to receive from the one who loves, because he does not keep this blessing to himself but communicates it to others" (CD II/1, p.276).

Indeed, God does not keep love and fellowship to himself, but imparts them to believers for them to create love and fellowship with fellow human beings in society. Definitely, every human being longs for love and fellowship from around society.

Barth, here, seems to have in mind a picture of our human behaviour, when we many times tend to keep ourselves closed up against others, not wanting to accommodate others in our love and fellowship. Love and fellowship toward others need to be created, and therefore, they are never automatic. If one decides not to love or not to share fellowship with others, it will be so.

Election

According to Barth, the doctrine of election is not to be regarded as an explanation of why certain persons believe, but as God's gracious decision to say "yes" in Christ to humanity, which he could justly have rejected (Thomas 1988: 252). Here, God is none other than the one who in his Son elects himself, and in and with himself elects his people (CD II/2, p.76; Webster 2000: 145). Therefore, Jesus Christ redeems human beings from being outsiders in the Triune God's partnership by electing (Thomas 1988: 252) them to relate to him as his covenant partners. Karl Barth says that:

> "It is his (God's) decision that there is a covenant-partner. It is also his decision who this partner is and what must befall him" (CD II/2, p.9)

He affirms election of human beings as the choice that God makes in his grace (Thomas 1988: 252) when God institutes, maintains and directs his covenant with human beings.

> "...that of the election in the sense of the election of divine grace, the choice which God makes in his grace, thus making this movement, and instituting, maintaining and directing this covenant" (CD II/2, p.9).

Barth describes God the Father, God the Son, and God the Holy Spirit as of the eternal being and character to fellowship with another reality and able to have a history (Webster 2000: 163, 164). That is why God, in his love and mercy, does elect another to fellowship with himself. According to Barth, God does decide to share his life with another reality because within himself he cannot know isolation, even though self-sufficient, because this free decision is the overflowing of God's love.

> "Speaking generally, it is the demonstration, the overflowing of the love which is the being of God, that He who is entirely self-sufficient, who even within himself cannot know isolation willed even in all divine glory to share his life with another, and to have that other as witness of his glory" (CD II/2, p.10).

He describes God as Creator, Reconciler and Redeemer, who "is the God of the eternal election of his grace" (CD II/2, p.14). Indeed, it was God's eternal decision to will human beings to election, salvation and life, and God himself to reprobation, perdition and death (McGrath 1998: 367). Hence, in his Son Jesus Christ, he stooped down from above in order that he has fellowship with another reality, human beings.

> "God's decision in Jesus Christ is a gracious decision. In making it, God stoops down from above" (CD II/2, p.10). "Encountering man is His free love, God becomes the companion of man. That is what he determined to do in Jesus Christ" (CD II/2, p.11).

Here, Jesus Christ is capable of fellowshipping with another reality by virtue of his participating in the Triune God's partnership and fellowship. In the Triune God's partnership, the Father has always been a partner of the Son as the Son has been a partner of the Father, in a relationship for which God the Father chose Jesus Christ. In turn, therefore, Jesus Christ relates to human beings, redeeming them from being outsiders in the Triune God's partnership, and hence, he elects them to become God's covenant partners in a free act of the overflowing of God's love. Here, Barth affirms this overflowing love of God as the deepest condescension ever to be made by God in Jesus Christ and in his grace.

> "This love of God is his grace. It is love in the form of the deepest condescension. It occurs even where there is no question of claim or merit on the part of the other. It is love which is overflowing, free, unconstrained, unconditioned...It is love which is merciful,

making this movement, this act of condescension in such a way that, in taking to itself this other, it identifies with its need, and meets its plight by making it its own" (CD II/2, p.10).

We did not elect Jesus, but Jesus did elect us. In his choosing and electing human beings, there was his free decision full of overflowing love of God. It is clear that God has elected human beings unilaterally and autocratically, without any cooperation upon human beings' part. Again, Barth understands Jesus as electing himself to stand in human beings' place and to make himself liable for human sin (CD I/2, pp.155-156; Princeton 1993: 21).

In the world today, the love of the other person is so much of the type that is never free but is conditioned, and many times such love is targeted toward where there is claim or merit on the part of the loved. This is not the type of love God has for us in Jesus. Jesus elects us as his companions even though there is no deservedness on our part because of our sinfulness. Hence, in turn and in our gratitude to God, we freely share our lives with other fellow human beings because they are human beings as we are, and despite any other differences with us. Moreover, human beings were not created lonely creatures right away from the beginning of their existence, but are social animals. This saying in Malawi supports the idea that human beings are social beings, "To be lonely in society is to be like a beast, but to relate with others in society is to be human." God himself is a free community in his Trinity. He did extend himself for more community - outside himself - in us when he created us, despite our corruption and sinfulness.

Calling to Christian discipleship

Barth affirms that Jesus Christ willed to suffer and die for human salvation, and as such, he calls believers to Christian discipleship (Barth, CD IV/2: p.544; CD IV/4: p.270ff; Webster 2000: 240-2410). That is, Jesus freely and willingly acted on human beings' behalf when he suffered and died on the cross to reconcile them to God and to share his benefits with them. Such a great act by Jesus does influence and empowers believers to willingly respond to their calling to discipleship, and hence, believers become ready to suffer for the liberation of those of their people in society who are in pains, oppression and other inflictions because. It is easy, in our world today, to turn a blind eye to what is happening in the world around us and to pretend as if nothing serious is happening to other people.

Faith

Karl Barth speaks about "faith" in connection with God's self-revealing. God chooses to reveal himself to whom his gift of "faith" is granted. And to whom the gift of "faith" is not yet granted, God remains veiled. As such, "revelation" and "election" are closely related in Barth's thought. For Barth, faith is a gift from God. It is God, by his Spirit, who creates faith in a believer in the event of his revelation in Jesus Christ. For example, in the Gospel narratives those in whom God has created faith are compelled to confess Jesus as the Christ.

Here, Barth conceives of God's revelation not just an event, but also precisely a decision corresponding to God's gracious decision for human beings in Jesus Christ.

> "...the being and activity of Jesus Christ in the power of His Holy Spirit awakening man to faith. As the event of a human act on this basis, faith is a cognitive event, the simple taking cognisance of the preceding being and work of Jesus Christ" (CD IV/1, p.758).

God's revelation decides whether an individual will respond to his election in faith and obedience or not. In this direction, therefore, Barth conceives of faith as human response to God's gracious decision for human beings in the person and work of Jesus Christ. Thus, faith:

> "...is the will and decision and achievement of Jesus Christ the Son of God that it takes place as a free human act, that man is of

himself ready and willing and actually begins to believe in him" (CD IV/1, p.744).

According to Barth, faith is not arbitrary human act since:

> "...the Holy Spirit is the power in which Jesus Christ the Son of God makes a man free, makes him genuinely free for this choice and therefore for faith" (CD IV/1, p.744).

Again, Barth says that faith does not go with passivity, but calls for "self-determination" (Webster 2000: 107). Faith means God chooses himself for human beings, and such corresponds to an act of human self-determination in which Jesus Christ chose himself for God and other humans.

Faith originated from God himself when in Jesus Christ he chose himself for human beings. Indeed, Jesus willingly and with love chose himself for other human beings in order that they can trust and depend on Jesus as their Lord and Saviour. In turn, therefore, these human beings, with love, will choose themselves for other human beings' trust, dependence, support and security, which all humanity needs.

The world at large is full of individualism and isolation, a world where it is just as difficult to find someone that you can trust and depend on. There are even fewer people who are ready and willing to choose themselves for others, in the manner described above. A good example of choosing oneself for others in society is what used to happen in the old Malawi. It used to be a tradition, then, that what would happen to one in a community would affect all members in that community. As such, there used to be trust in one another in every Malawian society such that everyone would feel cared for and defended by the rest of the society.

Justification

Barth understands justification as to say that human sin is covered and overlooked, and despised and disparaged by God, and therefore not worthy of further consideration (Gorringe 1999:

247). Hence, a justified person lives by the constant prevailing of the promised forgiveness of sins against the accusation from which he or she comes. Also for Barth, the right act of justification, which brings blessings to the sinner, has two aspects. One, justification means divine judgment. Thus, the human person is wrong, and as a wrongdoer cannot stand in the judgment of God and his righteousness, and hence, the righteousness of God means God's negating and overcoming and taking away and destroying wrong and human beings as the doers of it (CD IV/, p.597; Busch 2004: 210). Two, the justification of the human person is the establishment of his or her right, the introduction of the life of a new humanity who is righteous before God (CD IV/1, p.619; Busch 2004: 211).

It must be kept in mind that faith is very important for human beings' justification by God in Jesus Christ, despite their wrongdoing, in the sense that God does it all for their salvation. For Barth, everything depends upon the fact that Jesus who became a servant was and did all what he did for human beings, and hence, he fulfilled all righteousness, which means that he rejected freely where human beings maintain their innocence (Gorringe 1999: 228). In this direction, Karl Barth declares that sinful human beings are justified by "faith alone."

> "...the justification of sinful man is his justification by faith alone" (CD IV/1, p.614).

He defines justification, as God's pardon of sinful human beings that separates them from their past, and therefore, it is the cancellation of the sentence for human beings' sinfulness. That is, in their justification, God makes good (Busch 2004: 202) what human beings had spoiled. God makes good what the human person does wrong, not by validating but by condemning it (Busch 2004: 209). Now human beings, justified as they are, can go forward from their past to quite a different future.

> "...justification is therefore the divine pardon of sinful man. It is the sentence of God in virtue of which man is separated from that past and therefore the sentence of God on the man who can go forward from that past to quite a different future (CD IV/1, p.573).

Also, Barth discusses "the proud isolation of faith", the *sola fide*, to explain that human beings are justified by faith to the exclusion of all competing works – a notion based upon "the humility of faith".

> "But...this proud isolation of faith the *sola fide* and therefore the exclusion of all competing works can have meaning and truth only in the fact that it is based upon the humility of faith" (CD IV/1, p.627).

Here, faith eliminates the pride of human effort, because faith is not a deed that a person does. Instead, faith should exalt what God has done, not what people do. Faith should admit that human beings cannot keep the law or measure up to God's standards and that human beings need God's help. Therefore, justifying faith in Jesus Christ does exclude all works and denies the competence, the relevance, the power and the value of all human action.

> of human action in the matter of man's justification...It will and must be only faith" (CD IV/1, p.627).

However, Barth is quick to point out that justification ought to be traceable through what it does in the life of a justified human being.

> "And therefore human works as such cannot be regarded with contempt or indifference and rejected" (CD IV/1, p.627).

In the justified life, human beings move from a dead life without God into a lively life for God, and hence, human good works are necessary. Here, human works:

> "...are the (in itself) inevitable and good actualisation of the (in itself) good creaturely nature of man. They can and must be done. And faith itself would not be faith if it did not work by love..." (CD IV/1, p.627).

Definitely, justified human beings are those who are righteous by faith to the exclusion of all works, but at the same time, justified human beings are those who have set up righteousness in their life. Therefore, human beings can and must do good works – make peace with fellow human beings - because they are now at peace with God (justified) out of God's justice, mercy, love and grace, and through their faith in Jesus Christ.

Adoption

Karl Barth does not speak about our "adoption" into brothers and sisters of Jesus Christ. Instead, he affirms that Jesus Christ redeemed human beings from their broken relationship with God when he lowered himself to them in order to raise them up to himself and into the loving relationship of the Trinity, where they share knowledge about God.

> "When He raises us to Himself through the speech of this creature, He lowers Himself to us. All this is already true of the humanity of Jesus Christ" (CD II/1, p.55).

Barth then goes on to explain the existence of God as the Father, Son (Jesus) and the Holy Spirit, and that God does not exist in solitude, but seeks and creates fellowship.

> "...He is the Father, Son and Holy Spirit and therefore alive in His unique being with and for and in another. The unbroken unity of his being, knowledge and will is at the same time an act of deliberation, decision and intercourse. He does not exist in solitude but in fellowship" (CD II/1, p.275). "...He is God – the Godhead of God – consists in the fact that He loves and is the expression of His

loving that He seeks and creates fellowship with us" (CD II/1, p.275).

For Barth, there is a radical alteration of human beings by the establishment of fellowship between God and themselves.

> "This is the new creation of man, his liberation, his radical alteration by the established fellowship between God and himself" (CD IV/2, p.778).

Barth affirms the fulfilment of the act and work of God, which are the very act and work of the Holy Spirit in whom human beings are called and drawn by the Father to the Son and the Son to the Father.

> "In this calling and drawing of the Father to the Son and the Son to the Father there takes place the divine love by which man too is made one who loves" (CD IV/2, p.778).

That is - as sent by God - Jesus Christ lowered himself to sinful human beings in order that he raises them up into right and proper relationship with God – adoption into children of God. As followers of Jesus and privileged, Christians too must come down to those of their people who have been socially, economically and politically displaced, and to uplift them to their rightful place or level in society. Indeed, the socially, economically and politically displaced people in our societies do deserve dignity. In Malawi, for example, there are very many of our people who are poor and underprivileged and whose dignity has been eroded. These people need uplifting or empowerment that would be made possible at the expense and efforts of those who are privileged and well to do.

Sanctification

Karl Barth' discussion on "sanctification" is followed immediately by his discussion about the work of the Holy Spirit in building up the Christian community. Barth links sanctification of the justified sinner with the exaltation of the sinner, in terms of the being elected by God – and hence, it presupposes Jesus as the first elect of God. According to Barth, sanctification is about the disturbance of bourgeois complacency in which humanity does not cease to be sinners (Gorringe 1999: 249). Here, undisturbed sinners are always covenant breakers, not reconciled with God and unusable by him. That is, after the two dimensions of the working out of salvation (justification and sanctification) there is the dimension of vocation (Webster 2000: 107). Vocation is God's calling to discipleship[17] and gives rise to invocation as the right human response, and so the way of being both before God and in the world. The call to discipleship binds us not to an idea of Christ, a Christology or a Christocentric system of thought, but to the living Lord.

Barth says that the sanctified are human beings whom God has elected as his witnesses and called to discipleship in his salvation work in his Son Jesus, the first elect.

> "...discipleship is the particular form of the summons by which Jesus discloses and reveals Himself to a man in order to claim and sanctify him as His own, and as His witness in the world" (CD IV/2, p.534).

The elect as witnesses of Jesus in the world, thus, have their everyday succeeding works reflecting and rendering praise to God. The elect, here, do participate in Jesus' holiness that made him be capable of doing good works (Webster 2000: 150), which reflected and rendered praise to God. Here, Jesus' holiness, which made him capable of doing good works, constitutes a transforming power toward Christians (the elect) for them to do good works in relation to the community around them. Certainly, the succeeding works emanating from being the elect of God – human experience and action - are done in relation to the community around. That is, the elect as the justified through faith in Jesus Christ do put on new creation, and because of this, they have peace with God and fellow

---

[17] For Barth, the sanctified life involves the call to discipleship, the awakening to conversion, the praise of good works and the dignity of the cross.

human beings. Jesus, as himself the first elect of God, willingly became human and died on the cross to make peace with God on behalf of human beings, and therefore, he rendered praise to God, and peace in human beings toward God and amongst themselves.

Here, Barth understands anthropology as lived out as a practical anthropology in the Christian community, and in the lives of individual Christians in the midst of society and in opposition to all the inhumanity that reigns there (CD IV/1 pp.76ff; Webster 2000: 118).

That is, human life must be lived out in active service of a better human righteousness, which Barth calls "the subjective realization of the atonement". Moreover, the doctrine of the atonement as a whole is oriented to that clear knowledge, critique and overcoming of the regime of unrighteousness which we find in the "Christian Life" (Gorringe 1999: 224).

All in all, Barth would affirm that a justified human being is one whom God, in his Son Jesus Christ, has morally transformed, and therefore, righteous by faith to the exclusion of all works, but at the same time, a justified human being is one who has set up righteousness in one's daily works, in "discipleship as the particular form of summons of Jesus."

Setting up righteousness and putting on new creation in one's daily works is possible through what Barth calls "awakening to conversion"(Webster 2000: 183-184). Awakening to conversion involves compulsory and cooperation of all inner and outer forces of the sinner – the compulsory and cooperation of the sinner's whole heart and mind towards the sinner's relation with God.

> "We continue at once that in the conversion we have to do with the movement of the whole man. There are in his being no neutral zones which are unaffected by it and in which he can be another than the new man involved in this process" (CD IV/2, p.563).

Here, the conversion and renewal of the sinner affects also the sinner's relationship with other human beings, since it is inward as much as it is outward to include physical and social dimensions of the sinner's life as well. The human beings claimed by God are never without their fellow human beings.

> "We cannot interpret the conversion and renewal of man merely in terms of a relationship between him and God, to the exclusion of any relationship with his brother. To be sure, we are dealing with the fact that God is for him, and he is for God; with this reality as revealed truth, which forcefully sets him in motion. But he is not a man without his fellow men. How can this truth set him in motion if, as he makes this movement, it does not encroach at once upon his relationship with his fellows, necessarily involving the perishing of the old and the emergence of a new thing in this relationship" (CD IV/2, p.563).

Therefore, it constitutes a basis for Christians' relation to other human beings as objects of the eternal covenantal love of the Triune God, and therefore, Christians are called to see human beings in their suffering and in need of hope (Barth 1981: 270). Indeed, atonement is to be understood primarily as the confirmation and fulfilment of God's covenant with human beings, which is the free self-realization of God's being in relation (Gorringe 1999: 226). On the awakening to conversion, Barth is quick to point out that it belongs to that order of action, which is specifically divine - hence, it is a miracle and a mystery. In this direction, Barth rejects emphasizing divine grace at the expense of human freedom. It is not the work of the Holy Spirit to take away sinner's capacity as a human being. For Barth, genuine Christian love should allow for genuine human agency and freedom. Again, Barth rejects human freedom that is stressed at the expense of divine grace. God's grace by his Spirit does not mean repairing human capacity. Rather, it is meant for contradicting fallen human nature as a whole, with its capacities or incapacities, so that it actually transcends itself, despite its sinfulness.

The "praise of works" is so called by Barth in relation to the works of Christians, particularly in relationship to God.

> "In relation to the works of Christians, the praise of these works necessarily refers in some sense to their particular relationship to God, or concretely to Jesus Christ, who as the true Son of God and Son of Man is their Lord and Head, to whom they belong, and by whom they and the works are measured" (CD IV/2, 584).

They are "praise of works" by the fact that God praises them, affirming and acknowledging and approving them - or that the works praise God, affirming and acknowledging approving him (CD IV/2, p.584). Barth goes on to say that it is obligatory that Christians should do good works, without which they cannot be Christians and Christ cannot be their Lord and Head.

> "We may begin by saying in a general way, and without detailed elucidation, that it is obligatory that Christians should do good works in this twofold sense" (CD IV/2, p.585).

Good works are inevitable in the lives of Christians because they (Christians) have undergone through their calling to discipleship and awakening to conversion, otherwise, the whole event of reconciliation by God in Jesus has not fulfilled its purpose. Hence, Christians should witness of what God is and does for human beings. That is, they may and can and should reflect and practice God's being and acting for humanity.

According to Barth, in human beings' calling to discipleship, the cross is the most concrete form of the relationship between Jesus Christ and the Christian.

> "It is by the fact that He (Jesus) bore and suffered His cross that they (Christians) are sanctified and called to discipleship, and set in conversion and freed for doing of good works" (CD IV/2, p.599).

Hence, it is by the same fact that Christians come to bear and suffer their cross. Jesus Christ was rejected and died in human beings' place, and as such, he exalted human beings toward God. In turn, therefore, Christians will come to bear and suffer their cross for others in the world.

> "...it is necessary and good for the Christian, and serviceable to sanctification, to be kept in the humility which is not natural to any of us, or rather to be continually recalled to it, by the cross which he has to bear" (CD IV/2, p.607). "...for the Christian it is also helpful to sanctification that he should accept the punishment which in some real if hidden punishment for him and for the whole world...the cross which is really taken and carried by the Christian is a powerful force to discipline and strengthen his faith and obedience and love" (CD IV/2, 608).

Hence, Christian victims of the ongoing course of the world, those suffering under the many and complex forms of human unrighteousness and disorder, have seen the Lord of human righteousness (Barth 1981: 260-261). They have the freedom and joy, but also hear the command, to lift up their heads and call upon him to come. Hence, their humble, but rigorous use of the freedom to call upon God in this way is their true and essential revolt against the unrighteousness and disorder.

We are created to conform to the image of God

Karl Barth speaks about Jesus as the Son of God sharing everything with God, when he means to explain about creation of human beings in the image of God (Webster 2000: 167, 168). He affirms God as having created human beings in his own image, but non-deity, so that the difference therein can be a real partner that is capable of action and responsibility in relation to him (CD III/1, pp.184-185). Here, Barth means to say that human beings were originally meant to mirror God's own being in Jesus Christ, capable of loving and relating to others, despite any differences there may be.

Indeed, God originally created human beings in such a way that it corresponds to his own compatible or analogous eternal being of relatedness to another reality. Here, human beings' earthly being must relate to God and their fellow human beings, signifying that they belong to God who, himself, relates to others in Jesus Christ.

In so doing, human beings will prove that they are covenant partners with God.

What happens if the image of God gets affected in any way? For Barth, any fault with the image of God in human beings would result into sloth of human beings – human beings will distrust God, will not know God, will not have God, will not have any dealings with God and will defy their covenant with God.

> "In its form as man's tardiness and failure, sloth expresses much more clearly than pride the positive and aggressive ingratitude which repays good with evil. It consists in the fact, not only that man does not trust God, but beyond this that he does not love him, i.e. that he will not know Him and have Him, that he will not have dealings with Him, as the One who first loved him, from all eternity (CD IV/2, p.405).

Hence, human beings will tend to give up the meaningfulness of personal experience and human history and the world in which they live.

How does God restore his image in human beings? Barth affirms that God restores his image in human beings through Jesus Christ his Son. Here, Barth conceives of God as being the Father, the Son Jesus Christ and the Holy Spirit, existing in their relation of love. Jesus Christ, as the Son of God, shares God's own inner self-relation. And because Jesus corresponds to and shares God's own eternal self-relation of love, he therefore participates in God's own eternal being, that of relating to another reality and able to have history. Thus, God is for Jesus his Son as much as Jesus is for God his Father. Here, as Jesus Christ becomes a human being, he is for God in his definite form of humanity - that of being for other human beings. This means that Jesus Christ relates to God and human beings, and hence it signifies that he belongs to God in whom he participates in God's own eternal inner self-relation.

Certainly, on his becoming a human being, Jesus restored humanity's broken relationship with God, inasmuch as he participates in and shares in humanity's creation in the image of

God. In so doing, by his Spirit Jesus encourages and empowers believers to restore broken relationships with others in society inasmuch as they will also share their relation and fellowship with them. Moreover, it is not good that a human being be alone but needs company and fellowship. The root cause of broken relationships and isolation in our world today is carelessness toward each other and deliberate selfishness intended to degrade the other person. If only all human beings would be willing to see others as deserving relationship and fellowship, and not deserving isolation. There is no one who can be without the other people in society. We all need others to complement what we are. In Old Malawi, there used to be interdependence among our people. It used to be a terrible thing to be excommunicated from a society in those days. Society was more of a family than just a group.

Solidarity through the Spirit (in the church)

Karl Barth speaks about believers' "awakening to conversion", which is consistent with believers' solidarity through the Spirit (in the church).

> "The Christian community, the true Church, arises and is only as the Holy Spirit works – quickening power of the living Lord Jesus Christ. And it continues and is only as He sanctifies men and their human work, building up them and their work into true Church (CD IV/2, p.617; Gunton 2003)."

He affirms that in the awakening to conversion of sinners, believers live a "life of communion" that mirrors the communion in God's Holy Trinity in Jesus Christ. For Barth:

> "Communion is an action in which on the basis of an existing union (*unio*) many men are engaged in a common movement towards the same union. This takes place in the power and operation of the Holy Spirit, and the corresponding action of those who are assembled and quickened by Him" (CD IV/2, p.617).

Here, Barth refers to "the life of communion in God's Holy Trinity" as believers' participation in the koinonia of the Trinity in Jesus Christ (CD IV/1, pp.149, 150, 150f.153, 643-739; CD IV/2, pp.614-726; CD IV/3, 681-901; Webster 2000: 188, 190, 191):

> "On the basis of the grace of the incarnation, on the basis of the acceptance and assumption of man into unity of being with God as it has taken place in Jesus Christ, all this has become truth in this man, in the humanity of Jesus Christ…He is the eternal Son of God, there is promised to us our own divine sonship, and therefore our fellowship in His knowledge of God" (CD II/1, p.252).

Koinonia of the Trinity is where eternal God exists in community of the eternal Father, the eternal Son, and the eternal Spirit. The eternal Son, here, is not only the eternal God, but he is also the human being Jesus of Nazareth by the incarnation. Hence, it is in the *koinonia* of the community that the work of the Holy Spirit is fulfilled.

> "The work of the Holy Spirit…is the inner upbringing of the community…The Holy Spirit is not a private spirit, but the power by which the Son of God (*Heid. Cat. Qu. 54*) "has from the beginning of the world to the end assembled out of the whole race of man and preserves and maintains, an elect congregation""(CD IV/1, p.149).

Again, Barth refers to members of this communion as "saints" who exist in the world, but do not conform to the world as it were.

> "It is saints who are and act in this communion. The saints are men who exist in the world, and after the fashion of the world, but who, in virtue of the fact that they come from the union presupposed in the event of their communion and move forward to its revelation, are integrated and engaged in self-integration" (CD IV/2, p.642).

Hence, Barth goes on further to describe the life of communion by believers as being in three distinct forms – with Jesus Christ, with God's Holy Trinity, and with one another as humanity. Here, the

Holy Spirit is the one who mediates and unites believers with Christ, through whom they participate in the eternal communion of the Holy Trinity - while at the same time they also find communion with one another. Barth says that such is possible because the Holy Spirit is communal in content in Jesus, such that it is capable of bringing and holding together that which is different.

> "The work of the Holy Spirit, however, is to bring and hold together that which is different..." (CD IV/3, p.761).

Thus, the Holy Spirit serves as the unifying ground for the incarnation when it holds together the otherwise desperate realities of deity and human in Christ's person, and therefore, the communion of one another amongst believers.

> "These men – the – saints = who live and act in the communion of the one Holy Spirit, and therefore in communion one with another are Christians" (CD IV/2, p.642).

Definitely, the incarnate Jesus Christ, as a sharer of everything with God, is a participant in the communion of the Holy Trinity, such that he incorporates human beings into communion with the Holy Trinity of God by his Spirit (the Holy Spirit) - at the same time the incorporated human beings do become members of one another with other human beings, in their daily lives.

Summary

According to Barth, God eternally exists in a relation of Father, Son and Spirit, which extends to human beings, through Jesus Christ the Son of God, as an external expression of the fact that this triune God himself exists in a relation of love. Hence, human beings are made capable of existing structurally in relation.

Jesus willingly died at the cross for the salvation of human beings. At the cross, Jesus Christ was in solidarity with sinful human beings when he did right at the very place where human beings had done wrong, marking his supreme exaltation and human beings', and hence, human beings are made into people who can and will be in solidarity with the poor, the suffering and the vulnerable in society, in their daily lives. In his death on the cross Jesus willingly humbled himself and endured God's rejection of human beings' sin in order that he satisfies God's justice by accepting the responsibility for human beings' sin. Hence, Christians are encouraged and empowered not turn away from justice for all in society on account of any trials they can experience.

On the third day of his burial Jesus rose from the dead. The resurrection is the exaltation of Jesus and the exaltation of human beings, the new creation of human beings' new form of existence. Hence, the death and resurrection of Jesus is a springboard for Christians to stand up for the dignity of others in society, in their daily lives.

Jesus is capable of exalting human beings to new creation because in the first place he united them onto himself. Human beings are united with Jesus in terms of their participation in the eternal love and fellowship of the Triune God. Moreover, God does not keep love and fellowship to himself, but imparts them onto human beings. Hence, Jesus' union with humanity, in the Trinity's eternal love and fellowship, enables Christians to seek love and fellowship with others in society, in their daily lives.

Because of the existence of a unity between Jesus and human beings, Jesus is capable of ascribing on to human beings his election, salvation, and new life – and to himself, he ascribes reprobation, damnation and death. Hence, there is Jesus' transformative power, here, that effects Christians to look to the cause of other fellow human beings, in the midst of the world's hardships and evil, in their daily lives. Jesus, thus, looks to human beings' cause by calling them through his suffering and death and unto his benefits, despite their sinfulness. He thus calls human beings to care for one another in society, despite any differences there may be amongst them. Moreover, God chooses himself for human beings that are different from him in their sinfulness, and such corresponds to an act of human self-determination in which Jesus Christ chose himself for God and other humans in their sinfulness. Hence, Christians must be willing to choose themselves for God and other human beings by doing good works. Human beings can and must do good works because they have peace with God (justified) out of God's justice, mercy, love and grace, through faith in Jesus Christ - and hence, such must be consistent with the making of peace with fellow human beings.

By doing good works, human beings demonstrate that they are called by God to love other human beings. Definitely, in the calling and drawing of the Father to the Son and the Son to the Father there takes place the divine love by which a human person, too, is made one who loves. Here, the calling and drawing of the Father to the Son and the Son to the Father makes every human being into one who will draw into another's love.

Indeed, we cannot interpret the conversion and renewal of human beings merely in terms of a relationship between them and God, to the exclusion of any relationship amongst themselves. As such, Christians ought to see other human beings, as objects of the eternal covenantal love of the Triune God. Indeed, Christians are affected by the Triune God's transformative power and called to see other human beings in their suffering and need of hope, through their good works. Good works are inevitable in the lives of Christians because they have undergone through their calling to discipleship and awakening to conversion. Otherwise, the whole event of reconciliation by God in Jesus has not fulfilled its purpose. Hence, Christians must witness of what God is and does for human beings in their daily lives. Christians may, can and should reflect and practice God's being and acting for humanity.

How can human beings reflect God's being and acting in their daily life? Believers should look onto Jesus as their model. Jesus shares everything with God, and his participation in our image of God is genuine and original in the sense that his humanity is as God had originally intended it to be - belonging to God through relating and fellowshipping with others. Hence, Jesus' belonging to God through his relation and fellowship with others calls for Christians to relate and fellowship with other human beings as a proof of their covenant partnership with God. Moreover, Jesus Christ, is a sharer of everything with God and a participant in the communion of the Holy Trinity, such that he incorporates human beings into communion with the Holy Trinity of God by his Spirit. In so doing, Christians are encouraged to become members one of another with other human beings, in society.

AFFIRMATIONS ON THE REFORMED VIEW OF ATONEMENT

In the light of the atonement views by Anselm, John Calvin, Karl Barth and the *Westminster Confession of Faith*, it may probably be legitimate to develop the following broad consensus of a classic Reformed view of the atonement to be used as a heuristic framework in the rest of the study, in order to describe and understand the situation in the Reformed Church in Malawi (in chapter 3) and to respond to the original questions motivating and guiding this research (in chapter 4).

Covenantal faithfulness of God and God's love for all human beings

The "covenant" is God's decision to elect and save human beings by his grace. This decision came from within God's Holy Trinity's relation of love and partnership. That is why the covenant of God is also known as "the covenant of grace". "Covenant" begins with God himself in his Holy Trinity. God in his trinity has always existed, and still exists in covenant as Father, Son, and the Holy Spirit relations – a relation of love and partnership.

The making of the covenant was recognition that, if a society is to work, it requires a common structure of law to give framework for living. The covenant, therefore, was produced to give a pattern for life. It is as if God is saying, "You belong to me; this is how I want you to live" - "Pattern your life on mine" – "You belong to me, and I want you to live like Jesus my Son." Again in the covenant, Jesus caught up all humanity into his life and was himself caught up into God's equation of justice, by his becoming a human being. He was the bridge in the reconciliation between God and humanity.

In the covenant, also, there is God on one side that does not will to be God without humanity, and on the other side there is humanity that is failing to receive the covenant with God. Therefore, Jesus comes in and addresses the situation with the love from God in him. With the love from God he comes to be with humanity, and hence, humanity comes to be with Jesus.

The incarnation

The "incarnation" is the "becoming flesh" of the divine *Logos* in Jesus Christ. In the incarnation, God assumed mortality of human beings in the person of his Son Jesus Christ. In so doing, Jesus Christ was both human and divine. Jesus assumed human mortality in order that he uses it for reconciliation and redemption of sinful human beings. How did human beings become sinful? Originally and in his grace, God had created human beings without sin so that they honour and obey him. Unfortunately, human beings dishonoured and disobeyed God, and therefore, sinned. As a result, human beings, in their sinfulness, were incapable of honouring and obeying God, except if God himself would come to rescue and free them from their sinfulness.

Certainly, God in his eternal grace, love and compassion rescued human beings from sinfulness by himself becoming a human being, in his Son Jesus Christ, in the incarnation. In the incarnation, therefore, it was crucial for Jesus not to remain above humanity, up in heaven. Neither as God alone could Jesus feel death, nor as man alone could he overcome it.

Again, in the incarnation God's Son Jesus Christ, though divine, did bear humiliation and weakness of the human body, and identified with us sinful humanity, satisfying what we humans owed God. Also, in the incarnation, Jesus acted as God when he acted as a human being. He was the very God and the very humanity. Here, Jesus did unite human essence with his divine essence in order that he addresses the two – one on the other, especially the divine to the human.

Also, because of the incarnation, Jesus Christ was capable of perfectly satisfying the justice of God his Father by his perfect obedience and sacrifice of himself in his death, and hence, purchased reconciliation and everlasting inheritance in the kingdom of heaven for human beings.

The cross as acceptance of those who do not deserve anything (justification), and as a transformative power not to turn away from justice

God does feel bad about human sinfulness. However, in his mercy and love, God continues to love sinful human beings so much that he does not want them suffer the consequences of their sin, the death punishment. It is because of this that God, in his Son Jesus Christ, had to take up the place of sinful human beings by dying on the cross. Here, Jesus was innocent. Jesus Christ, innocent as he was, died once, just like innocent animals that would be sacrificed again and again by shedding of blood, in place of the sinful person making an offering in the Old Testament times.

Jesus had to suffer and die on the cross in order that he makes a proper, real and full satisfaction of his Father's justice on behalf of humanity. He thus did exert a transformative power onto Christians for them to assist in the up-keeping of justice among fellow human beings in the society that they live because human beings need justice for the well-being of their society. It took so much courage, endurance and love for humanity for Jesus to die such a terrible death on the cross. Moreover, he did not violate God's justice himself, but human beings did.

Some people do not understand how a good God would target wrath toward his people because of their sinfulness. However, even though God had wrath against his sinful humanity, but he also had his mercy for his people such that he saved them his Son's death on the cross - and hence God gave humanity room for their rehabilitation in Jesus.

On the cross, it was not humanity that died, but Jesus. Jesus deeply humbled himself by suffering human beings' punishment of sin and died on the cross, and hence, he redeemed them of their sin, once for all. Jesus struggled for God's justice in his suffering and dying on the cross. He thus did suffer God's judgment – humiliation – in humanity's place, but also at the cross he did receive exaltation together with humanity.

If there should have been death of Jesus only, then we should have not been talking about hope or a new form of existence of human beings in the resurrection of Jesus. However, the resurrection is not only the exaltation of Jesus, but is also the exaltation of human beings. The resurrection is the new creation of human beings' or the new form of existence in Jesus Christ.

The resurrection as power of renewal of human life

Human beings were of original perfect body at creation by God. Unfortunately, human beings disobeyed and dishonoured God, and hence, they lost their original perfect body. The result was that they became imperfect, sinful, corrupt and vulnerable. Here, if human beings are to be restored to their original perfect body, as it was at creation, they must be restored with the very body in which they were created and live in this life. That is why Jesus Christ willingly assumed the mortal and vulnerable human body so that he would live human life. In so doing, Jesus did experience a life of humiliation (such as living under the Law of God) and a life of indignities of the world, which he did perfectly fulfil and persevere. Indeed, Jesus Christ went through a life of humiliation in human beings' place and willingly endured God's rejection of human sin. Here, Jesus did accept the responsibility for human beings' sin and death penalty for that sin, so that on his resurrection from the dead he would exalt human believers inasmuch as God his Father would exalt him. Definitely, because Jesus Christ underwent such humiliation and indignities of the world so successfully, God raised him from the dead and exalted him from being a servant to being

Lord of all, which he did as a public person, and the head of the Church.

Without the resurrection of Jesus Christ, therefore, only weakness appears in his death and burial. But Jesus was resurrected so that believers' faith must leap over death and burial to something hopeful that will enable their faith attain its full strength. This "something hopeful" is Jesus Christ's endurance of the shameful death on the cross through his joyful anticipation of his exaltation by God his Father. Certainly, Jesus died on the cross, as human beings were dead for corruption and sin. Therefore, Jesus rose up from the dead on that Easter Sunday to assure all believers of their resurrection with incorruptible and sinless bodies from the dead at some future time.

Union with Jesus Christ

Jesus is a sharer of the eternal Holy Trinity's communion, a virtue that makes him capable of uniting human beings with his person, as much as he is capable of uniting the human beings with the rest of Holy Trinity's communion. It is because of this that Jesus Christ does cleave to believers by an indivisible bond of fellowship in the union with him. With a wonderful communion, day by day, Jesus Christ grows more and more into one body with believers, taking them into fellowship with him, incorporating them into God's kingdom - as much as he gives them fellowship in his knowledge of God, up until he becomes completely with them. Here, believers' union with Jesus becomes effectual in his death and resurrection from the dead. Therefore, Jesus is capable of communicating his perfect satisfaction of God's justice, persuading them to believe and obey the mystery of salvation.

Also, in his union with believers, Jesus was capable of effectually applying and communicating his graces onto them. Because of their union with Jesus Christ, therefore, believers can claim that what belongs to Jesus belongs to them, too.

Again, in his union with human beings, Jesus took into himself human sinfulness and punishment by God and shared the pain therein, of which he so persevered unto death on the cross in anticipation of the benefit of being exalted by God. All in all, in our union with Jesus Christ, as believers, God demonstrates that he does not keep his love and fellowship to himself, but willingly imparts them to his human beings. In his union with humanity, therefore, God calls human beings to live a life of love and fellowship amongst themselves, as much they love God and fellowship with him.

Our election in Jesus Christ by God, despite our failures and weaknesses

Election is God's grace whereby he chooses individuals or groups for a specific purpose or destiny. The election of individuals or groups for a specific purpose by God stems out from the behaviour and character of God as the Father, the Son, and the Holy Spirit, in which God has always been capable to relate to another reality – able to elect and have a history. In temporal terms, election occurs outside of time, and that suggests that it is not itself temporal. Election occurs before the foundation of the world. It occurs eternally in the mind of God. The first election of such kind took place in God's Son Jesus Christ. God the Father elected the Son Jesus in a partnership relation. It is because of this that the Father has always been a Partner of the Son, and the Son has always been a Partner of the Father. Certainly, Jesus Christ himself is very important for human beings' election by God. Moreover, Jesus was the first to be elected by God his Father in order that he becomes Mediator between God and human beings by virtue of his righteous living. Truly, Jesus lived under the Law of God, which he perfectly fulfilled and proved righteous. In so doing, it proves the point that Jesus was made first elect of God in order that he might afterwards elect human beings and share his gifts of righteousness with them. Therefore, Jesus is both the electing God and the elect in his capacity as God-Man.

Indeed, Jesus does elect human beings to become his companions - even though human beings do not deserve it because of their sinfulness. Moreover, human beings were not created lonely creatures right away from the beginning of their existence, but are social animals. Hence, Jesus does elect human beings as his companions by living a life acceptable to God his Father on their behalf. That is, as much as Jesus did live a life acceptable to God his Father, even so he did it for human beings' election and human beings' redemption from all unrighteousness by his application of his righteousness onto them.

All in all, Jesus Christ as Mediator was both God and human in one person in order that he elects humanity for reconciliation with God – through proper works of each nature that might be accepted of God for humanity.

Our calling

God wilfully and effectually calls sinners to discipleship, inviting them to freely will that which is good by coming to Jesus Christ. It is because of this that God grants grace and gifts appropriate to the diversity of callings in life so that each one can carry out his or her appointed duties. Such gifts are to be exercised in faithful service to Jesus Christ so that the restoration of his kingdom is promoted. Jesus Christ taught believers what it means to live one's calling through his experiences of pain and suffering on the cross and in the rest of his earthly life. On the cross and in his life, Jesus teaches believers what it means to live one's calling when, in their midst, he willingly humbled himself in perfect obedience to God's law and justice for their sake, sinful as they are, because he loved them from the heart. However, those that God does not will to call, the reprobate, do wilfully neglect God's calling, and therefore, are contempt of God's grace offered to them, and do never truly come to Jesus Christ. Whilst the elect, despite their sinfulness, are effectually called in Jesus Christ and do partake justification, adoption, and sanctification in this life.

In the calling to discipleship, there is moderation which serves to guide believers in the proper use of creational gifts, given them freely by God, with a humble spirit - and, hence should make them capable of loving their neighbours from the heart. How tempting are creational gifts that we may discover to possess, which are given us freely by God, and hence, one tends to feel full of esteem as frequent use of such gifts grows. Nevertheless, Jesus as a human being had recreational gifts that he used in his life to care for others around him.

Our faith

Faith is connected with God's self-revealing to human beings. God reveals himself in his Word, and hence, faith is having permanent relationship with the Word of God. Here, the Word of God is like a mirror in which human beings gaze upon God himself. Once they see God, they can confidently trust him. Here, it is God who creates faith in human beings in the event of his revelation by his Spirit. He chooses to reveal himself to whom his gift of "faith" is granted, and to whom the gift of "faith" is not yet granted, God remains veiled. God's revelation decides whether an individual will respond to his election in faith and obedience or not.

Faith as a gift from God does enable the Christian to accept the authority of God as he speaks and reveals himself in his Word. In his Word, God speaks to the elect to believe in his salvation for all humanity in Jesus Christ. Hence, faith is response to God's gracious decision for human beings in the person and work of Jesus Christ. That is the reason why Jesus Christ is the Mediator in human beings' relationship with God.

Faith originated from God himself when in Jesus Christ he chose himself for human beings. Indeed, Jesus as Mediator between God and human beings willingly and with love chose himself for other human beings such that we can trust and depend on him as our Lord and Saviour.

As Mediator, Jesus is both the author and finisher of believers' faith in terms of growing up and victory in faith, and therefore, faith does not go with passivity, but calls for "self determination". When granting faith on to human beings, God does choose himself for human beings. Such corresponds to an act of human self-determination in which Jesus Christ chose himself for God and other humans.

Justification in light of who we are

Calvin rejects the efficaciousness of human merit in justification and elaborates on the idea of justification by grace only (*sola gratia*). He insists that the human will plays a passive role in salvation (Kang 2006: 47). For him, justification begins with sinners' faith in God. It begins with the sinners when they begin relating with God and foresee the nature of judgement God has for them. Thus, when sinners come to believe that God will fulfil their promises, even though they do not see those promises materializing yet, they demonstrate true faith. It is by such kind of faith that justification takes place, by which God accepts sinners into his favour as righteous persons. Here, God justifies sinners by virtue of the righteousness of his Son Jesus Christ so that those that are not righteous in and by themselves may be reckoned as such in Jesus. Here, Calvin's doctrine of justification has the synthetic view that for the justification of the sinner something must be added to the sinner: the imputed righteousness of Christ (Kang 2006: 45-46). It is because of this that human justification by God is by "faith alone" in Jesus Christ. For their justification, therefore, Jesus Christ redeems sinners by making them, unconditionally and without merit, accepted by God his Father, in spite of sinfulness and alienation from God. Here, by virtue of his righteousness, Jesus Christ justifies sinners so that they that are not righteous in themselves may be reckoned as such before God. As justified, they now can rest in Jesus Christ because he completely satisfied God's demands and standards of his justice. Indeed, after being justified, believers now become free from slavery of sin, a state that had restricted them from willing and doing freely that which is good and pleasing to God. They now move on from a dead life without God into a lively life for God. Definitely, as justified by God, they are righteous by faith to the exclusion of all works, but at the same time, as justified they are those that have set up righteousness in their lives. Definitely, Jesus justifies sinners by his graces so that they may have peace with God and neighbours.

Justified sinners are those who are righteous by faith to the exclusion of all works, but at the same time, justified human beings are those who have set up righteousness in their life. Therefore, human beings can and must do good works because they are now at peace with God (justified) through God's justice, mercy, love and grace in Jesus Christ.

In the justification of sinners, therefore, Jesus Christ sets an ethical example of compassion and mercy according to our nature as human beings – that of sparing the wicked, and therefore, save the wicked that in justice might be destroyed.

Our adoption

Human beings were of the original status as children of God in their first parents Adam and Eve, before their fall into sin, but lost that status at their fall into sin. Hence, at their fall into sin, all human beings lost the status of being children of God together with Adam and Eve. At the fall, all human beings became children of humanity. However, human beings can regain their former glory as children of God only through a new relationship in God's Son Jesus Christ.

Jesus Christ is a sharer in the Holy Trinity's loving relation, and is himself the first and proper human subject of the knowledge of God. Therefore, only Jesus is capable of adopting human beings into becoming children of God once again. In believers' union with Jesus, he lowers himself onto them, raising them up and taking them into the Holy Trinity's fellowship, where, besides sharing knowledge about God with him, they participate in his love, in which as the Father he loves the Son and as the Son loves the Father.

Certainly, Jesus Christ redeems human beings from being outsiders in God's family, and hence, God make them partakers of his grace of adoption in Jesus Christ. As adopted children of God in

Jesus Christ, therefore, believers are entitled to enjoy the liberties and privileges of the children of God. The liberties and privileges comprise of their putting on of God's name as God's children, their receiving the Spirit of adoption, their having access to the throne of grace with boldness, their being pitied, protected, provided for, and chastened by God as a good father, and inheriting God's promises as heirs of everlasting salvation.

Obedient following of Jesus Christ through renewed life of practicing justice (Sanctification)

There is no sharp line between "justification" and "sanctification." On one hand, "Justification" of a sinner does provide the living context out of which the Christian life lives and grows. Here, the context for Christian living and growth is only possible through believers' union with Jesus Christ. That is, at being justified sinners are empowered to practice true holiness by all saving graces in Jesus Christ's death, resurrection, his Word and the indwelling Spirit. After justification of sinners, therefore, follows an unbroken and continued process towards the exaltation in Jesus Christ of believers.

But "sanctification" is the living and growing process of believers' life towards their exaltation in Jesus Christ. In the process, Jesus Christ makes believer's evil desires, bondage in sin or love of sin die with him in his death on the cross, so that by his resurrection he enables radical transformation of the believers' sinful heart to understand and embrace God's moral order for their life, as powered by the regenerating work of the Holy Spirit.

Regeneration

"Regeneration" is the work of the Holy Spirit in sinners what has already been accomplished in Jesus Christ. The Holy Spirit, here, is an agent for regeneration, therefore, communal in content. It is capable of bringing and holding together that which is different. It serves as the incarnation's unifying ground. The Holy Spirit holds together the otherwise desperate realities of deity and human in Jesus Christ's person.

In "regeneration" are the death and burial of the sinners' old way of life, in the death and burial of Jesus Christ - leading to the sinners' rising up from the dead into new life in the resurrection of Jesus Christ from the dead. Once the sinners' old life is dead and buried, the sinners now have a powerful motive to resist sin. The sinners are now capable of resisting sin because they can now consciously choose to treat the desires and temptations of their old nature as if they were dead.

Indeed, Jesus Christ applies salvation to believers not only for their sanctification, but also for their regeneration. In regeneration, Jesus Christ comes into the hearts and lives of the elect on earth by his Spirit to grow up together with them into one body. Here, as Jesus Christ lives in the hearts of the elect, he connects them to sharing in his graces. It is because of the graces, which Jesus shares with believers, that the elect are capable to practice true holiness.

We are called to conform to the image of God in Jesus Christ

According to the first narrative in Genesis, God created human beings in his own image (Genesis 1:26, 27). Creation of human beings in God's image distinguishes them from all other life forms. Here, the centre of the image of God in human beings is their "soul." Hence, "soul" in Hebrew means *nephesh* – living souls. Since to live is to relate, therefore, the notion of human beings as "living souls" prescribes their relation to God, to their fellow human beings and to the rest of created world.

Certainly, human beings reflect the image of God when they relate and act. Moreover, God's eternal being is that which is capable of acting and relating to another reality and able to have a history. God the Father, the Son, and the Holy Spirit has always been acting and relating, even before the advent of creation. Truly, God wanted his glory in the Holy Trinity, that of acting and relating, to be held in human beings as in a mirror. And human beings do mirror God's acting and relating when they live freely and gladly in relationships of mutual respect and love (in their relation with God, and in their relation with other creatures). Here, the concept of the image of God has something to do with God investing human beings with the rational nature of discernment, so that they might be capable of relating to God, to their fellow human beings and to the rest of creation. It includes human beings' ability to make good judgements in life and to refrain from complaining about struggles. Instead, human beings must see struggles as opportunities to grow in character to God's glory.

However, when the image of God in human beings became effaced and worn away by sin, at the fall of Adam and Eve, humanity became faulty of acting and relating. Human beings willed not to have any dealings with God, and human beings defied their covenant with God. It is because of this that human beings tended to give up the meaningfulness of personal experience, human history and the world in which they lived. Human beings could not even know moral truth, were not drawn to it, and would not choose to practice it.

Nevertheless, God with his mercy and love came to human beings' rescue in his Son Jesus Christ, who became a human being. Jesus Christ shares everything with God. Hence, when Jesus became a human being, he was truly a human being created in the image of God, genuine and original in the sense that it was as God had originally intended it to be. Jesus as the true image of God was successful in making good judgements in life and never complained about the struggles he had in life for human salvation. Therefore, when Jesus obeyed God his Father and suffered and died on the cross for human beings' salvation, he proved that he belonged to God. He willingly maintained his obedience to God his Father by upholding God's truth and justice in life and word, of which he so persevered unto his death on the cross. Hence, the renewal of the image of God in human beings was accomplished through the redemptive work of Jesus Christ, and is the goal of the Christian life.

On his becoming a human being, Jesus restored humanity's broken relationship with God, inasmuch as he participates in and shares in humanity's creation in the image of God. Moreover, it is not good that a human being be alone but needs company and fellowship. Our neighbours deserve dignity, our respect and our protection from any harm or danger as our own flesh - and once again, this characteristic Reformed conviction, at the heart of the doctrine of atonement, will prove to be of extreme importance.

Jesus is the true image of God to which Christians are called to conform. Here, there is the outward aspect of believers' imitation of the death of Jesus Christ in bearing the cross, which involves accepting the hardships, and difficulties that God brings into our lives, both the afflictions we share with all human beings and those undergone for the sake of the gospel and the cause of righteousness.

Solidarity through the Spirit (in the church)

God the eternal Father, the eternal Son and the eternal Holy Spirit exists in solidarity as community (*koinonia*) of the Holy Trinity. The eternal Son became human in the incarnation as Jesus of Nazareth, yet he still existed in solidarity with the Holy Trinity. Here, on his becoming human, as Jesus of Nazareth, he did incorporate believers into himself, making them partakers in communion with the Trinity. In so doing Jesus makes believers partakers in his graces of suffering, death, resurrection and glory.

It is the eternal Holy Spirit, here, which fulfils believers' participation in the *koinonia* with the Holy Trinity. Here, by his Spirit, Jesus Christ unites believers onto himself in order that he gathers them up as a community of faith, builds them up in love and sends them out into the world in hope. In so doing, human beings find themselves members of one of another with other human beings, in their daily lives.

Again, Jesus gathers his Church by his Spirit in the Sacraments of Baptism and the Lord's Supper. He has dedicated and sanctified the Sacrament of Baptism to form believers as the firmest bond of their union and fellowship with him and with other members of Jesus' Church. Jesus did, also, dedicate and sanctify the Sacrament of the Lord's Supper for believers' mutual sharing of his broken body (his Church), his love and one another's love as members of the one Church of Jesus Christ. The sacraments are integral to the means by which the Spirit keeps believers in connection with Christ and with one another – and therefore it is crucial for a Reformed understanding of the atonement that any form of disregard for the dignity of the brothers and sisters contradict our participation in baptism and the Lord's Supper, which, vice versa, make the sacraments powerful instruments in the service of human rights. Here, for example, the Lord's Supper produces a life together in mutual sharing and love as Christians – and therefore Christians to anticipate, in the midst of present suffering, God's promise of a new, liberated, and reconciled humanity in a new heaven, a new earth and a new community. Here, our lack of love in our human society as believers may contradict our participation in the Supper.

All in all, only those that are united with Christ does he gather to form the "Communion of Saints", such that they find themselves uniting to one another in love, having communion in each other's gifts and grace and being in solidarity in times of suffering and need – hence such is solidarity of the Spirit.

JESUS CHRIST'S ACTIVE AND PASSIVE OBEDIENCE

From the classic Reformed view of the atonement that has been formed in this research study, above, it is very important for this section, therefore, to go on to discuss what is called in this tradition Jesus' active obedience and Jesus' passive obedience, before giving special attention to the Reformed notion about Jesus Christ's active obedience to God his Father, which is capable of impressing on the Christian believers Jesus' ethical examples for their renewed life (in 2.8).

Jesus Christ's "passive" obedience and Jesus' "active" obedience are the two core notions, in the Reformed tradition and theology about human salvation by the Lord Jesus Christ. While in one sense Jesus Christ was passive in his obedience toward his Father, in the sense that he suffered and died on the cross for human salvation - in another sense he was actively obedient toward his Father when he willingly and perfectly fulfilled God's law in his offering himself as an atoning sacrifice for sin, as a high priest (Hebrews 7:27). Because the terms "active" and "passive" are a bit confusing, some theologians prefer using the terms "preceptive" and "penal" to describe Jesus' work.

In his "passive obedience," Jesus did satisfy the penal requirement of the law by his suffering and death on the cross. He suffered and died on the cross in human beings' stead to pay the just penalty of human beings' sin. His passive obedience means believers' guilt is gone on the basis of Jesus' finished work on the cross, and hence, the righteousness of Jesus is imputed onto the believers at that point in time. But if all that Jesus had done for human beings were merely to remove from them the guilt of their past sin, it would then have been to believers' own efforts to go forward in righteousness through their own satisfaction of the law, an expectation that all human beings are incapable of.

Therefore, God in Jesus came to human beings' rescue. By his "active obedience", Jesus' perfect obedience to the law satisfied all the law's "precepts". He was righteous because he did what the law of God required. By this perfect life of righteousness Jesus, thus, makes a perfect positive righteousness available by imputation to all who believe. His active obedience means that believers have positive righteousness with God. Based on Jesus' active obedience, believers' are clothed with the perfect righteousness of Jesus. This far, Jesus has not merely paid the penalty of Adam's first sin, and the penalty of the sins, which human beings individually have committed, but also he has positively merited for believers new and eternal life. He has, certainly, paid the penalty of sin for believers, but, also, he has stood the probation for them in their new life with him (and hence, their life is sanctified by the Holy Spirit and they are called to discipleship, they are adopted into children of God, they are called to live a life of regeneration, they are called to live a life of conformation to the image of God with Jesus as their example and they gather as one church of Jesus Christ, powered by the Holy Spirit of God. Here, believers, thus, respond by doing good works out of gratitude for what God has done for them in Jesus. In so doing, those who have been saved by Jesus not only are righteous in the sight of God, but they are beyond the possibility of becoming unrighteous.

While theologians do correctly make distinctions between Jesus obedience in fulfilling the law as precept and penalty, the Bible itself does not make such clear-cut distinctions. Instead, the Bible simply speaks of obedience of Jesus – the whole obedience of Jesus, which includes his active and passive obedience - as the basis of justification of sinful human beings. Nevertheless, the active (preceptive) and passive (penal) obedience of Jesus are but different aspects of the same thing. This distinction is not so presented in the Bible as though the obedience of Jesus answered one purpose, and his suffering another and distinct purpose. However, the distinction becomes important only when it is denied that Jesus' ethical obedience is any part of the righteousness for which the believer is justified, or that his whole work in making satisfaction consisted only in expiation or bearing the penalty of the law.

However, this twofold obedience of Jesus lies at the heart of the atonement, and that this obedience, which transforms believers, reveals the more comprehensive dimensions of the atonement. These more comprehensive dimensions of the Reformed view of the atonement lay theological foundations for the involvement of churches in the building of a human rights culture.

All in all, the distinction is very important for this research study as it gives special attention to Jesus Christ's active obedience to God his Father, and what it is capable of impressing on the Christian believers as Jesus' ethical examples for their renewed life. The implications for the pursuit of human justice and for the respect for human dignity are immediately obvious – particularly if it can be shown that the life and ministry of Jesus' own obedience and fulfilment of the law, his call to discipleship, and therefore his union with believers through his resurrection and through the Spirit, including the sacraments, include precisely such a pursuit for justice and respect for the divine image in other human beings, our own flesh, in John Calvin's words.

JESUS' ACTIVE OBEDIENCE AND ITS TRANSFORMATIVE EFFECT

After the discussion about Jesus' active obedience and Jesus' passive obedience, above, this research study, therefore, gives special attention to Jesus Christ's active obedience to God his Father, according to the Reformed view of the atonement, which is capable of impressing on the Christian believers as Jesus' transformative power for their renewed life. As much as Jesus Christ is actively obedient to God his Father, in the light of the Reformed view of the atonement, also, Jesus by his Spirit influences and empowers believers to mirror him and his obedience to God his Father, in their daily lives, as people of a covenant with their God.

Indeed, Jesus' active obedience to God his Father was meant for God's covenantal faithfulness to his human beings. Hence, human beings' response as their active obedience to God - as regards to Jesus' transformational power that affects believers - is not done in isolation. Here, Jesus' transformational power over believers for their renewed life does stem out of Jesus' active obedience to God for the demands of God's law, without which their response as active obedience to God would be baseless, and therefore, meaningless.

Again, Jesus' active obedience to God is so called because it stems out of God's divine and human work for salvation of human beings. Indeed, Jesus' active obedience towards God is so amazing, and is full of God's grace, love, care and compassion because it is done for human beings' good - so sinful and corrupt as they are - such that they are forcibly moved to embrace Jesus as their ethical example for their renewed life, in which they love and care for God and others in return. As the analysis of the thinking of John Calvin, Karl Barth and the Westminster Confession shows, Jesus' Christ's active obedience to God and his work toward human beings' renewed life can serve as framework to describe and understand the situation and the contemporary challenges regarding justice, dignity and rights in the Church of Central African Presbyterian, in Malawi.

1.   Jesus as a transformative power for human beings to be capable of self-giving and entering into communion with God and other human beings, in God's covenantal faithfulness to his people

In his covenantal faithfulness God decided to elect and save human beings in his grace, a decision that came from within his Holy Trinity's relation of love and partnership. Therefore, in the fullness of time God extended himself to human beings through his Son Jesus Christ in the bid to save them, an external expression of the fact that he exists in the relation of love and partnership. Here, Jesus, sinless as he is, willingly actualises God's covenant of grace in time and space.

As a true image of God, Jesus relates to human beings that are different from him because of their sinfulness, and hence, as new beings in Jesus Christians ought to exist structurally in relation with other human beings, despite any differences there may be. Therefore, as human beings are created in the image of God, they are not just something, but are people called by grace to covenant with the Creator God, and therefore, capable of self-giving and entering into communion with God and other human beings.

2.   Though divine, Jesus willingly became fully human in body and soul in the incarnation in order that he might unite and fellowship with other human beings

In the incarnation, God assumed human body in the person of his Son Jesus Christ. Here, Jesus, though human, belongs to the very same existence and life of God. In so doing, Jesus was both human and divine. Though divine, Jesus willingly became fully human in body and soul, and therefore, became of a common human nature and fellowship with other human beings. He willingly became fully human in body and soul so that through that he might unite himself and fellowship with other human beings. As followers of Jesus Christ, believers ought to affirm their union and fellowship with other human beings in society.

3. *By giving himself to die on the cross, Jesus, thus, did set an ethical example for Christians not to turn away from justice on account of any trials they can experience*

Human beings had violated the justice of God, and therefore, became sinful. God does feel bad about human sinfulness. However, in his mercy and love, God continues to love human beings such that he does not want them to suffer consequences of their sin alone. Therefore, God sent his Son Jesus Christ to take up the place of sinful human beings and to die on the cross. Jesus, thus, made a proper, real, and full satisfaction of his Father's justice in behalf of human beings when he willingly died on the cross as a sin offering. By giving himself to die on the cross, Jesus did strive to see God's justice prevail, which is Jesus' call impressed upon Christians, by the Holy Spirit, not to turn away from justice on account of any trials they can experience.

4. *Through his resurrection, Jesus Christ invites human beings to strive after newness of life*

God originally created human beings of perfect body. However, at the fall into sin, human beings became imperfect and vulnerable. Hence, if human beings are to be restored to their original perfect body, as was it at creation, they must be restored with the very body in which they were created and live in this life. Therefore, God in Jesus willingly assumed mortality of human beings' body when he became a human being, and hence, lived a life of humiliation unto death. Jesus, thus, willingly endured God's rejection of human beings' sin and accepted the responsibility for human sin and death – and hence, humiliated himself. However, on his resurrection from the dead, God his Father exalted him inasmuch he did exalt all human beings unto new life in him – and hence, Jesus invites human beings to strive after newness of life in his resurrection.

What does "new life in Jesus' resurrection" mean? New life in Jesus' resurrection means that human beings enter a life in which they think and act, as they never did before. Once they were dead in sin and buried with Jesus Christ, but now have risen to life with Jesus. This new life in the resurrection of Jesus is something foreign to their former fallen nature. Their new life, besides pointing towards their resurrection from the dead after this life, it is here and now, in this life, swayed by new motives; their new life, besides their having a hope of immortality, it causes them to purify themselves in this life, here and now, in preparation for its realization. Once, they lived to please themselves in this life, but they now live this life to please God. Once they lived for what they could get for themselves in this life, but now their conduct in this life is controlled by the rule of the heart-searching God.

5. *Jesus Christ unites with human beings as an external extension of his love and fellowship with other human beings*

Jesus Christ is a sharer of the Holy Trinity's communion and fellowship, and therefore a virtue that made him capable to relate and unite with human beings. By his Spirit and by grace alone, Christ engrafts human beings into his life. Once engrafted into Jesus Christ, human beings participate, through faith, in his relationship with the Father and in the benefits of his life, death and the resurrection, endowed him by the Father.

Therefore, when Jesus willingly took onto himself the very curse, pain and suffering of the cross, God declared his love to all persons, the benefit of which falls forever upon those who adhere to his Jesus Christ. Jesus' union with human beings, therefore, enables the human beings to participate in his righteousness before God, inasmuch as he becomes the bearer of their sin. Jesus, thus, affirms that he does not keep love and fellowship to himself, but imparts these to human beings by the power of the Holy Spirit. Christians, too, ought to seek love and fellowship with others in society, in their daily lives as new beings in Christ.

6. *Jesus elected human beings when he willingly lived a life acceptable to God his Father for them*

Jesus is the Head of human beings' election. It is in Jesus that human beings are elected, and it is their election that they are in Christ. They are "chosen in him". They are elected into him. Formerly, human beings were in themselves, but now the love and Grace of God, into Jesus Christ, calls them out of themselves. When in themselves, they were wicked and depraved in darkness and sin, and they had no desire for God or the things of God. But they are now in God, and they have his righteousness. Now, they have desire for God and things of God.

But why are human beings elected? First, we should keep in mind that God, first, elected his Son Jesus Christ in order that he might afterwards elect human beings to share in his benefits of his life, death, and resurrection. Indeed, Jesus did this when he willingly lived a life acceptable to God his Father for human beings. In so doing, he elected human beings to live a life acceptable to God for other human beings. Therefore, human beings that have been chosen by Jesus "should be holy and without blame before God by love". "Holy" conveys the thought of being different and being separate. Elected human beings should be different from other human beings that are not elected in character and behaviour. "Without blame" refers to the sacrificial animals that were without blemish or defect. Elected human beings are called to live a spotless life, a life full of love for other human beings – and hence, God-like love in his Son Jesus Christ – a life possible by the work of the Spirit of Christ.

7. *Jesus called and drew human beings to himself in order that they be made into people who love God and other human beings*

Calling began with God himself when the Father was called and drawn to the Son, and when the Son was called and drawn to the Father, in a divine love. In turn, Jesus called and drew human beings to himself and his love when he willingly humbled himself in his experiences of pain and sufferings on the cross and in the rest of his earthly life, in human beings behalf and for their satisfaction of God's justice. Jesus' calling and drawing into his Father's love calls for transformation in the lives of believers as they, too, are drawn into Jesus' love and that of his Father God. It is because of this that Jesus makes human beings into people who love other human beings without conditions. This affirms that it is "love" that matters most of all, in being a follower of Jesus.

Jesus calls human beings to live a life of "loving God" and "of loving and caring for other human beings." "Love" is the opposite of selfishness, of showing off, of competing and trying to show up and shut out other human beings. "Love" is not the constant focus on the self, but instead, it is a focussing on Jesus, a being centred in him.

8. *Jesus justifies human beings in order that they love other human beings, in spite of who they are and their being different*

God in Jesus Christ is the author and finisher of human beings' faith, sinful as they are. As an author of faith, Jesus chose himself for God and other fellow human beings, and as a finisher of faith, he grows up human beings' faith to the point of applying his righteousness on to them for their resting in him, despite their sinfulness. Hence, it is human beings' justification.

In justification, Jesus Christ redeems human beings by making them, unconditionally and without merit, accepted by God his Father, in spite of who they are and their alienation from God. In their justified life, human beings have the justice of God, which is the same as the justice of Jesus. Therefore, a bond of friendship is created between God and human beings, and the resemblance and the image of the Son is now on them (Romans 8:29), and a relationship of love and friendship between God and human beings is established. At the same time, human beings, unconditionally and without merit, will in gratitude be capable of loving other human beings and doing them the same justice they received from God through Jesus.

9. *Jesus Christ adopts human beings into his love, and that of the triune God, in order that they love other human beings with a spirit of adoption*

By virtue of his status as a sharer in the love and fellowship of the Holy Trinity, Jesus Christ, in justification, adopts human beings into love and fellowship with himself and into the love and fellowship of the rest of the Trinity. Jesus, thus, adopts human beings into his love, in which the Father loves the Son, and the Son loves the Father. Here, God's love for human beings in Jesus is not some vague instinct that happens automatically in God, rather but God invites each human being individually to become his chosen child. Hence, human beings' adoption into children of God in Jesus should make each and every believer into one who loves other human beings in society.

Again, the love of the three divine Persons for each other is not a natural instinct that just happens without anybody willing it. On the contrary, each of the divine Persons chooses to love the other divine Persons. It is as if these divine relationships must be renewed at each instant or the Trinity would fall apart. That seems unthinkable, and it is. It is unthinkable, however, because the Trinity's intentional love is so intense that one cannot imagine God having a change of heart over his intention to love everybody. And so, must human beings, whom Jesus adopts into the love of God, are drawn into willing to choose to love other human beings in relationships that must be renewed at each instant.

10. *Jesus Christ, by his Spirit, transforms human beings' sinful hearts to understand and embrace God's love, moral order and justice for their lives in society*

In the person of Jesus, the Son of God, human beings are sanctified and therefore, renewed. This is possible because Jesus Christ himself is the "last Adam" or "second Adam" (cf. 1 Corinthians 15:45, 47). He is the first born of all creation, and a source of new humanity. Therefore, salvation involves participating in that new humanity, so as to live the human life now as God refashioned it in his Son Jesus Christ (cf. Colossians 3:10). This understanding of humanity as made new in Jesus, by God's transforming power, throws light on the New Testament affirmation that, while human beings are not saved because of works, they are created in Jesus for good works (Ephesians 2:8 ff). Good works are the fruit of the freedom God has given Christians in his Son Jesus.

In sanctification, therefore, Jesus Christ, by his Spirit, enables radical transformation of Christians' sinful hearts choose to understand and embrace God's moral order for their lives. This is not the natural freedom to choose between alternatives, but freedom to do God's will.

> "Jesus Christ has set me free from the law of sin and death... in order that the just requirement of the law of sin and death might be fulfilled in us" (Romans 8:2, 4).

Christians are, therefore, freed and enabled to keep the Commandments of God by the power of the Holy Spirit, to live faithfully as God's people and to grow in love within the discipline of the community, bringing forth the fruit of the Spirit - promoting love, moral order and justice in society.

11. *In regeneration, Jesus grows together with the elect into one body, sharing his Spirit with them, and hence, sets an example, whose pattern the elect ought to express in their daily life*

As the elect of God, Christians come away from condemnation to justification based on the righteousness of God's Son Jesus imputed on to them or charged to their account. This righteousness is the merit of Jesus' whole work of redemption for his followers.

Therefore, in regeneration, Jesus Christ, by his Spirit, imparts or gives a new principle of life and faith - the very life of God which is Jesus - into the hearts and lives of the elect on earth. Hence, Jesus grows up together with them into one body, sharing his Spirit with them. Here, Jesus, through whom the elect return into favour with God, has been set before Christians as an example, whose pattern they ought to express in their daily life. Therefore, this affirms that regeneration always results in a new way of living in society.

12.   In his redemptive work, Jesus accomplished the renewal of the image of God in human beings

God created human beings to conform to his image, enduing them with his knowledge, righteousness, and true holiness. Of course, in every way the image of God in Christians should be informed and governed by the character of the triune God, who is relational in his very being. Therefore, every bit of a Christian should mirror and represent God. As a mirror reflects, so Christians should reflect God. When Christians are what they ought to be, others should be able to look and see something of God in them. Here, Christians are not just what they are, but are also what they do. As God, in his relational character and being to his creation, is kindness and goodness, so must Christians be what they ought to be through their kindness and goodness to God and other human beings. Only, then can it be said that human beings are indeed the image of God and are reflecting God.

However, when the image of God in human beings became effaced and worn away by sin, human beings were no longer related to God. That is, when this chief relationship left, the straightening and informing effect on all other acts and relationship left, too. Nevertheless, God came to human beings' rescue in his Son Jesus Christ. Jesus Christ is thus the true image of God (Colossians 1:15). Looking at Jesus, therefore, Christians are able to see what they should be like in terms of the true image of God. As one among the triune God and as himself a true image of God, Jesus shares everything about God's relational character of kindness and goodness to own being and to his creation. That is why Jesus was wholly directed toward God and neighbour, in his whole life (Matthew 26:39; Mark 10:45; John 15:13). Again, in his redemptive work, Jesus was capable of accomplishing the renewal of the image of God in human beings, which is the goal of the Christian life. As the goal of the Christian life, therefore, Jesus Christ's life is set before Christians as an example, whose pattern they ought to express in their lives, that of being wholly directed toward God and other human beings. Here, Christians are not to consider that other human beings merit of themselves, but instead they should look upon the image of God in all human beings to which they owe all honour and love. To honour and love the divine image impressed upon other human beings is to embrace own human flesh.

13.   *Jesus willingly unites with human beings into himself when he gathers his Church through the Spirit (in the church)*

Jesus Christ gathers his Church by willingly uniting human beings into himself by his Spirit (the Holy Spirit's power). Here, the Holy Spirit is not a private spirit, and therefore, he gathers the Church. The Holy Spirit, hence, presupposes community, and community presupposes individuals. Of course there cannot be one without the other. Again, Jesus willingly gathers his Church in his death through the Lord's Supper. The Lord's Supper signifies human life in togetherness of mutual sharing and love. Hence, Jesus and his death constitutes a transformational power that effect Christians to live a life of mutual sharing and love with other human beings in society, in their daily life.

SUMMARY AND EVALUATION

This chapter tried to argue for the Reformed view of the atonement, but within the atonement notions of Anselm of Canterbury, John Calvin, Karl Barth, and the Westminster Confession of Faith. Special attention was given to Jesus Christ's active obedience to God his Father. In the course of the discussion about Jesus' relation to God his Father, in salvation of human beings, the chapter demonstrated that Jesus Christ's active obedience to God his Father is so amazing, so full of God's grace, love, care and compassion for human beings – even though human beings are so sinful and corrupt - such that the human beings are forcibly moved to embrace Jesus as a transformational power for their renewed life, in which situation they will find themselves in love and care for God and others. Again, the chapter demonstrated that, Jesus' active obedience to God and Jesus' earthly life, by the power of the Holy Spirit, does impress transformation in the lives of believers - both of which do stem out from the emphasis on Jesus Christ's deity and humanity by the Reformed view of the atonement. Jesus' active obedience to God his Father, thus, does lead to Jesus' transformational effect for believers' renewed lives, in the sense that it is a revelation of the kind of renewed life that the believers are called to participate in. Definitely, here, Jesus Christ does become believers' measure and transformational power with which they are able to relate to God and others in society. The question is what kind of implications this typically Reformed understanding of the atonement could and should have for Reformed churches and believers in Malawi, especially for the participation in life and in society, today?

CHAPTER 3

THE REFORMED VIEW OF THE ATONEMENT IN CONTEMPORARY MALAWI

INTRODUCTION

Chapter 2 tried to argue for the classic Reformed understanding of atonement, particularly in the notion of Jesus' active obedience and Jesus' transformational power for our renewed life, in this tradition. Hence, it was concluded that there is, in Jesus' active obedience to God his Father, Jesus' love, care and compassion for his fellow human beings - so sinful and corrupt as they are - such that these human beings are forcibly moved by the Holy Spirit to embrace Jesus for their renewed life, in which situation they will find themselves in love and care for God and others. Therefore, this chapter will investigate whether and how the Church of Central Africa Presbyterian in Malawi did receive or did not receive the Reformed view of atonement in Chapter 2, and especially whether or not they did receive or did not receive Jesus' active obedience and Jesus' transformational power, through the Holy Spirit, for a renewed life.

The organization of the chapter is in four sections. The first section is the background, and hence, explains the history of the Church of Central Africa Presbyterian. The second section discusses the Church of Central Africa Presbyterian's official views of the atonement, in terms of the same categories that were found in the description of the classic Reformed understanding. The third section discusses Jesus Christ's active obedience and the Christian life with a view to Malawi, today, and contrasts findings about the popular views in sermons and in the church with these official positions. The fourth section is the conclusion.

BACKGROUND

The Church of Central Africa Presbyterian, popularly known as "General Assembly of the CCAP", herewith, in this research study, also referred to as the Reformed Church in Malawi, has its roots from the Church of Scotland. The Scottish missionaries planted this church in Malawi between 1875 and 1876, as they were responding to David Livingstone's [18] appeal for evangelisation and economic transformation of that part of Africa, in addition to fighting slave trade, which was still going on there despite its abolition in Europe and America (Ross 1996: 18, 39, 65; Paas, Steven 2006 (b): 188-198). There were two mission groups of the Church of Scotland that came to Malawi (Sinclair 2002: 17). One group was from the Free Church of Scotland (popularly known as "Livingstonia Mission") that came to Malawi in 1875 and settled in the Northern Region of Malawi (Ross 1995: 41). The other group was from the Established Church of Scotland (popularly known as "Blantyre Mission") that came to Malawi in 1876 and settled in the Southern Region of Malawi (Ross 1995: 43).

Although these were two divided groups, all along they worked together until they eventually emerged to become one church in Malawi in the year 1924. And in 1926, the Dutch Reformed Church of South Africa missionaries in the central region of Malawi joined the union, as a third partner to the church, to become one local Church of Central Africa Presbyterian, independent of their mother churches in Britain and South Africa, and having its own constitution. The Church of Central Africa Presbyterian, being Presbyterian and Reformed, is a member church of the World Alliance of Reformed Churches (WARC) through its regional membership to the Southern Africa Alliance of Reformed Churches.

Hence, the Church of Central Africa Presbyterian's Reformed view of the atonement, under investigation in this chapter, is

---

[18] David Livingstone, from Scotland, did many explorations of Africa in the 19th century, at a time when the African continent was known as "the Dark Continent". He visited Malawi in 1859.

contained in the following confessions: the Nicene Creed, the Apostles' Creed, the Westminster Confession of Faith, the Westminster Shorter and Larger Catechisms, the Heidelberg Catechism, the Belgic Confession of Faith, the Canon of Dort, the Church of Central Africa Presbyterian's Confession of Faith of 1924, the Church of Central Africa Presbyterian Synods' catechisms and the Constitution of Church of Central Africa Presbyterian.

THE CHURCH OF CENTRAL AFRICA PRESBYTERIAN'S VIEW OF THE ATONEMENT

Does the Church of Central Africa Presbyterian share the classic Reformed understanding of the doctrine of the atonement? In order to answer this question, it is helpful to begin with the views expressed in these official confessional documents of the Church. The different categories that came to the fore in the earlier analysis of the classical Reformed view of the atonement may again be used as a framework in terms of which to summarize the official positions of the Church of Central Africa Presbyterian.

Covenantal faithfulness of God

In these official documents, the Church of Central Africa Presbyterian affirms that God willed and intended to save human beings from their sins, in his Son Jesus Christ, from way back in the eternity, before creation – and hence,

> "In the fullness of time - after God had completed his work of creating the world - God sent his Son Jesus Christ to save all humanity from their sins in his covenant of grace" (Synod of Blantyre Larger Catechism, Question 45).

Jesus Christ is the only way to God. He is God's love and salvation for all human beings. As the Son of God, Jesus is the only authentic "Mediator" between God and human beings in this covenant of grace. There is a saying in Malawi that says, "A good friend is the one who attends and supports you in times of hardships or trouble." Hence, the Reformed Christians in Malawi would understand Jesus, here, as a friend indeed in the sense that he came at the right time, when human beings were still troubled by their sinfulness. In traditional Malawi, the ancestral spirits (like Jesus) acted as the servants of the Great Spirit, and were regarded as having power from the Great Spirit – God - to be in charge of the people's affairs (Hara 2008: 173). Such did have a transformative effect on the people, which resulted into thanks-offerings by the people, towards the spirits, as a gesture. In this direction, a Tanzanian theologian has it that Christ is our ancestor (Nyamiti 1984: 7; Wendland & Hachibamba 2007: 350). Hence, Jesus, just like the ancestral spirits, has a transformative effect on Reformed Christians in Malawians to assist others in society in times of need, disasters and other hardships. Moreover, others in society are just as human as the Christians are.

There have been times when some of our people in Malawi have been hit by such disasters as floods, and their properties destroyed or washed away. Sometimes, in such situations the Malawi government has been unable to cope with the gravity of disasters alone, and has had to call upon non-governmental charity organizations to assist. Interestingly, some amongst such charitable organizations are Christian that depend on local donations, particularly from the individual Christians in Malawi, and they trust that Christians will at least give generously.

Again, the covenant of grace in Jesus Christ has always been administered after one and the same manner. Both the Old Testament and the New Testament have Jesus Christ as their focal point, but with two different administrations. Here, Jesus Christ who was to come was fore-signified by the Law in the Old Testament. That is, the prophets in the Old Testament taught people the Word of God to build them in faith in the promised kingdom of God in Jesus Christ. Here, in practical life of the Church of Central Africa Presbyterian, many members conceive of their pre-Christian ancestors as having known God. Dr. Handwell

Yotamu Hara, in Malawi, comments that a traditional Malawian (pre-Christian Malawian) was very religious and he or she carried religion wherever he or she went (Hara 2008: 173). The traditional Malawian knew God as "the Great Spirit" (*Mulungu*) who gave Malawian ancestral spirits great power to be in charge of the people's affairs. That is, God did love the pre-Christian ancestors in Malawi, just as God loved the Old Testament believers who lived in the time when the message of Jesus Christ was not there, and whose faith God targeted toward the Messiah who was to come – and hence, experienced salvation (Ross 1998:42, 43). The church in Malawi holds the belief that Jesus Christ as Logos has been active in human life and history from the beginning and that all people have access to God in Jesus Christ through the best of their tradition – the classical Christian teaching of the *logos spermatikos*. The incarnation, therefore, does not bring something totally discontinuous with previous experience, but rather the fulfilment of the antecedent traditions, which reflect the presence of the *logos spermatikos*.

Incarnation

The Church of Central Africa Presbyterian affirms that human sinfulness against God prompted the incarnation.

> "On our own and in our sinfulness, we were not worthy to stand before God as righteous people, and hence, we deserved punishment. Therefore, it should have been unfortunate for us if there had been no-one righteous and sinless to perfectly fulfil the law of God in our behalf. Indeed, there was none among us to stand for us all, until the Son of God Jesus Christ, our Lord, was born of Mary by the power of the Holy Spirit" (*Synod of Nkhoma Catechism*, p.60).

The Lord Jesus Christ was born of the Virgin Mary, a true human being and true God, yet without sin.

> "The Lord Jesus Christ, being conceived by the power of the Holy Spirit, and born of the virgin Mary yet without sin, was true man and true God" (CCAP. Constitution 2000: 20). "Jesus Christ humbled himself by stripping off himself the divine glory, by being born of the Virgin Mary and by living on earth as a true human being, but without sin" (*Synod of Blantyre Larger Catechism*, Question 46).

It is culturally right in Malawi that any outsider, whether holding a high position where he or she is coming from or not, needs to humble oneself and in so doing be able to assimilate into the Malawian society. Once assimilated, it is believed that the foreigner will learn from the people – their failures or successes – at the same time the foreigner is capable of respecting and appreciating them. If need arises that the foreigner wants to assist, he or she will have been knowledgeable already about the gravity of the problem, and hence, will be able to assist appropriately. Hence, the Church of Central Africa Presbyterian affirms that Jesus Christ was born both divine and human in order that he might appropriately reconcile God with human beings (*Blantyre Synod Larger Catechism*, Question 48). Most Reformed Christians in Malawi would understand the notion of God in Jesus, who stripped off the glory of his divinity and putting on humanity as proper for himself if he was to assimilate into the human community and be capable of bailing out the humanity from their sinfulness. Hence, the Anglican Bishop James Tengatenga, in Malawi, describes Jesus in the incarnation as the visible presence (sacrament) of God to the world (Tengatenga 2006: 196). Such a conviction would also make sense to Reformed people in Malawi.

Truly, human beings were sinful against God, and incapable of saving themselves (*Synod of Blantyre Larger Catechism*, Question 59). They could only be saved by the grace of God through the redeeming work of Jesus Christ, and the regenerating and sanctifying work of the Holy Spirit (*CCAP. Constitution* 2000: 20).

Therefore, the Church of Central Africa Presbyterian goes on to explain that Jesus Christ,

> "...as a human being lived a humble and poor life as a servant, teaching people about the kingdom of God, healing the sick, raising the dead, did good works wherever he travelled and finished his work by dying on the cross on behalf of human beings" (*Synod of Blantyre Larger Catechism*, Question 49).

In so doing, Jesus Christ became Mediator of sinful human beings.

> "As we were worthy of experiencing sufferings and death because of our sinfulness, Jesus our Lord took all this upon himself on our behalf. By taking these upon himself on our behalf, he became our Mediator, sinless, holy, righteous and capable of taking upon himself in his being punished on our behalf" (*Synod of Nkhoma Catechism*, p.44).

Jesus perfectly fulfilled the Law of God in behalf of human beings so that they who were sinful should be righteous in him.

> "In his life on earth the Lord Jesus loved God and his fellow human beings, and hence, perfectly fulfilled the law of God. Here, his divinity made him capable of fulfilling the law of God" (*Synod of Nkhoma Catechism*, p.61).

In the incarnation, therefore, Jesus humbled himself by stripping off himself the divine glory and was born and lived as a true human being, and hence, was capable of fulfilling the Law of God on behalf of human being. Jesus, thus, bailed out human beings from their misery in sin.

Jesus Christ's death on the cross

The Church of Central Africa Presbyterian affirms that humanity's violation of the Law of God led to its sinfulness, and hence, all humanity deserved the curse and punishment of the law. However, God in Jesus Christ died for human beings on the cross, taking upon him all their sins – and hence saved and justified them.

> "Jesus Christ died on the cross for us, taking upon himself all our iniquities, for our salvation and justification" (*Synod of Blantyre Larger Catechism*, Question 50).

Here, the Church of Central Africa Presbyterian conceives of Jesus Christ as offering himself on the cross once, a true and perfect sacrifice, unlike the animal sacrifices that were offered in Old Testament times. As sinful human beings, God should have punished them. However,

> "...the sufferings that were meant for us were afflicted on the Lord Jesus. He suffered because of our sins when on the cross he lamented, "My God, my God, why do you forsake me?" (*Synod of Nkhoma Catechism*, p.61).

Therefore, he offered himself on the cross a true and perfect sacrifice on behalf of all humanity.

> "Certainly, we would not have been saved without Jesus dying for us. The death of Jesus was humbling and shameful, because he entered a place of sinful people in order to save them" (*Synod of Nkhoma Catechism*, p.61).

This is a familiar scene in Malawi whereby the uncle as the head of the clan takes upon himself all iniquities that each one of the members of the clan comes across. The uncle is answerable to all questions and problems regarding each and every clan member. For example, if a young man in the clan has gone out and impregnated a girl from another clan, it is up to uncle to stand in for the young man, and meet the uncle from the other clan. That is, the uncles from clans the two clans will sit together to find a way forward, particularly on damages made. It is common in Malawi that uncles are true and right people to represent their clan members and also to carry their burdens or iniquities. In the same way, Jesus did suffer death on the cross - carried human burdens or iniquities.

The resurrection of Jesus Christ from the dead and hope

The Church of Central Africa Presbyterian briefly affirms that Jesus Christ died on the cross, was buried, and rose again from the dead.

> "...died, was buried, and rose again from the dead... (*CCAP. Constitution* 2000: 21). "Jesus Christ was buried and on the third day he rose again from the dead... (*Synod of Blantyre Shorter Catechism*, Question 10; *Synod of Nkhoma Catechism*, p.62). "

Hence, Jesus destroyed the power of Satan, death and sin by his resurrection from the dead.

> "The Lord Jesus was raised from the dead by the power and life from above, for death was unable to hold prisoner the life of God in Jesus. On his resurrection, he destroyed the power of Satan, death and sin (1Corinthians 15:55-57; *Synod of Nkhoma Catechism*, p.63).

For many Reformed Christians in Malawi, Satan is real and his supernatural power is real, too. At the same time these Reformed Christians do believe in the supernatural powers of Jesus, particularly in his death and resurrection, and hence, they would treat Jesus a hero, similar to those that have been in the lead in different struggles in Malawi. The late Dr. Hastings Banda was given the title of *"Ngwazi"* - which means "hero" – for his leading role in Malawi's struggle for independence. Reformed Christians in Malawi would call Jesus a hero – *Ngwazi*[19] – in the sense that he led his people in the struggle for their salvation.

Therefore, the life that Jesus had been raised from the dead with, God gives to those believers that receive Christ's death and resurrection as their own. Hence, believers die with Christ and rise up with him, and at the same time, they receive a life of victory over sin[20] and power to give glory to God (Romans 6:5; *Synod of Nkhoma Catechism*, p.63).

Union with Jesus Christ

The Church of Central Africa Presbyterian affirms the Holy Spirit of God who works faith in us, and that he unites us with Jesus Christ, and hence, brings about salvation in us.

> "The salvation thus wrought for us in Christ is applied to us by the Holy Spirit, who worketh faith in us, and thus unites us to Christ, enabling us to receive Him as He is offered to us in the Gospel, and to bring forth the fruits of righteousness" (*CCAP. Constitution* 2000: 21).

Here, Jesus unites us to himself by his Spirit (the Holy Spirit), and enables us to receive him as he is offered to us in the Gospel, and to bring forth the fruits of righteousness. Jesus' enabling act, here, causes a transformative effect in Christians to open up their lives to others in order that they share and enjoy with them the fruits of righteousness, which they received from Jesus Christ. In Malawi, it

---

[19] In 2009, President Bingu wa Matharika was conferred the title of the "Ngwazi by the *Ngonis* in Malawi," a title which many opposition leaders and other Malawians are disputing to say that it belongs to the late President Banda alone.

[20] According to the Ten Commandments, sin is ill-will against God and fellow human beings.

is a popular notion that "birds of the same feather flock together." It is normal in Malawi for parents to encourage their children to continue being friends with those children who are well-behaved and who come from well-behaved families. These parents believe their child will turn to be well mannered, and hence, be capable of behaving nice toward others in society.

In the case of our unity with Jesus as human beings, Reformed Christians in Malawi would see and treat Jesus as well-behaved and a loving person toward others in society, and hence, worthy to relate to very closely in terms of participating in what he does. Therefore, because Jesus loves them, the Reformed Christians in Malawi, in turn will show the same love they received from Jesus, toward others in society. Moreover, Christians are people in whom the Holy Spirit works faith and unites them to Christ in order that they bring fourth the fruits of righteousness in the society they live in.

Again, the Church of Central Africa Presbyterian affirms that in our being united with Jesus Christ, the Holy Spirit uses all means of grace onto us, especially the Word, Sacraments (Baptism and the Lord's Supper) and prayer.

> "Baptism signifies our union with Christ - the forgiveness of our sins - our being born again by the Holy Spirit - and our engagement to be the Lord's. The Lord's Supper signifies the death of Christ for our remembrance, and that all partakers experience fellowship in his body, and blood, signifying their love and faith for Christ" (Synod of Blantyre Larger Catechism, Question 92, 97).

Hence, in Baptism we were brought into the family of God where we share in one another's life as members of the same family, and again, our remembrance of Jesus' death at the Lord's Supper does have a transformative effect on us to fellowship in one another in love as human beings, as much as we experience fellowship in Jesus' body. This is a familiar scene in Malawi culture where people who are enemies would neither dare have a bath at the same spot along a river or river, nor will they be able to sit around the same table and eat together. For the Reformed Christians in Malawi baptism and the Lord's Supper symbolize close family ties. Therefore, baptism and the Lord's Supper do constitute a transformative effect for Christians to form strong family- like bonds toward others in society because they share the same world with them.

Election

Officially, the Church of Central Africa Presbyterian is silent about our election by God. But, the classic Reformed view of the atonement affirms that Jesus Christ, as God and man in one person, and in his mediatory role, elected human beings for reconciliation with God, through proper works of each of the two natures that might be accepted of God for human beings.

There is a lot of mediation going on in Malawi communities. There are traditional leaders, besides the courts, that mediate disputes. The communities in Malawi trust their traditional leaders in the sense that they are there to support and protect every member of a community. As such, these traditional leaders will try as much as possible to settle disputes fairly in a bid to find a lasting solution and reconciliation. In such processes, traditional leaders will, in the first stage, try to evaluate carefully the position of each and every party by reasoning with each, and hence, pave way for reconciliation with one another – a kind of electing the parties for reconciliation.

Here, the Reformed Christians in Malawi would see Jesus as a trusted leader when he elected human beings for reconciliation with God through proper works of his natures, the divinity and humanity – a kind of evaluation of the position of each nature. By his Spirit, Jesus, here, would impress the quality of his leadership onto Christians for them to live a life worthy of trust by members of society - a life capable of influencing reconciliation and lasting solution among members of society. The idea of trust by members of society onto Christians might not be true in other parts of the world, but in Malawi members of the society have trust in the Christian church that it is capable influencing reconciliation and solution, as was the case in the case of struggle for democracy in Malawi between 1992 and 1994.

Calling

The Church of Central Africa Presbyterian is also silent about our calling by God. But the Reformed view of the atonement affirms that Jesus Christ's life on earth was full of transformative power on believers, and this is an example of what calling should embody. Christ lived a life acceptable by God, and therefore, lived a life of love and compassion for other human beings. That is, on the cross and in his life, Jesus willingly humbled himself in perfect obedience to God's law and justice in our midst and for our sake because he loved us from the heart, despite our sinfulness and corruptedness.

In Malawi society there is the notion of living together as people, in the sense that "one needs others as much as others needs one" in order to have a very productive and supportive society. Again, Malawians culturally do believe in the saying, "I am, and therefore, we are." Also, in Malawi there is saying about killing lice, "One finger cannot kill lice, but two fingers." It all expresses the idea that we all need each other to achieve something in society.

Therefore, in his perfect obedience to God's law and justice on humanity's behalf, Jesus did demonstrate that he loved human beings from the heart – love and compassion - because they are human as he is, despite their sinfulness. Jesus thus does call on Christians to live a life of love and compassion for others in society – love from the heart - because they (others in society) are human as the Christians are.

Faith

The Church of Central Africa Presbyterian affirms that faith is a gift from God, who, by the Holy Spirit in Christ convicts human beings of their sin - and hence, enables them to recognise God's love for them in Jesus Christ. Here, Jesus Christ by his Spirit helps and supports us by convicting us of our sin, and enabling us to recognise God's love for us in him.

> "The Holy Spirit helps us to believe in Jesus Christ by teaching us that Christ wants to save us, and by making us freely will to be Christ's so that we worship him, obeying him and following him in all his ways" (*Synod of Blantyre Larger Catechism*, Questions 60).

Jesus' convicting us of our sin by his Spirit, and his enabling act for us to recognize God's love for us, here, calls for Christians' willingness to help and support others in society because of their true love (Christians') them. True love is an internal entity in the human being and needs to be externalised onto others in society, who in turn will recognise it. In Malawi, people do talk about some people who will just uncover their teeth pretending that they are smiling with love, when in fact they are not. True love in a person is recognisable in the sense that others will experience the person's willingness to help and support others – "the fruits of good works" that come out of a lively faith.

Here, the Church of Central Africa Presbyterian affirms of lively faith that bears the fruits of good works, even though good works do not bring salvation in human beings.

> "Faith is lively and acts. Where there is faith, there are good works, such that believers prove their faith and good works (James 2:18-20; *Synod of Nkhoma Catechism*, p.98).

Therefore, faith without works is dead, and a good tree is known by its fruit, and hence, such is a basis for Christians to be known by their good behaviour and character towards fellow human beings in society. John Mbiti has it that the African Christian concept of faith reflects that of the Bible which is always expressed in actions and has specific works (Mbiti 1986: 103). That is, a person who has that kind of faith will express it in actions. Moreover, the Holy Spirit makes Christians free to will to become Christ's in order that they participate in all his ways of good character and behaviour towards others in society.

Justification

According to the Church of Central Africa Presbyterian, God gave us his law for us to keep, and unfortunately, no one was able to keep it. Therefore, we all violated God's law, and deserved God's judgment and death. But God foreknew that we would not capable of saving ourselves from sinfulness, and hence, God had already improvised a plan to save us in his Son Jesus Christ.

> "In his knowledge of human beings' incapability to save themselves from sin, God in his mercy had already planned someone to pay the debt for their sins. This someone is Jesus Christ his Son, who satisfied the law of God by giving his life on the cross a ransom for all human beings. The power of his ransom comes from the fact that his death saved us from our violation of God's justice. Therefore, Jesus' work in keeping the law perfectly enables us to stand righteous before God. God, in seeing the ransom paid him by Jesus, receives it, and hence, forgives all those having faith in Jesus for their ransom" (*Synod of Nkhoma Catechism*, p.79).

Therefore, we are justified by God's grace through our faith in Jesus Christ who died for us on the cross, taking upon himself all our sins, saving us, and hence, scraped off all our sins (Murray 2005: 51-52).

> "Jesus Christ died on the cross for us, taking upon himself all our iniquities, for our salvation and justification" (*Synod of Blantyre Larger Catechism*, Question 50).

The Church of Central Africa Presbyterian points out that our good works have no place in our salvation.

> "...all our good works do not meet God's standards of his law because they are not good enough by virtue of our sinfulness..." (*Synod of Nkhoma Catechism*, p.80).

However, the Church of Central Africa Presbyterian is quick to say that we ought to do good works:

For our gratitude to God for his salvation to us in Jesus:

> "True Christians, with the knowledge about their salvation from their sins by God, will not sit down passive, but will do works in praise and glory to God with all their whole heart because of such salvation…"(Synod of Nkhoma Catechism, p.98).

As evidences of our lively faith:

> "Faith is alive when it brings forth fruits of good works. Where there is faith, there are good works (James 2:18-20)" [Synod of Nkhoma Catechism, p.98).

And for encouragement of others to come to Jesus Christ.

> "Jesus Christ came into this world to seek the lost and to take them to salvation, and hence, the saved, in turn, will assist Jesus in seeking others for salvation. We are saved in order to serve others, so that they, too, come to salvation. The Lord commissioned us to serve others before his ascension into heaven (Matthew 28:19)" [Synod of Nkhoma Catechism, p.99).

Here, our being served by Jesus in our salvation from sin is a transformative power for us to serve other in terms of good works in our society. Good works are thus done with a pure heart, and in consistent with the Word of God - done in glory to God and in the power of the Holy Spirit, and hence, leading to helping the needy and spreading the Good News about our Lord Jesus Christ (*Synod of Nkhoma Catechism*, p.101).

Justification in the Church of Central Africa Presbyterian, therefore, is transformative in the sense that "one will not do anything to despise the one from whom one received assistance and support." That is the reason why those people who do a lot of helping and supporting others in society do receive a lot of free and voluntary respect and honour from members of society. At the same time, the supported members of society are encouraged to return favour, not necessarily to the charity people from whom they receive support, but to others around them in the society they live. However, there are some ungrateful few who would not dare return favour onto others in society, in spite of receiving so much support from charitable organizations.

Yes, the Reformed Christians in Malawi do find the notion, that our good works do not save us in our being justified, difficult and therefore inadequate if there is not adequate explanation of the importance of human good works. For them, good works are inevitable in a sinner's justified life in the sense that Jesus has effected transformation onto the sinner, such that the sinner tends to return the free favour that he or she received from God in Jesus. This sinner will not want to defy God in any way and will do everything to please God. In Malawi, we have a saying that says, "You will not bite a finger that feeds you." This saying relates to feeding a baby. A baby does reach a stage when it is fed porridge, and the mother would use a finger, in the absence of a spoon, to scoop small lumps of porridge from the plate and feed the baby. If the baby was to bite the mother's finger, then it will be very difficult for the mother to do the feeding. In reference to God and us, "biting the mother's finger" would mean defying the God that saves and supports you by continuing living in sins. In the very old days, a traditional Malawian would give thank-offering as a gesture to the spirits and the Great Spirit – God for any success in life (Hara 2008: 173). For example, a hunter would offer part of the meat to the spirits whom he believed had helped him to be successful.

Certainly, Jesus' salvation work did justify us in order that we become capable and deserving of standing righteous before God. He thus did us good service, and hence, empowered us (by his Spirit) to serve others in society with love and compassion.

Moreover, every member of society freely and equally deserves love and compassion from others, as everyone else.

Our adoption into children of God

The Church of Central Africa Presbyterian affirms that those who receive Jesus and believe his name will surely become children of God (*Synod of Nkhoma Catechism*, p.306; Murray 2005: 39-41). Even if they fall again into sin they will not cease to be God's children, but will be disobedient children of God. Human beings are, of course, adopted into children of God in Jesus and by the power of the Holy Spirit:

> "The Holy Spirit convicts human beings of their sins, and hence, adopts them into children of God by new birth. In so doing, the Holy Spirit lives within them, renewing them and leading them" (Synod of Nkhoma Catechism, p.69).

Therefore, as much as they will become obedient children of God, in their adopted life, in Jesus and by the power of the Holy Spirit they will also become obedient children to one another amongst themselves. Here, the Holy Spirit lives within them, renewing them and leading them, and making them participate with Jesus in his obedience to God the Father.

The plight of orphaned children in Malawi is so great, as a result of the HIV-AIDS pandemic, and hence, the notion that Jesus by his Spirit does adopt believers into children of God by new birth would, in contemporary Malawi, be very well understood. Many families now are adopting orphans, children without parents, because the parents have died of AIDS. When a child without parents is being adopted into a new family, he or she is like re-born into this new family. This child now has equal access to the privileges that this family has for its other legitimate children born in it. Again, there are many HIV positive and AIDS infected men, women and children in Malawi. These people do need care, inclusion, support and sympathy from the rest of the Malawian society. Unfortunately there are many unsympathetic Malawians out there, who stigmatise and segregate these people. Time has come for the Reformed Christians in Malawi to take the lead in bringing back the dignity of these people. They, too, become equally adopted children of God with us in Jesus, and they also do become obedient children to one another with us, the HIV-negative. Therefore, when Jesus by his Spirit convicted human beings of their sins, and hence, adopted them into children of God by Birth, he thus invited them to participate with him in accommodating others in society into one's life, particularly orphans and the HIV-AIDS affected, because we need to care for one another as children of one society and as children of God.

Sanctification

The Church of Central Africa Presbyterian affirms that the Holy Spirit of God sanctifies us and renews our hearts in order that we turn away from sin.

> "The Holy Spirit sanctifies human hearts by turning them away from sin, and by sanctifying the inward of human beings and everything therein" (*Synod of Blantyre Larger Catechism*, Question 54).

Once in the human beings heart, the Holy Spirit convicts them of their sins in details, and therefore, human beings' sanctification takes place (Murray 2005: 57).

> "The Holy Spirit starts by pointing out those sins that are visible like stealing, polygamy, drunkenness, for human beings to stop doing them. Later, the Holy Spirit goes on to convict human beings of their hidden sins" (Synod of Nkhoma Catechism, p.71).

In sanctification, the Holy Spirit opens the eyes of human beings in order that they see their sins – which usually have negative impact on their fellow human beings - and hence, feel sorry about them.

> "In so doing, they will see their old self as an enemy" (Synod of Nkhoma Catechism, p.72).

Therefore, human beings, in their sanctified life, will not do anything that may harm their fellow human being.

Of course, it is by our union with Jesus Christ that we deserve sanctification by the Holy Spirit. This Holy Spirit is also known as the Spirit of Jesus, and therefore, by his Spirit Jesus sanctifies human hearts by turning them away from sins that are visible; these sins are very much connected with a negative human's life toward others in society. Jesus himself and by his Spirit did not do anything to harm other human beings in society, but rather suffered and died for their salvation. Hence, Jesus and his Spirit do call believers not to do anything that may harm fellow human beings in society because they themselves do not deserve to be harmed. Here, the Reformed Christians in Malawi will understand a sanctified life as positive moral life in community with others in society.

Regeneration

The Church of Central Africa Presbyterian affirms that those united with Jesus Christ do enter the grace of Jesus' life - that of regeneration (transformation).

> "Those united with Christ receive his life of grace, cleansing them of all weaknesses of their lives, encouraging their new reborn life..." (*Synod of Blantyre Larger Catechism*, Question 99).

Therefore, those united with Christ are born again, effected by Jesus' transformative power in his life of grace, in order that they do away with their old life and take on a new life in Jesus Christ. Hence, they show forth fruits of the Holy Spirit, mentioned in Galatians 5: 22, 23. Here, the nature of the fruits signifies that human beings must bear such fruits in society and targeted toward their fellow human beings.

Being "born again" became a very big issue in the late nineties when some of the members of the Church of Central Africa Presbyterian were disgruntled by the immoral behaviour that some of the church leaders tended to expose. For them, to be born again meant to become Christ-like in all daily affairs of human life, especially doing good works in society. These members tended to create a life of purity and this tendency still remains in the Church up to date. Indeed, they had in mind that in our being born again Jesus has impressed onto us a new reborn life that is free of all weaknesses.

We are called to conform to the image of God

The Church of Central Africa Presbyterian affirms that God originally created human beings in his own image.

> "He created human beings of good reasoning. In creating human beings, God gave them spirit, when he breathed into them his own breath in their nostrils. For God is spirit, therefore, he made human beings have a spirit. Therefore, the human being ware of good reasoning, capable of knowing their Creator God and of relation to God" (Synod of Nkhoma Catechism, p.37).

God created human beings in his own image in order to be like him in his righteousness and wisdom.

> "He created human beings righteous in order that they should not sin" (Synod of Nkhoma Catechism, p.37).

Unfortunately, human beings violated God's creation order when they sinned. Here, the Church of Central Africa Presbyterian discusses the sin of all human beings in terms of the first human parents Adam and Eve in the Book of Genesis.

As a result of the fall of Adam and Eve, therefore,

> "...the image of God in human beings was totally defaced, except for a very small remnant. The remnant in human beings assists the Holy Spirit the work of rebirth in them" (Synod of Nkhoma Catechism, 39).

How do human beings regain their createdness in the image of God? Here, the Church of Central Africa Presbyterian affirms Jesus as the one human beings' Mediator who suffered in their place, reconciling them with God (Synod of Nkhoma Catechism, 43), and hence, regained their createdness in the image of God for them. In their return to God, therefore, human beings must be like Jesus by showing fruits amidst society, which come with the Holy Spirit (Galatians 5:22, 23; *Synod of Nkhoma Catechism*, p.73). Here, Jesus is portrayed as the true image of God (and a transformative power) to whom human beings should conform. The Reformed Christians in Malawi treat Jesus as a genuine human being - a transformative power - in the sense that they learn from him how to behave in daily life as human being. They would understand Jesus' sufferings for human beings to regain their createdness in the image of God as a transformative power for Christians to dignify others in society because they are human as the Christians are.

Solidarity through the Spirit in the church

The Church of Central Africa Presbyterian conceives of "the church of Jesus Christ" as being those people who believe in Jesus Christ and obey him, together with their children (*Synod of Blantyre Larger Catechism*, Questions 79, 80, 81; *Synod of Blantyre Shorter Catechism*, Question 15). It goes on to explain that the church of Jesus Christ first came to be on the Day of Pentecost, during which Christ poured the Holy Spirit onto his disciples who had gathered together in the Upper Room.

> "The Church of Jesus Christ is gathering of Christians who have vowed to believe and obey Christ, together with their children. The Church of Jesus started on the Day of Pentecost when Christ poured his Spirit upon his followers who had assembled together in the Upper Room on that same day (*Synod of Blantyre Larger Catechism*, Questions 79, 80).

Today, by his Spirit Jesus sends out believers into the world to invite others to come to Jesus for their salvation (*Synod of Nkhoma*

Catechism, p.279). Hence, by the Holy Spirit, Jesus Christ gathers and grows his church in this world today. He so pours his Holy Spirit on those believers who go out to spread the Good News of the kingdom of God.

> The Church of Jesus Christ grows in this world amongst those who receive the Holy Spirit, and go out to spread the Good News of the kingdom of God and teaching people of all nations (*Synod of Blantyre Larger Catechism*, Questions 81).

Again, the Church of Central Africa Presbyterian affirms that Jesus, by his Spirit, gathers his church through the Sacrament of Baptism:

> "On being baptised people vow that they are not their own but God's" (Romans 7:4; Synod of Nkhoma Catechism, p.83).

Therefore, as much as they have vowed to belong to God, they also find themselves belonging to one another in Jesus Christ's body. Jesus gathers his church through the Lord's Supper. The elements used in the Lord's Supper are bread and wine, and hence, the Lord Jesus is the bread of God, coming down from heaven, and hence, giving all the world life (John 6:33; Synod of Nkhoma Catechism, p.83). Therefore, as members of the Church sit around the communion table they commune in one another as a family of God. The sharing of the elements at this table does cement the relationship in fellowship of the people sitting around it (Tengatenga 2006: 196).

All in all, the Church of Central Africa Presbyterian affirms that the visible sign of the Holy Spirit of God in people filled with it is love, happiness and peace.

> "We know the Holy Spirit because we can see its work and signs, which are works of love, works of happiness and works of peace in and among believers" (Synod of Blantyre Shorter Catechism, Question 15).

And hence, sharing of the elements at the Lord's Supper, therefore, means Christians' to extension of love, happiness and peace towards other Christian members or other human beings in society.

JESUS' ACTIVE OBEDIENCE AND THE CHRISTIAN LIFE

But is the Reformed notion about Jesus' active obedience and his transformative power of his life, a "pattern" for Christian life? Definitely, yes, because Jesus' active obedience to God and his transformative power for our Christian life, in Chapter 2, were drawn from the Reformed tradition's emphasis on Jesus Christ's deity and humanity, especially from his birth through his life on earth, up to his death on the cross.

In his human life, Jesus at all times did what God required of his law. In his death on the cross, Jesus willingly paid the penalty of sin for believers and stood the probation for them in their new life with him. Jesus was, thus righteous, and hence, such is his active obedience. In his active obedience to God, therefore, Jesus affirmed by the Reformed tradition is making a perfect positive righteousness available by imputation to all who believe in him. That is, by his active obedience, Jesus is capable of clothing believers with his perfect righteousness.

Jesus actively obeyed God his Father for the wellbeing of believers - in his life and death. In so doing, believers are constrained to respond in wonder and gratitude to God for their justification in Jesus. Moreover, Jesus has justified them in order that they love other human beings - in spite of who they are. Definitely, Jesus is, now, their example whose pattern they ought to express in their daily life. By his Spirit, Jesus transforms their sinful hearts to understand and embrace God's love, moral order and justice for their lives in society. Jesus, thus, called and drawn them to himself in order that they might be made into people who love God and other human beings. In other words, Jesus has elected them to live a life acceptable to God his Father. It is because of this that the Holy Spirit sanctifies believers' life and thus believers are called to discipleship - and hence, they are called to caring for other human beings. They are, now, capable of caring for other human beings because, they have been adopted into children of God by Jesus' righteousness. Jesus Christ adopts sinful human beings into his love, and that of the triune God, in order that they love other human beings with a spirit of adoption. Here, they have been gathered as one Church of Jesus, and they are going through a life of regeneration, powered by the Holy Spirit. In regeneration, Jesus grows together with the elect into one body, sharing his Spirit with them. Because they are, now, united with Jesus, they are striving after the newness of life in the resurrection of Jesus from the dead. Here, Jesus unites with them as an external extension of his love and fellowship with other human beings.

Likewise, in the Constitution, Confessions of Faith and catechisms of the Church of Central Africa Presbyterian, above, we identified a similar emphasis on the deity and humanity of Jesus Christ to that of the Reformed view of the atonement in chapter 2, from which we were capable of drawing out Jesus' active obedience to God – Jesus' transformational power on to believers for their Christian life. However, in his survey of Malawian sermons and the general impression left by the Malawian preachers on their listeners, Kenneth Ross' [21] has discovered that there is relatively little emphasis on the deity and humanity of Christ in the practical lives of the Reformed Christians in contemporary Malawi. Instead,

---

[21] Kenneth Ross has worked with the Church of Central Africa Presbyterian for many years as a missionary from the Church of Scotland. He may be amongst the pioneers in research about contemporary life and impact of these mainstream churches in Malawi. He made a very broad survey encompassing three different Malawian churches, Presbyterian, Anglican and Roman Catholic that fall within the category of "mainstream". He made a study of each one of these mainstream churches on its own, followed by a comprehensive and comparative study. His general objective was to provide a survey and analysis of the general message being preached and its effects in the life of the people of Malawi (Ross, *Gospel Ferment in Malawi*, p.82).

there is but more emphasis on the works of Christ than they do with features of God the Father or God the Holy Spirit (Ross 1995: 85; Wendland 2000: 18; Mijoga 2000: 114). Such looks like it is limiting the Reformed view of the atonement way of drawing up Jesus' active obedience to God – Jesus' transformative power onto believers for their Christian life. If such is the case then, therefore, it makes the Church of Central Africa Presbyterian in Malawi look like it wants to strictly keep its Reformed view of the atonement - evident in its traditional confessions, catechisms, and constitution - as were first introduced by the Church of Scotland Missionaries, but in practice the church fails to live up to those standards or expectations. Again, Ross' survey shows that more sermons dwelt substantially on either the need for personal conversion or duties of the Christian life (Ross 1995: 87). He has it that an extreme strong emphasis on law-keeping and good works, gives the impression that believers by good works contribute to salvation (Paas 2006: 42). Of some significance too, Matthew, John, Luke, Acts, Mark, and Romans, were the five most commonly chosen books by Malawian preachers in the whole of the New Testament - whilst "practical" James and "moralistic" 2 Timothy were the more commonly chosen rather than the more doctrinal Ephesians and Colossians (see table A below).

OLD TESTAMENT	PROMINENCE	NEW TESTAMENT	PROMINENCE
Genesis	34	Matthew	48
Isaiah	23	John	36
Exodus	21	Luke	33
Psalms	17	Acts	25
Proverbs	11	Mark	22
Jeremiah	10	Romans	21
1 Kings	9	Revelation	11

Deuteronomy	8	1 Corinthians	9
2 Kings	7	2 Timothy	9
Ezekiel	6	James	8
Jonah	5	Ephesians	7
Joshua	5	2 Corinthians	6
Malachi	4	Hebrews	5
Numbers	4	1 John	5
1 Samuel	4	Galatians	4
Leviticus	3	2 Peter	4
Micah	3	Philippians	4
Daniel	2	1 Timothy	4
Job	2	Colossians	2
Amos	1	1 Peter	2
1 Chronicles	1	Philemon	1
2 Chronicles	1		
Habakkuk	1		
Hosea	1		
Judges	1		
Lamentations	1		
Nehemiah	1		
Obadiah	1		

Table A

Nevertheless, such seems to affirm that theology ought to be constructed out of a committed engagement with the contemporary life of the church (Ross 1998: 16-18; Fiedler 1999: 23). Here, one's view of God and one's relation to God goes along with one's view of society and its customs (Ross 1996: 65). Hence, the actual knowledge of God from which theology may be constructed is not an idealistic or mystical form of knowledge but rather one that is worked out in personal discipleship and social praxis. It is the Bible as it is read and internalised, and found application in the life of the community that creates the field within which the theologian can operate. Hence, there is no theology that is culture free (Fiedler 1998: 10). We cannot artificially create an African theology or even plan it, but it must evolve spontaneously as the church teaches and lives her faith and in response to the extremely complex situation in Africa (Bueta ed. 1968: 332). Unfortunately, there has been a lot of scholarly attention as to the origin of the Church of Central Africa Presbyterian and other mainstream churches in Malawi, but by contrast, their contemporary life and impact seem to have attracted little in a way of systematic study (Ross 1995: 81).

However, the findings that the Gospels of Matthew, John, Luke, Mark are among the five top most commonly chosen books of the New Testament, seems to suggest that the Reformed Christians in Malawi put much emphasis and importance on the oral material, that is, the preaching and teaching of Jesus Christ in the Gospels. In this direction, Ross' survey revealed that preaching in Malawi, by and large, attempts to explain, amplify, illustrate, and apply a given passage of scripture into the lives of the people (Ross 1995: 86). Hence, such affirms why all answers to Kenneth Ross' question about the most important rules or laws for a Christian to follow, fell into the one answer that Jesus gives in the Gospels: "Love God" and/or "Love your neighbour[22]" (Ross 1995: 88).

In the Gospels of Matthew, John, Luke, and Mark are Jesus' life, sayings and parables, from which Malawian preachers draw out examples for application into the lives of their listeners - and hence, such are oral examples by Jesus Christ. Hence, such seems to affirm that in Jesus' life, sayings and parables (in the Gospels), Reformed Christians in Malawi are able to trace Jesus' active obedience to God his Father and Jesus' call for participation with him, in their renewed life. So, too, are the "practical" James and

---

[22] "Love your neighbour" tends to be very prominent in the Reformed church in Malawi and definitely it originates from what the Roman Catholic Father John Ambe describes as "an African strong sense of community," which he detected among the Bafut society of Cameroon, good to enrich the Sacrament of Reconciliation (Ambe 1992: 37-38).

"moralistic" 2 Timothy, being the more commonly chosen rather than the more "doctrinal" Ephesians and Colossians, seem to serve as complements and support for "oral" examples in the Gospels that Jesus gives for the renewed lives of Reformed Christians in Malawi.

Indeed, for a Malawian Reformed Christian, Jesus' life, sayings, and parables, are very important, crucial and have a transformative power for the development of Christian duties in one's life. Certainly, Jesus' life, sayings, and parables, act as a base for Malawian Reformed Christian duties, stemming out of what Jesus said, and hence, Jesus' oral example for their renewed lives – without which, Malawian Christian duties would be isolated, and therefore, unworthy of God's justice. Therefore, Kenneth Ross' survey (see table B below) shows that "duties of the Christian life" has very high prominence in contemporary Malawian preaching.

THEME	PROMINENCE
Need for personal conversion	35
Duties of the Christian life	25
God's judgement	21
Christ's power to save/heal today	14
The life to come	12
Mission and evangelism	7
Christ's finished work	9
God's creation	9
Growth of Christian character	7
The incarnation	5
The deity of Christ	4
Marriage and family life	2
Importance of the sacraments	1
The humanity of Christ	2
Social renewal	2

Table B

Definitely, Jesus' pattern of life for the renewed life of the Reformed Christians in Malawi does stem out of Jesus' obedience to God for the demands of God's Law on behalf of human beings, as affirmed in his gospel teachings, sayings or parables. In the same way, the Reformed view of the atonement affirms that Jesus' transformative power for believers' renewed life does stem out of Jesus' active obedience to God for the demands of God's law in his deity and humanity. Hence, it demonstrates that Jesus' transformative power, as affirmed by his gospel teachings, sayings or parables, for the renewed life of the Reformed Christians in Malawi, is consistent with Reformed view's active obedience to God by Jesus that is affirmed in his deity and humanity.

Certainly, Jesus' transformative power in the Gospels for the renewed life of the Reformed Christians in contemporary Malawi remains faithful to the proclamation of God's grace because such does stem out from Jesus Christ's works and spoken words in the Gospels, and hence, reflects the true image of God in the lives of Reformed Christians in Malawi. Of course, humankind reflects the image of God when it relates and act in everyday life, upholding God's truth and justice. Jesus himself willingly maintained his obedience to God his Father by upholding God's truth and justice in life and word, of which he so persevered unto his death on the cross – hence, he demonstrated a life of conforming to the image of God.

The Malawian Reformed view of atonement, therefore, seems to affirm that from Jesus Christ's life, sayings or parables, there is Jesus' active obedience towards God his Father for human salvation, which is truly consistent with Jesus' deity and humanity. Hence, in the Gospels the Reformed Christians in Malawi do find so much proclamation of God's grace in the life of Jesus, such that they are constrained to respond in wonder and gratitude to God – leading to their "love of God' and/or their "love of neighbour" as the most important rules or laws for them to follow (Ross 1995: 89). Thus, Jesus' "active obedience to God his Father in the Gospels" does present Jesus' transformational power for the renewed lives of the Reformed Christians in Malawi, in the sense that it is a revelation of the kind of renewed life that they are called to participate in. Hence, whatever Jesus Christ portrays as ethical, in his life, sayings or parables, becomes the measure with which the Reformed Christians in Malawi are capable of relating to God and to others in society.

CONCLUSION

This chapter tried to investigate whether and how the Church of Central Africa Presbyterian in Malawi did receive or did not receive the Reformed view of atonement in Chapter 2, and more specifically whether or not they did receive or did not receive Jesus' active obedience and Jesus' ethical life for our renewed life. The investigation revealed that the documents in the Malawi church do include most of the broader view of the classic Reformed doctrine of atonement, if not all – Covenant, Incarnation, death, resurrection, union with Christ, Faith, Justification, Adoption into children of God, Sanctification, Regeneration, Image of God and called into community by the Spirit. Also, the investigations revealed the extreme strong emphasis on law-keeping and good works by the Reformed Christians in Malawi, which gives the impression that good works can contribute to salvation. But, this research study shall serve as an eye opener for this church in Malawi to keep itself within its traditions and beliefs, and this includes the message that is preached in its pulpits. Nevertheless, it became clear in the investigation that in the justified, sanctified and regenerated life of the Reformed Christians in Malawi, Jesus Christ's life, sayings and parables do offer a transformative power for their renewed life, and that, in them, Jesus does fulfil the demands of God's Law. The transformative power by Jesus, for the renewed life of the Reformed Christians in Malawi, does stem out of the Gospels, and hence, does lead to Christian duties – love of God and/or love of neighbour. Moreover, the visible sign of the Holy Spirit in people that have been justified, sanctified and regenerated is love, happiness and peace. Hence, Christians are called to extend love, happiness and peace towards other human beings in society. This takes us to the next chapter (Chapter 4), which will make a case about the active obedience that is expected of Christians, where Jesus Christ is used as a transformational power that affect believers (in the Gospels) - in the broader view of the atonement – and leading to a different view, on the part of the Reformed Christians in Malawi, concerning human dignity and human rights.

CHAPTER 4

HUMAN RIGHTS IN MALAWI IN THE LIGHT OF THE REFORMED VIEW OF THE ATONEMENT

INTRODUCTION

Chapter 3 investigated whether and how the Church of Central Africa Presbyterian in Malawi did receive or did not receive the Reformed view of atonement, especially Jesus' active obedience for the transformative effect on believers' renewed life. Hence, the chapter demonstrated that the Church in Malawi has, indeed, received not only the Reformed view of the atonement but the broader one. But the impression that good works can contribute to salvation by Reformed Christians in Malawi was noted and shall be put to check as one of recommendations to the church in Malawi, by this research study. However, it became clear that Jesus Christ's life, sayings and parables in the Gospels, do constitute much of Jesus' transformative power for the Reformed Christians' renewed life in Malawi. Here, Jesus' active obedience does fulfil the demands of God's Law, and, at the same time, it has a transformative effect in the lives of the Reformed Christians in Malawi as their active obedience that is expected of them in their justified, sanctified and regenerated life by God. It is because of this that this Reformed Christians' response does result into Christian duties – love of God and/or love of neighbour.

Therefore, this chapter will, in light of the Reformed view of atonement, make a case of the active obedience that is expected of Christians, the kind of active obedience that is effected by Jesus Christ's transformative life and ministry - and therefore, leading to a different view concerning human rights, on the part of the Reformed Christians in Malawi. And since more and more members of the Reformed Christians in Malawi are seeking to support a human rights culture in democratic Malawi, this chapter will, therefore, argue for the impact and the difference the

Reformed view of the atonement could and should make in the lives of the Reformed Christians in Malawi, in their reception of human dignity and human rights.

The chapter is organized in four sections. The first section is about human rights in Malawi. The second section discusses Jesus Christ's transformative life and ministry, in the Gospels, as a pattern for the renewed life of the Reformed Christians in Malawi. The third section is about human rights in Malawi in light of the Reformed view of the atonement. The fourth is the summary and evaluation.

HUMAN RIGHTS IN MALAWI

Malawi, then Nyasaland, used to be a British protectorate until 1964 when it became independent under the leadership of Dr. Hastings Kamuzu Banda. Interestingly, Dr. Banda was raised as a Presbyterian, and spent many years as a medical general practitioner in Scotland and England, before coming back to Malawi in 1958. Banda became a Medical Doctor, after studying medicine in the United States (Forster 2003: 149). But in order to practice medicine in territories of the British Empire he was required to get a second medical degree from the University of Edinburgh in Britain in 1941. Later, he established medical practice in London, England, where his office became a meeting place for exiled African leaders. He returned to Africa in 1953, and set up a medical clinic in Kumasi, Ghana, before coming back to his homeland Malawi in 1958 (Forster 2003: 157), to campaign against the federation of Nyasaland with the two Rhodesia's (now Zimbabwe and Zambia). In 1961 Banda's Malawi Congress party won a sweeping election victory. Nyasaland, which he led as prime minister, became independent as Malawi in 1964.

Barely a month after independence, Malawi suffered a cabinet crisis (Forster 2003: 159). Several of Banda's ministers presented him with proposals designed to limit his powers. He had already been accused of autocratic tendencies. Banda responded by dismissing four of the ministers, and two others resigned in sympathy. The dissidents fled the country. Under a new constitution, Banda became president in 1966. Increasingly autocratic, Banda made himself president for life in 1971 (Forster 2003: 164). His regime oscillated to some degree between harsh, violent repression and a more paternalistic form of authoritarianism, and all executive authority was concentrated in the office of the Life President (Phiri & Ross. Eds. 1998: 10). Opponents were routinely jailed and some killed. The most severe human rights abuses characteristic of the Banda regime included assassination, torture, long-term detention and exile of opponents.

The church in Malawi, too, was not let alone, during the one-party era from 1964-1993. There were severe restrictions on the church's public witness on political issues by Dr. Banda's government. In his book, *Gospel Ferment in Malawi*, Kenneth R. Ross comments that these years were repressive, during which church leaders, with a few exceptions, refrained from addressing the Word of God critically to political life of the country (Ross 1995: 49-52). The church's message was concerned with personal spirituality and morality. In other words, the church's message was concerned with preparing people for the next world. Hence, the atoning work of Christ was not understood as having a direct bearing on the direction and conduct of political life of the people of Malawi.

However, change had to come to Malawi. The end of the Cold War triggered the sudden and widespread changes in Eastern Europe and sub Saharan African countries when authoritarian governments were toppled peacefully. Churches and civil society in Malawi re-examined the political structure that had lasted three decades and yet had failed to deliver either liberty or the minimum of economic prosperity(Mayaya 2005: **Error! Hyperlink reference not valid.**). The Roman Catholic Bishops wrote their most celebrated March 8th, 1992 *Lenten Letter*[23], that turned out to be

---

[23] Full version of the letter can be found in *Christianity in Malawi, edited by Kenneth R. Ross* (Ross. ed. 1996: 204-215).

an eye-opener for many Christians in Malawi in realizing that their faith had much to say in relation to political issues (Tengatenga 2006: 9). For the first time, the Church of Central Africa Presbyterian[24] leaders with the support of leaders from the World Alliance of Reformed Churches, came out of their shell and met the former President of Malawi, the late Dr. Hastings Kamuzu Banda, to discuss issues of national concern [25]that had been reflected in the Malawi Roman Catholic Bishop's *Lenten Letter*. The intention of the *Lenten Letter* was to address human rights problems - the increasing gap between rich and poor, censorship of reading materials, poor education and healthcare, and others (Ott 2000: 122). After meeting Dr Banda, the Church of Central Africa Presbyterian leaders worked towards forming an umbrella organization called the *Public Affairs Committee* (PAC) to carry out dialogue with Dr. Banda's *Presidential Committee on Dialogue*. Its membership included the Roman Catholic Church, and other major denominations in Malawi (Tengatenga 2006: 13). *Public Affairs Committee* played a crucial role in the drafting of the new constitution of Malawi, particularly the Bill of Rights and guiding the civil society through a turbulent period.

After the formation of the *Public Affairs Committee*, and between 1992 and 1994, the Church of Central Africa Presbyterian played a great role in fighting for human dignity in Malawi, besides fighting against the dictatorial regime of the late Life President Hastings Kamuzu Banda[26]. Eventually, Dr. Banda bowed [27]to the

---

[24] It is popularly known as "CCAP."

[25] It must be noted here that Synod of Blantyre, a member of the Church of Central Africa Presbyterian did, earlier on in 1958, write a statement in support of political change in Malawi, and was signed by the Rev. Allan Thipa, the Moderator of Synod of Blantyre at that time (Ross, ed. 1996: 195-201). It was a time when Dr. Hastings Banda had come back home to lead black majority in the struggle for Independence from British colonial rule in Malawi (then Nyasaland).

[26] Malawi had its first democratic elections in 1994, ending 30 years of dictatorial rule by Dr. Hastings Kamuzu Banda.

church's and Malawian people's demand for democracy, respect for human rights and multi-party politics in Malawi. However, the Church of Central Africa Presbyterian has always tended to be supporting human rights culture in principle, but in actual specifics, it has been very cautious so as not to contradict with its Christian teachings and traditions (Mayaya 2005: **Error! Hyperlink reference not valid.**) especially its Reformed tradition's atoning work by Jesus Christ, which is the main theme amongst Christian teachings. Here, Human rights culture means people asking questions in their struggle for human dignity and a more just dispensation. In addition, the doctrine of atonement (Christ's atoning work) in these evangelically minded circles means the work Christ did in his life, death and resurrection to earn human salvation (Grudem 1994: 568). Sometimes the doctrine is used in evangelical thought to refer only to Jesus dying on the cross and paying for human sin. The joint result of the historical development in Malawian politics and the widespread spirituality in the church circles was that believers often supported the new human rights culture, but without being able to relate it with their understanding of the gospel. In fact, the church made their understanding of the gospel concentrate exclusively in the atonement of Christ as spiritual reconciliation between God and sinners.

Now that Malawi is more than ten years of democracy, more and more members of the Church of Central Africa Presbyterian are seeking to support a human rights culture. However, as much as these members would like to see the church's support for their venture, there is a strong resistance coming from the church itself. Increasingly, these members have had to turn to their church's code of conduct for guidance and support. Unfortunately, while the church's code of conduct is available, members find a lot missing, which would help them support the human rights culture

---

[27] Dr. Hastings Kamuzu Banda allowed a national referendum to take place in June 1993 in which the people of Malawi voted in favour of multi-party system of government.

as Christians. The church's Reformed view of the atonement tends to have some implications often leading in the opposite direction. It tends to deny them understand Jesus as restoring their lost human dignity in the present (as it is in the future). What the members are primarily concerned with is the more illusive but in some ways more significant matter of their actual Malawian belief, outlook and practice (Ross 1995: 67). They are looking forward to the day on which their church would see Christ's saving work as having something to do with their present life. May be, then, human rights would at least have a chance to be related with something in the Christian church. Indeed, we live in times of cultural dynamics where theology and theologians are challenged to re-read and to re-understand the Gospel and of the churches' presence in the world (Ott 2000: 155). As Christians we need to link up contemporary challenges with the rich our rich tradition, interpreting God's care for Malawi within the history of salvation. Moreover, the gospel of our Lord Jesus Christ has always been transforming society ever since it came into being just as human rights do. Just as human sin creates conflict within the world, tearing its social fabric apart, so the gospel of our Lord Jesus Christ, in seeking its remedy, creates a ferment of transformation not only in the church but also within society (De Gruchy 2002: 20-21).

It is good for Malawi that, as a nation, it protected human rights by law on 17th May, 1994, for the first time, when its National Assembly adopted an Interim Constitution, soon after its first ever multiparty democratic Presidential and Parliamentary General elections (Phiri & Ross 1998: 353). Prior to the adoption of this new constitution, the opposition political leaders attacked the Malawi Congress Party government for the social, economic, cultural and political crimes it committed against the people of Malawi during its thirty years in power, and hence, called for a new Constitution (Ott 2000: 92). The opposition political leaders saw that the one-political party system of government in Malawi was harbouring evils, including violations of human rights Phiri & (Phiri & Ross 1998: 92). The eight Roman Catholic Bishops, too, in their letter that was read in all Roman Catholic parishes, attacked the social, political, cultural and economic injustices and gross abuse of human rights by the Malawi Congress Party government. It is because of this that they called for immediate change of the entire superstructure, since the independence Constitution had no legal guarantees of human rights (Phiri & Ross 1998: 356). The independence Constitution was no more than a symbol of *a de facto* transfer of power, which had already occurred at constitutional talks. But Malawians saw the new Constitution as a means by which they would free themselves from a repressive past, and appropriate the virtues of democracy with its emphasis on the rights of the individual and responsibilities of the state (Phiri & Ross 1998: 320).

It is evident, here, that all along the fight for democracy in Malawi, condemnation for human rights violations was so much targeted towards the Malawi Congress Party government. Yet, human rights violations were, and still are, rampant amongst people at local level in Malawi. Even as it is more than ten years of democracy in Malawi now, there still are large numbers of complaints of human right violations. For example, the 2005 United States Report on Human Rights in Malawi announces that the Malawi Human Rights Commission handled 1,136 complaints of human rights violations in Malawi society in 2004, compared to 587 complaints in 2003 ((United States Department of State Report of 2005). Again, the Malawi Human Rights Commission handled 867 complaints of human rights violations during the year 2006 (United States Department of State Report of 2006). The Malawi Human Rights Commission was established under Chapter XI of the 1995 Constitution of the Republic of Malawi in order that human rights may be well maintained in Malawi. The Malawi Human Rights Commission acts as a human right information source, promotes awareness and respect for human rights, assists teaching and research on human rights and addresses human rights violations in Malawi (Malawi Human Rights Commission). In so doing, it has a broad mandate of promoting and protecting human rights in the broadest sense possible and to receive violations of human rights on its own motion or upon complaints received from any person, class of persons or body.

Besides itself, the Malawi Human Rights Commission maintains a directory of Human Rights Institutions that lists more than seventy institutions and organizations dealing with diverse issues of human rights such as women's and children's rights, rights of persons with disability, the situation of orphans or education. It was during the "Referendum" that the human rights organisations surfaced (Phiri & Ross 1998: 244). The first one was the "Civil Liberties Committee" (CILIC) that was launched in February 1993, and followed by "Legal Resources Centre" (LRC). By the various institutions for the upholding human rights in Malawi, members of the general public, government, academic institutions and other non-governmental institutions are assisted on specific human rights needs and issues, which they want to be addressed.

Churches, too, have institutions that handle human rights issues. The Roman Catholic established a "Justice and Peace Desk", which received departmental status as of 1996, and Synods of Blantyre and Livingstonia of the Church of Central Africa Presbyterian established a "Church and Society Desk" each (Phiri & Ross 1998: 117-118). However, in Malawi the modal approach to church parish work treats social ministry as secondary, as evidenced by the outcome from Church and Society of the Synod of Blantyre, which works through the church ministers and lay leaders to bring human rights issues to the local level (Phiri & Ross 1998: 118-119).

Here, the Presbyterian church ministers' and lay leaders' tend to emphasize more on spreading the gospel, deepening people's understanding of their faith or helping people meet Christ as their Saviour, than the way they are doing it to bring human rights issues to the local level. Their understanding of the gospel is more of a spiritual change than it is of a social change. They tend to leave matters of social change in the hands of the state. Yet there is interconnectedness between the church and state, and the church must be very much involved in civil affairs (Tengatenga 2006: 28). The Presbyterian or Reformed tradition, itself, lays down the principle that the church ought to be interested in all sides of life, spiritual and social.

> "Troeltsch observed that the Presbyterian or Reformed tradition...is marked by 'a systematic endeavour to mould the life of society as a whole...it lays down the principle that the church ought to be interested in all sides of life'" (Nzunda & Ross, *Church, Law and Political Transition in Malawi 1992-1994* 1995: 39-40).

JESUS' LIFE, IN THE GOSPELS, AND A PATTERN OF LIFE FOR THE REFORMED CHRISTIANS IN MALAWI

From the picture we have of the Church of Central Africa Presbyterian in Malawi, it is evident that Jesus' life on earth, Jesus' sayings or parables in the Gospel narratives (Paas 2004: 137-138), are sometimes misunderstood or insufficiently applied, by the Reformed churches, for believers' renewed life in Jesus Christ. Such is an insufficient application of salvation by grace through faith in Jesus Christ. However, Jesus Christ as our Mediator, sent by God to accomplish our reconciliation and salvation, did offer active obedience to God such that he effected transformation and participation in us in our renewed life, not only from his death on the cross, but also in his incarnation and through his life of obedience all the way to his resurrection from the dead. Indeed, what Jesus said or encountered in his human life on earth, or what we read in the Gospels, was definitely consistent with God's moral justice, his intrinsic nature as the Son of God, and his mission as the saviour of sinful humanity.

The Reformed Christians in Malawi do believe that in the Gospel narratives Jesus teaches them who God is, as much as he demonstrates his life in human society, to them, for them to participate in their renewed life. That is, on reading the Gospels, one does find oneself filled with admiration, overwhelmed with emotion and taken captive by the record of Jesus' life, parables and sayings - besides his death. Here, Jesus' life, teaching, parables and sayings do penetrate more deeply into the mysterious reality of human condition. Therefore, by noting Jesus' conduct and his words, recorded in the Gospels, believers are able to learn what God is like, how he acts, what human beings could be and ought to be, and hence, this evokes their participation.

Certainly, in the parables and sayings, Jesus does illustrate who God is, sometimes using imaginary characters, for his practical life in human society, in order that he will impress a pattern of life in our renewed life with him. Hence, these were "passive parables" in the sense that Jesus Christ did use imaginary characters to assist in conveying his message about God onto us, as his transformational power for our new life in him. Indeed, Jesus' own life and actions do constitute "active parables", in the sense that he himself is, but acting out real and genuine human life worthy of transformation and participation by believers in their renewed life. In these active parables, Jesus' deeds do complement what he says – and hence, these parables and deeds do have a transformative effect in the lives of believers. This section, therefore, will discuss Jesus' real and genuine human life in the Gospels, which is capable of effecting transformation in believers and as commonly and popularly understood by the contemporary Church of Central Africa Presbyterian in Malawi, with a view to their potential relevance for a culture of human rights.

Jesus felt compassion for people in need, and was inclusive of women and children in his life

When we read the Gospels, we are struck by the fact that large crowds always followed Jesus, in his public ministry. Wherever Jesus went he was in the midst of people. That is, Jesus was very fond of welcoming other people into his life. Therefore, it was not surprising to see him in the synagogue, at the temple festivals, at weddings, at funerals, near sick beds, eating with publicans, sinners or with prostitutes.

The people who gathered around Jesus were not people of status in society, but the local people on the street and in villages. These were people with needs, desires, hopes or longings. They followed Jesus with different motives and desires, and hence, they behaved differently at different times. For example, those that followed Jesus included those with a feeling of the burden of heavy taxation, the experience of the cruelty of the Roman rule of the time, hard-pressed life and alienation from the temple religion, sickness, hunger and thirsty, homelessness, destitute life, marginalized life or those that wanted to hear about the coming rule of God and the establishment of the kingdom of God.

Interestingly, Jesus knew very well that the people who followed him were sinners, and that not all that followed him did that purely for spiritual reasons. Nevertheless, Jesus' heart was moved with compassion every time he saw a crowd. Here, compassion simply means a human heart taking upon itself the suffering of another human being for comfort, without consideration of any returns from the human being. How did Jesus bring others, around him, into his comfort? Jesus seems to have been born in a middle class family of his father Joseph and his mother Mary. His father was a carpenter. Even though Jesus had come from such a middle class family and had no appreciable disadvantages himself, he willingly and intentionally mixed socially with the disadvantaged in order that he alleviates their suffering and anguish. That is why, over and over again, in the gospels, Jesus says to the needy around him, "Do not worry," "Do not cry" (Luke 7:13), "Do not be afraid" (Matthew 10:31), or "Do not let your hearts be troubled" (John 14:1). Jesus was moved with compassion, and therefore, he set out to liberate people from every form of suffering and anguish. Whoever did not have food to eat, Jesus would find food on their behalf. Jesus would pray for the sick and they got healed. He had the deeds of others at heart and was always willing to help.

Again, we read in the Gospels that out of his compassion for people, Jesus healed people with physical impairments, those that were considered as unclean, and hence, there always took place a restoration of their relationship with their families and their society. In the Hebrew Bible, purity and cleanliness are shown to be important to the religious life of the community. Those who were considered to be unclean by the community, such as those with physical impairments, were removed from society until such a time as they could be classed as clean. For some time, however, unless a miracle occurred, they would always stay stigmatized and excluded from society. Therefore, by touching those considered unclean and by willing to spend time with those whom society had rejected, Jesus showed that he considers all people equally valuable. Where once people would have been isolated and alone, Jesus brings them back to their families and communities. Nevertheless, although physical healing was important for restoration of earthly relationships, Jesus offered the physical impaired the opportunity to be spiritually healed. The opportunity to be restored spiritually is the most important relationship of all because it is the restoration of a relationship with God. That is why Jesus said, "Your sins have been forgiven," most of the times he healed a person.

In the Gospels, also, we see Jesus Christ having special relationship with women. Jesus accepted women in his life, in contrast to what was happening in the Jewish religion at the time. There are such examples as the healing of Simon's mother-in-law who was in bed with fever (Mark 1:29-31); the healing of the woman with the haemorrhage (Mark 5:24-34); the healing of the Syro-Phoenician woman's daughter (Mark 7:24-30); the raising of Jairus' daughter (Mark 5: 35-43); Jesus compassion for the widow of Nain whose son he raised from death (Luke 7:11-14); Jesus affirmation of the woman with spinal deformation as a daughter of

Abraham (Luke 13:10-17), that is to say, one of God's chosen people.

Again, in the Gospels Jesus accepts personal service of women. Good examples are those of Martha (Luke 10:38-42; John 12:2), who welcomed Jesus into her house and served him with a meal, and a sinful woman who anointed Jesus with oil (Luke 7:36-50).

There is also evidence that some women, whom Jesus had healed, participated in his public ministry together with his twelve disciples. These women are Mary Magdalene, Joanna, the wife of Herod's steward Chuza and Susanna (Luke 8:1-3).

In the Gospels, also, there are traces of Jesus having concern for women when he uses women as examples in his teachings. Jesus admires a poor widow's generous giving (Mark 12:41-44); he grieves for daughters of Jerusalem (Luke 23:28); he uses women in some of his parables, such as the parable of a woman's search for a lost coin (Luke 15:8-10).

Also, in the Gospels we read that Jesus had a special place for children in his life. At one point in the gospels, it seems Jesus' disciples did not think children were important enough for Jesus to take time with them (Mark 10:13-16). After all, many important men, like religious leaders, were coming to Jesus and asking him questions. Maybe the disciples thought Jesus had more important things to do, or maybe it had been a long day and they did not want Jesus to get tired out. But Jesus was angry with his disciples when they tried to stop the children from coming to him. Here, Jesus cares so much about children and he was serious with his disciples about not hurting the children's feelings. The disciples had a wrong attitude about children, which may have been the way most people back in those days thought of their children. But Jesus treated these children with utmost importance as he would treat adults. In fact, Jesus did not leave that place until he had held them, laughed with them, played with them and prayed for them.

Again, in his teaching, Jesus linked children with eligibility to receiving the kingdom of God (Luke 18:15-17). Of course, the passage does not explicitly state what it means to receive "the kingdom of God like a child". Some have suggested that it has something to do with children's exemplary life of openness, willingness to trust and dependence. Also, Jesus links children with greatness in Luke 9:46-48. Jesus' good news for his disciples was that greatness could not be pursued and possessed. While in Matthew 21:12-17, Jesus affirms the validity of children's worship of him despite the condemnation of the chief priests and teachers. Here, those who had great religious training failed to see what children ably recognized.

Jesus' presence among people was the good news for the poor and the vulnerable, and hence, affirms that God is already in the midst of human beings, empowering them to liberate themselves from the shackles of depression and despair through serving one another. Here, Jesus' presence among the people and his compassion for people do evoke human beings' participation, to truly love one another, to accept one another for who they are, and to grow together, unified and equal. All this is possible through human beings' willingness, as believers, to share what they have with the poor, to feed the hungry and to care for the vulnerable or relieve the oppressed in the society they are living. Moreover, in a justified life a believer has been graciously set free to love and obey God in loving his or her neighbour (Brinkman 1996: 47).

In short, according to the way that the Gospels are commonly and popularly read and preached in the CCAP, one would expect that this compassion of Jesus and this obvious inclusiveness of his ministry would inspire congregations and believers in Malawi to look on to Jesus' life and behaviour as a pattern they ought to apply in their lives, in their support or cultivation of human rights.

Jesus' transformative power that affects human beings to willingly serve those in need

In the Gospels, Jesus physically died on the cross as a sacrifice so that God might forgive human beings of their sins, and hence, Jesus willingly did a great service to all human beings. At the Last Supper Jesus predicted his death as he affirmed of his pouring out of his blood for many for the forgiveness of their sins (Matthew 26:27; Mark 14:24; Luke 22:26). Human beings themselves were unable to save themselves from sin. In this direction, John the Baptist affirms of Jesus as the Lamb of God who takes away the sin of the world (John 1:29). Moreover, Jesus himself knew no sin. The angel that came with a message of God, about Jesus birth, to Mary, describes Jesus as "the holy one to be born" (Luke 1:35). However, Jesus became sin, taking on the sins of all human beings onto his shoulders, so that he might make sinful human beings saints.

By his death on the cross, Jesus Christ reconciled the world with himself, liberating needy humanity from all their pretensions and releasing them for historical actions in the ambiguities of daily history (Brinkman 1996: 50-51). Because of what Jesus endured on the cross, every human being is now reconciled with God and to one another through serving one another. Such is the transformative power in Jesus, which does effect believers to the point of willingness to serve those that are in need by taking onto their shoulders their sufferings and miseries. That is, this widespread understanding of Jesus' self-giving, according to the Gospel accounts, of his life and death has transformative effect on believers as a "pattern" they ought to apply in their own lives and for the support and practice of human rights in society.

The very nature of Jesus Christ is that he came to serve others, and for believers to walk with him with gratitude by willingly serving others

In the Gospels, Jesus affirms that God forgives human beings their sins because God is merciful, and hence, human beings become justified. Here, there is an automatic or natural connection between the justification of the sinner and his or her desire and ability to perform good works (McGrath 1988: 122). Therefore, in their justified life human beings are called to do other human beings the same justice they received from God. The parable of the unforgiving debtor (Matthew 18:21-25) is one such example. In this parable, Jesus means to call upon believers to participate in producing a free and generous attitude of forgiveness toward others in society, especially those who repent and seek forgiveness, realizing how completely God in Jesus has forgiven them (Matthew 18:25). That is, because God had forgiven all their sins, when they expressed repentance, they should not withhold forgiveness from others who repent. Here, repentance and forgiveness are very important in God's justice towards human beings. In the Rustenburg Declaration of black and white, South African church leaders expressed their awareness "that without genuine repentance and practical restitution we do not appropriate God's forgiveness and that without justice true reconciliation between people is impossible (Brinkman 1996: 45).

Again, the Gospels speak about Jesus reconciling human beings with God, and Jesus sending human beings the Holy Spirit. In other words, the Gospels speak about human beings entering into reconciliation with God in Jesus Christ, which brings his Holy Spirit to work in human beings here and now. The Holy Spirit, thus, sanctifies human beings by working in them the very nature of Jesus Christ. The very nature of Jesus Christ is that he came to serve others, and for believers to walk with him, and hence, they willingly participate in serving others with Jesus out of their gratitude for what Jesus has done for them. Moreover, Jesus tells believers that if they love him they will do what he has commanded them to do, Again, Jesus tells believers to learn from him, as he is lowly and humble (Murray 2005: 68-71). Hence, he affirms that the more lowly believers become and do service to others, the greater they become in the eyes of God. For the popular sermon readings in the CCAP, this "doing service to others" message in the Gospels' account of Jesus is fairly obvious – and it is a transformative power that should effect Reformed Christian believers in Malawi towards a human rights culture.

Jesus' Passover meal and command to Baptism is transformative power that effects believers to commune in one another as members of one family of God – the Church

The Gospels portray Jesus Christ as willing to gather his church. One such example is Jesus appeal to his disciples for them to unite in harmony and love as the Father, Son and Holy Spirit do (John 17:1, 21-24). Hence, Jesus prayed to ask his Father in heaven to gather all human beings as his one Church, in the oneness of the Holy Trinity.

In the Gospels, also, Jesus called on his disciples to make disciples of all nations, and that they baptize everyone to signify everyone's obedience to Jesus' command and entry into this Church of Jesus Christ (Matthew 28:19).

Again, the Gospels tell of Jesus' gathering of his Church through the Last Supper – the Lord's Supper (Matthew 26:26-29; Mark 14:22-25; Luke 22:17-20). Each time believers use the Lord's Supper it brings out a different dimension to it. It is the Lord's Supper because it commemorates the Passover meal Jesus ate with his disciples, but it is Holy Communion because through it believers commune with God and with one another as they sit around the one communion table. This is like a traditional Malawian meal, where a family would sit around the one table, and eat from the one big plate of food, and drink from the one big cup of water. Hence, it signifies unity in harmony and love of the family. If for some reasons members of this family have sour relationship among themselves, they would resort into eating from different tables and from different plates, and drink from different cups of water.

JESUS' PATTERN OF LIFE FOR BELIEVERS AND HUMAN RIGHTS

This section, therefore, will seek to affirm how Jesus' active obedience to God may lead the Reformed Christians in Malawi toward the protection and upholding of human rights and freedoms, in their renewed lives. The point of departure achieve this goal will be the pattern of life that believers get from the obedience of Christ (in the foregoing section 4.3). In this process, also, a more specific theological basis for human rights – based on the Reformed doctrine of atonement – will be provided than has often been provided in church discussions, and it is one that should resonate well with believers in the CCAP in Malawi, helping them to overcome a still widespread reluctance and even resistance, often based on misunderstandings of the Reformed proclamation of atonement. Once again, the wide range of aspects of the classical Reformed understanding of the atonement will be used to describe such a broader theological basis for a culture of human dignity and human rights.

The covenantal faithfulness of God to his people

Jesus Christ is the actualization of God's covenant of grace in time and space. The apostle John affirms that in Jesus God's love for human beings is made complete (1 John 2:5), despite their sinfulness. No wonder the Gospels do affirm of Jesus as being very fond of welcoming other people into his life of a human being - no matter whether and how much these other people were different from him in their sinfulness. Jesus, thus, did not discriminate against anyone, and therefore, in their participation with Jesus Reformed Christians in Malawi ought to welcome other human beings in society into their lives by virtue of their being human, in their renewed life.

In Malawi, it is the person's right not to be discriminated against (*Malawi Constitution* 4.20.1-2). The right guarantees all persons in Malawi equal and effective protection against discrimination on grounds of race, colour, sex, language, religion, political or other opinion, nationality, ethnic or social origin, disability, property, birth or other status. Christian believers, themselves, depending on the covenantal faithfulness of God should easily recognize the correspondence between their faith and this fundamental human right in society.

The incarnation

Jesus Christ, in his immortality, risked his life by crossing the barriers between infinite and finite in order that he assumes the mortal human body. He assumed mortality of human beings so that by his immortality he might uplift human beings from their miseries, sufferings and death that had been caused by their sinfulness. The apostle Paul says that when the mortal has been clothed with the immortality, then the saying that is written will come true: "Death has been swallowed up in victory" (1 Corinthians 15:54). That is why the Gospels describe of Jesus as a mortal human being who lived on earth to experience sufferings and even death for the sake of delivering vulnerable human beings from their miseries and sufferings. By his Spirit, Jesus thus influences and empowers Reformed Christians in Malawi to do something about the problems and sufferings, which others in society are affected with, because they are community together with them, and that when one member of society is affected by a problem, the problem also affects the rest of members in that society, in some way.

In Malawi, it is the person's or a group's right to claim, without fear, that a fundamental right or freedom guaranteed by the Malawi Constitution has been infringed or threatened (*Malawi Constitution* 4.46.2). Many human rights abuses in Malawi go without being dealt with because some people lack the courage and sacrifice to claim, either for themselves or other people, the rights that have been infringed or threatened. Christians, who, themselves are continuously surprised by the love of God for human beings so powerfully demonstrated in the incarnation, should immediately see the importance of respecting, upholding, protecting, and if necessary defending the dignity of others.

Jesus' death on the cross as the acceptance of those who do not deserve

Human beings were still sinful and corrupt when Jesus Christ sacrificed his life and died on the cross for the justification (acceptance of those who do not deserve) of sinful human beings and for the upholding of God's justice. The apostle Paul affirms that while human beings were still sinners, Christ died for them as a sacrifice, justifying them by his blood and saving them from God's wrath through him (Romans 5:8, 9). The Gospels, too, speak of Jesus as having died and shed his blood on the cross for human sin. Jesus, thus, rendered his life as a sacrifice acceptable and meaningful to God and sinful human beings. In so doing, Jesus took human beings' death punishment, shame and their blame – which human beings deserved - and hence, Jesus clothed them with his innocence and purity that they did not deserve.

In so doing, Jesus does affect the Reformed Christians in Malawi, by his Spirit, not to turn away from struggle for justice for all in society on account of any humiliation, suffering, trials or even death they may experience – but to render their lives as a sacrifice acceptable and meaningful to God and their neighbours - because, as community, they all stand together as dignified human beings.

In Malawi and through the assistance of the courts, the Ombudsman, the Human Rights Commission and other organs of the Malawi Government, it is the right of all persons in Malawi to seek the promotion, protection and redress of grievances in respect of human rights for all (*Malawi Constitution* 4.15.2). There are some people in Malawi who still think that the responsibility in enforcing protection and upholding of human rights remains in the hands of the Malawi Government. The right, therefore, means to say that it is everyone's duty to see to it that human rights are protected and upheld.

d) Jesus' death and resurrection means human uplifting from lowliness

Jesus died on the cross and was buried. He was in the grave up to the third day, on the Easter morning, when he rose up from the dead. Here, not only do believers share in Jesus' death in their union with him, but that Jesus does also assure believers of their own resurrection by receiving a guarantee, substantiated by his. It is because of Jesus' death and resurrection that believers are lifted up from lowliness to exaltation and made new creation, and hence, it is their new form of existence as faithful covenant-partners with God. In his death, Jesus, thus, identifies with human beings in their sinfulness in order that he uplifts them up into newness of life by his resurrection. The apostle Paul affirms that if we are united in Christ in his death, certainly we will also be united with him in his resurrection (Romans 6:5ff.). We can, therefore, enjoy our new life in Christ because of our union with him in this manner. Our former evil desires, bondage to sin, and love of sin, have since died with Jesus. Now, that we are united by faith in Christ in his resurrection life, we have unbroken fellowship with God and our neighbours, and freedom from sin's hold on us.

The resurrection is not only the exaltation of Jesus, but is also the exaltation of human beings. The resurrection is the new creation of human beings' or the new form of existence in Jesus Christ that makes them capable of looking on beyond human struggles for justice and better society - to a new and better world for all. By looking beyond such life struggles, it makes a vision or a goal real, and hence, it is very encouraging. Moreover, everyone has a right to development in that better world. In Malawi, it is everyone's right to development and therefore to the enjoyment of economic, social, cultural and political development of all (*Malawi Constitution* 4.30.1).

To this end, there has not been enough done in the development of the poor, the vulnerable and suffering in Malawi society political leaders in Malawi. Most politicians in the Malawi House of Parliament do not seem to identify with their poor genuinely in the constituencies that they lead, and hence, they tend to divert away from most of development items on the agenda in Parliament. Such behaviour divides the House so much that it tempts most of the Parliamentarians to commit most of their time to petty political parties' issues, aimed at degrading each others' political parties. Hence, there is very little hope for a better Malawi for many Malawians. Hope for a better Malawi can only be instilled in the Malawi people, especially the poor, the vulnerable and suffering, through empowering them to develop in different sectors of their lives, whilst in their present situation of life's struggles. The Parliamentarians in the Malawi House of Parliament can make this possible only through serious debates on development issues. Based on their faith in the atoning work of Jesus Christ, Christians and the churches, too, should support and embody this special care for the suffering and poor, also by public appeals and examples.

Our union with Jesus Christ

Jesus Christ willingly and intentionally unites with believers in order that he shares their sinfulness and the consequences thereof, and thereafter he uplifts them from the agony of sin. It is because of this that believers are eligible for partaking of what Jesus has benefited for them in his suffering, death and resurrection (Jesus' graces). Therefore, in uniting with believers and sharing in their sin and its consequences for their up-lifting, Jesus thus makes the Reformed Christians in Malawi capable of sympathizing with the oppressed and suffering around them in society in a bid to uphold justice in that society, and in a bid to uplift the lives of those people so that they may fully enjoy the privileges that they themselves enjoy in society.

The apostle Paul urges all believers be devoted to one another in brotherly love, honouring one another above self (Romans 12:10). As believers, we honour people because they are our brothers and sisters in Jesus Christ, and because they have a unique contribution to make to Christ's church, in spite of their being needy, suffering or vulnerable.

In Malawi, it is the right of all persons to development and therefore to the enjoyment of economic, social, cultural and political development, with the vulnerable such as women, children and the disabled given special consideration in the realization of the right (*Malawi Constitution* 4.30.1-2). The right protects women, children and the disabled, who, in the Malawi society, are still under-represented in decision-making forums for development. This has resulted to inequality of opportunity for all in the access to basic resources, education, health services, food, shelter, employment and infrastructure.

Again, Jesus Christ's union with believers makes him mortal, and hence, a sharer in their misfortunes of sin and its consequence in the divine and human unity of being, enabling believers to partake of his graces in his suffering, death and resurrection. Hence, it presupposes believers' sharing of God's power, might and wisdom which enables them to stoop down and to accommodate the vulnerable in the society that they live, in their lives, in such a way that what they (the Christians) are – dignified - others become also. In Philippians 3:10, the apostle Paul as sinful human being willed to be united with Christ so that he would partake in his graces, and experience the power that raised Christ from the dead. In the same way, if Christians are willing to identify with the needy, vulnerable and suffering, there will be a great experience of power of social justice and equality in the lives of these needy, vulnerable and suffering.

In Malawi, the vulnerable have the right to experiencing power of social justice and equality. That is, it is the vulnerable persons' (especially women, children and the disabled) right to development, with measures taken to introduce reforms aimed at eradicating social injustices and inequalities in society (*Malawi Constitution* 4.30.1,3). Hence, the right puts the needy, vulnerable and suffering at equal level with everyone else in Malawi society. Unfortunately, some people in Malawi treat the needy, vulnerable and suffering as if they are not worthy of some of the privileges in economic, social, cultural and political development. Worst of all, there are not many people in contemporary Malawi who take it as their responsibility to uplift the lives of others.

God calls us in Jesus as his covenant partners

Jesus Christ calls men and women for making them covenant partners to look to the cause of fellow human beings in a world of corruption and evil. In Romans 5:8, the apostle Paul says that while we were still sinners, Christ died for us. Here, we were weak and helpless because we could do nothing on our own to save ourselves from sin and death. Someone had to come and rescue us, and that is Jesus Christ. The apostle Peter says that it is God who, in Jesus Christ his Son, has made us participants in his divine nature and escape the corruption in the world (2 Peter 1:4). Jesus, thus, protected and upheld our dignity, and hence, he made us participants with him in looking to the cause of others in our daily lives – leading to our protection and upholding of dignity for all in society.

Not everyone, in our world today, is capable of ensuring the promotion, protection and redress of grievances in respect of rights for self. Hence, many human rights abuses go unchecked. Nevertheless, it is the right of all natural or legal persons, in Malawi, to seek the assistance of the courts, the Ombudsman, the human Rights Commission and other organs of the Malawi government to ensure the promotion, protection and redress of grievances in respect of rights for themselves or others (*Malawi Constitution* 4.15.2). Unfortunately, there are still people in Malawi who think that protection and upholding of human rights is none of their business, but remains in the hands of the Malawi Government and other agencies, whilst some women think that it is the duty of men to promote and protect human rights. This right, therefore, means to educate and empower all people in Malawi (men and women) that in every generation there shall be violations of human rights and that it is everyone's duty to assist without fear and partiality in the enforcement of those rights through the agencies mentioned above. There is a tendency by some people in Malawi society that, for fear of getting involved, they do not care when someone's rights are at risk.

In addition, Jesus Christ teaches us what it means to live our calling. In the first letter of John (3:16a), "Jesus Christ laid down his life for us." Jesus loved us from the heart, such that he lived a sacrificial life of fellowship and service with us, in his union with us and vulnerable as we were in our corruptedness and sinfulness. In so doing, Jesus thus is calling the Reformed Christians in Malawi to discipleship, and to be ready to suffer for the liberation of those of their people in society who are in pains, oppression and other inflictions because they need freedom and joy as they (the Reformed Christians) do. It is easy, in our world today, to turn a blind eye to what is happening in the world around us and to pretend as if nothing serious is happening to other people. Reformed Christians in Malawian Christian must be willing to lay down their lives for others in society (1 John 3:16b). Since there is a tendency by many people to degrade the vulnerable in our world today, Jesus seems to say, here, that special attention should be given in empowering the vulnerable of society for fellowship and service.

For example, many men in Malawi would degrade women to the point of denying them participate in certain roles traditionally meant for men only in Malawi society. Certainly, Jesus would say, here, that all men, in their daily lives, ought to empower women for fellowship and service, in spite of their sex – leading to their lifting women up from the agony of degradation and servitude.

In Malawi, it is women's right to full and equal protection by the law, and the right not to be discriminated against because of their gender or marital status (*Malawi Constitution* 4.24.1-2). It includes the right to be accorded the same rights as men in civil law. Some people in Malawi society still feel that women are not equally capable of doing certain things as men. In the Church of Central Africa Presbyterian in Malawi, too, there are still some members who think that subordination of women to men is divinely sanctioned (Phiri 2000: 55). They do insist that the creation story in Genesis is but the biblical foundation for the subordination of women. Here, Genesis 3:16 is taken to be the divine law that man should be the head of the woman - arguments further strengthened by Paul's teaching in the New Testament, especially his words addressed to the church in Corinth in 1 Corinthians 14:34-35). While there is insistence on subordination of women to men on biblical grounds, there is also insistence on subordination of women on cultural practices (Phiri 2000: 61). Thus, there are some people in Malawi today that are of the opinion that women should not be entitled to certain things equally with men because they are female, and hence, they feel that women are inferior to men. The right, therefore, lifts women up from a life of inferiority, indignity and fear, to a life of equal dignity with men. Moreover, men and women should work together as bondservants of Jesus Christ and his righteousness. Jesus' yoke and bonds, here, are of love and not fear (Sinclair 2002: 227).

Again, God in Jesus Christ teaches us what it means to live one's calling. In his first letter, the apostle John affirms that God loved us and sent his Son as an atoning sacrifice for our sins (1 John 1:10). With love from the heart, on the cross and in his life, God's Son Jesus willingly humbled himself in perfect obedience to God's law and justice (God's will) in the midst of human beings and for human beings' sake. He did all this in spite of human beings' sinfulness, and hence, such did impress on the Reformed Christians in Malawi to do God's will in society and for the sake of others, in their daily lives – leading to their being capable of caring for one another in society, despite any differences and shortfalls.

If Christians in Malawi would respect the right of each member of a family to enjoy full and equal respect in Malawi, out of doing God's will and for the sake of others in society, everyone should, thus, be protected against all forms of neglect, cruelty or exploitation, despite who they are, man, woman or child (*Malawi Constitution* 4.22.2).

This right seems to educate married couples in Malawi in the upholding full and equal respect of one another, or of the children, as partners in a family, in spite of any differences. Right now, African women, including Malawi, are asking for partnership in family, society and in the church (Phiri 2000: 159). Many times, disagreements arise in a marriage just because one or both are trying to turn one into being the other - and hence, such is being disrespectful of each other. There are certain things family members need to tolerate of each other - as long as it does not have a negative impact on anyone.

God's justice in Jesus his Son

In Romans 3:25, the apostle Paul describes God as presenting his Son Jesus as a sacrifice of atonement, through faith in his blood, in order that he demonstrates his justice. Hence, Jesus Christ sacrificed himself for God and for human salvation in order that he satisfies God's justice. In the first place, God is justifiably angry with sinful human beings. They have rebelled against him and cut themselves from the life-giving power of God. But God declares Christ's death to be the appropriate and designated sacrifice for human sin. Christ then stands in human beings' place, completely satisfying God's demands, at the same time, paying the penalty of death for human sin, giving the Reformed Christians in Malawi a pattern of the life of determination in the struggle toward the liberation of those of their people that are under oppression of some kind and whose dignity is threatened, and even give up their lives in the struggle. In the words of the Lutheran tradition, justification is God's radical, liberating grace, which is given to human beings in Jesus and brings down the walls that separate human beings from God and each other. Here, God's grace not only allows human beings to be reconciled with each other, but it also compels them to seek proper social justice (Lutheran World Federation).

Here, as much as Malawian Christians would live their lives to exalt God and his justice, at the same time they would be exalting their fellow human beings, seeking proper social justice and putting them at their right place in society – respect of the dignity of all persons. In Malawi, all people are called to respect the right to the dignity of all persons (*Malawi Constitution* 4.19.1). The right protects everyone in Malawi from acts of injustice and indignity on one another.

We are justified freely by Jesus' grace

Apostle Paul affirms that we have all sinned and fall short of the glory of God, and are justified freely by Jesus' grace through redemption that came by him (Romans 3:23, 24). That is, by his grace Jesus Christ justifies believers, giving them rest on himself and his righteousness, despite their undeserving and vulnerability. In turn, the Reformed Christians in Malawi ought to mirror Jesus Christ into their lives, and should seek to be in solidarity with those people in society that are undeserving and vulnerable.

In Malawi it is the right of all persons to an effective remedy by a court of law or tribunal for acts violating the rights and freedoms granted to all persons (*Malawi Constitution* 4.41.3). The right protects all persons from any indignity, in spite of any vulnerability, and hence, all persons deserve equal recognition before the law as persons.

In addition, in justification and by virtue of Jesus Christ's righteousness, and not good works, human beings, that are not righteous in themselves, are reckoned as such before God. In gratitude, therefore, the Reformed Christians in Malawi will be capable of doing others the same justice they received freely from God – leading to their protection and upholding of the dignity of other human beings in society, despite their undeservedness.

In Malawi, it is the right of all persons to equal recognition as a person of dignity, before the law (*Malawi Constitution* 4.41.1). Traditionally and culturally, many people in Malawi tend to priotize the moral demands to the deserving such as those closest to them, particularly members of their own family, extended family or immediate community – and hence, are gracious to others by judging them as deserving. The right, therefore, means to encourage people in Malawi to recognize each other as people of equal importance and worth, and hence, they must be gracious towards one another without discrimination of any kind.

In their justified life, believers are dead into sin and risen into newness of life with Jesus. They are empowered, thus, by the regenerating work of the Holy Spirit to hate sin and to do good works acceptable to God in the world. In the newness of life with Jesus, therefore, believers are expected to embrace God's moral order for their daily lives – leading to their doing good works of justice in the world. All natural and legal persons in Malawi are called to doing good works of justice, in particular, the respect and uphold human rights and freedoms (*Malawi Constitution* 4.15.1). If only many people in Malawi were able to embrace moral order for their daily lives, there will be very little respect for human rights and freedoms in Malawi. The right means to call on all people in Malawi to embrace moral order for their lives according to the human rights chapter of the Malawi Constitution.

Our adoption into children of God

Apostle Paul affirms that God in his love predestined human beings to be adopted as his children through Jesus Christ, in accordance with his pleasure and will (Ephesians 1:4-5). Though divine, Jesus Christ willingly and freely lowered himself onto human beings when he became a human being himself in order that he raises human beings, adopting them into becoming brothers and sisters with him. Jesus, thus, willingly and freely called sinful human beings to become adopted children of God, in order that they become capable of experiencing and reflecting God's love in him - in which God the Father loves the Son, as God the Son loves the Father. Here, as a reflection of God's eternal love, Jesus calls and takes human beings into his fellowship with the Holy Trinity, where, besides sharing knowledge about God with Jesus, human beings will participate in Jesus' love with the Father.

In their fellowship with Jesus, in the Holy Trinity, the Reformed Christians in Malawi, therefore, find themselves capable of reflecting God's eternal love. That is, in fellowship with God and his Trinity, Christians are made into those who may and will freely love fellow human beings in return, to the point of adopting those whose dignity is threatened, into their lives.

In Malawi, the law shall prescribe criminal penalties for violations of human rights (*Malawi Constitution* 4.46.5), and hence, all persons in Malawi must respect the rights of other people as an obligation. But, as Christians, Malawians will go beyond the idea of an obligation, and will be capable of respecting the rights of others willingly and not out of fear of the prescription of criminal penalties for violations of those rights. This will be possible by the virtue of their being in fellowship with God as Trinity. As a result, a great many persons in Malawi shall feel dignified and secure not only amidst one's family, but also strangers or enemies. Here, a Malawian Christian is encouraged to set up dignity and security for others, beyond family loyalties, in return for the fellowship with God.

Our election

God in Jesus does freely elect human beings, out of his grace, to do works acceptable to God through looking to the cause of others in a world of corruption and evil, God's purpose of election. In Romans 9:11-12, the apostle Paul says that human beings are, thus, capable of doing good works by God who calls them to election, in order that God's purpose in election might stand. That is why, in his public ministry, as the first elect of God, Jesus felt compassion for people around him, and hence, he did works acceptable to God when he looked to the cause of other human beings. Jesus calls the Reformed Christians in Malawi, therefore, to participate with him in fulfilling God's purpose of election through looking to the cause of their fellow human beings freely, in the midst of corruption and evil in society.

In Malawi, by law and without prejudice, all persons should not place any restrictions or limitations on the exercise of any rights and freedoms provided for in the Malawi Constitution (*Malawi Constitution* 4.44.2). But, in order that God's purpose in election might stand Reformed Christians in Malawi will be capable of looking to the cause of other human beings – leading to their avoidance to placing restrictions or limitations on the exercise of any rights and freedoms provided for in the Malawi Constitution.

We are called to conform to the image of God

All human beings are called by God in Jesus to conform to his image by way of being a mirror of God's character and behaviour. Being a mirror of God's character and behaviour includes human beings' ability to make good judgements in life and to refrain from complaining about struggles. Instead, human beings must see struggles as opportunities to grow in character to God's glory and betterment of their fellow human beings. Jesus himself was capable and successful in making good judgments with other human beings, in his human life, and never complained because he is a genuine image of God. In his public ministry and as a human being, Jesus did not turn away from the justice he owed God his Father, but went ahead to alleviate sufferings and misery in people he came across, no matter such did bring him suffering and death. In Colossians 1:22, the apostle Paul speaks of God reconciling us on to himself in Jesus, who did not turn away from God's justice, but went through death and suffering in order that God presents us holy in his sight, without blemish and free from accusation.

Therefore, Jesus is an example for the Reformed Christians in Malawi, whose pattern they ought to use in their lives, for them not to turn away from justice they owe God because of any trials they can experience – leading to their protecting rights and freedoms of other human beings. Moreover, Malawian Christians have the support of the law in Malawi, which says that the courts shall have the power to make any orders that are necessary and appropriate to secure justice where the enjoyment of human rights and freedoms that have been unlawfully denied or violated (*Malawi Constitution* 4.46.3).

Again, Jesus' createdness in the image of God is genuine and true in the sense that his humanity is as God had originally intended it to be - belonging to God through relating to others. The apostle Peter urges his readers, as people belonging to God, to practice good relationship and good deeds when living among nonbelievers, despite hostility by these nonbelievers, so that on their seeing such good relationships and good deeds the nonbelievers will glorify God (1 Peter 2:12). For this reason, the whole of Jesus' public ministry was full of good relationship, love and compassion for other people around him in society, despite their hostility caused by sin, for them to see his good deeds and glorify God.

The Reformed Christians in Malawi, too, are called to practice good relationship and good deeds in the society the live in - relationships of mutual respect and love - despite any differences, say, in opinion, ideology or belief with others in society. Such is consistent with every person's right to freedom of conscience, religion, belief and thought (*Malawi Constitution* 4.34).

Jesus gathers us by his Spirit in the church

Jesus gathers believers as his Church by his graces in his sufferings, death, resurrection and glory, and makes them partakers with him in Holy Trinity's communion in the heavenly realms, through their fellowship with him by faith, in spite of their being vulnerable to sin and corruption. In so doing, Jesus makes them members with each other despite any differences among them. The apostle Paul affirms that it is by Jesus' grace that we have been raised up by God, even when we were dead in our transgressions, and that we sit with him in the heavenly realms (Ephesians 2:5, 6).

By the Holy Spirit, therefore, Jesus calls the Reformed Christians in Malawi to indiscriminately become members with others in society, in their daily lives - leading to their sharing in each other's gifts and graces in society, and are obliged to performance of such duties (public or private) for their mutual good.

Also, Jesus gathers his Church by his Spirit in the Sacraments of Baptism and the Lord's Supper. In Baptism, Jesus forms the firmest bond of union and fellowship between himself and believers, and believers amongst themselves in his Church. And in the Lord's Supper, Jesus makes believers capable of sharing of his broken body (his Church) in mutuality of love - a practice that enables the Reformed Christians in Malawi to become members one of another in their differences, and to love one another as members of the one Church of Jesus Christ.

John Calvin affirms of the Lord's Supper as a place of love. He explains the intention of Jesus about the Lord's Supper as that of exhorting Christians to purity and holiness of life, and to love, peace and peaceful relations among human beings (Calvin, *Institutes*, 4.17.38). Therefore, Calvin conceives of Jesus as communicating his body to Christians, so as to become completely a unity with them, and them with him. The bread in the sacraments represents this unity. Since bread is made up of many grains - so mixed together that one cannot be distinguished from another - so does Calvin believe that it is fitting that in the same way Christians should be joined and bound together by such great agreement of minds that does away with any disagreement or division. Hence, Christians will not allow other human beings to be despised, rejected, abused or offended in any way because they are the same body of Jesus. Christians ought to take the same care of other human beings' bodies as they take care of their own bodies. Here, any injury, despise and abuse of other human beings would mean injury, despise and abuse of Jesus Christ himself. For Christians, one cannot love Jesus without loving other people in society.

In Malawi, it is all persons and peoples' right not to be discriminated against – leading to the passing of legislation to address inequalities in Malawi society (*Malawi Constitution* 4.20.1-2), which is aimed at loving and serving one another as human beings equal in dignity. In his letter to the Galatians, Paul builds a case for Christian liberty for love and service. Because believers are saved by faith, and not by keeping the law (Galatians 5:1-12), they have Christian liberty. Christian liberty means that believers are free to love and serve one another, and not to do one another wrong (Galatians 5:13-26). That is, Christians should carry each other's burden and be kind to each other (Galatians 6:1-10). Moreover, Jesus suffered and died on the cross, and hence, carried human beings' burden of sin. In Jesus' death believers have put to death their sinful nature, and therefore, truth, love and peace should mark Christians' lives (Colossians 3:9-15). Here, their love for Jesus Christ, for his dying for them, should translate into love for other human beings (Colossians 3:16-4:1).

SUMMARY AND EVALUATION

Given the fact, which was mentioned in the hypothesis of this research thesis (in Chjapter 1), that many Reformed Christians in Malawi are seeking to support human human rights and dignity in democratic Malawi, but that they see the classic Reformed doctrine of atonement as not assisting them in doing that, this chapter therefore, demonstrates that only the broader view of the atonement can contribute to a more positive view of human rights and dignity. Hence, the chapter showed how Jesus' active obedience as a full human being and as protrayed in the Gospels, is consistent with the broader view of the atonement (Covenant, Incarnation, Union with Christ, Calling, Justification, Adoption into children of God, Election, Image of God and Community in the Church by the Spirit). In each case Jesus sets an example whose pattern the Reformed Christians in Malawi ought to express in their renewed life in Jesus. If only these Reformed Christians in Malawi will be able to take Jesus seriously and as their pattern of life, along the lines of the broader view of the atonement above, there cannot be any great impact or difference the Reformed view of the atonement can make in their lives, in their reception of human rights and freedoms in Malawi.

Indeed, the Gospels are full of life experiences, sayings and parables by Jesus, worthy participation by Reformed Christians in Malawi in their new life in Jesus. That is, Jesus' acts as a human being on earth, Jesus' sayings or parables in the Gospel narratives are of much relevance in the lives of the Reformed Christians in Malawi, particularly as a power for transformation of their new life in Jesus. Hence, this is consistent with the Reformed view about Jesus Christ's graces in his death and his resurrection, onto believers – even though salvation is not by good works, but by grace through faith in Jesus Christ. Definitely, Jesus' compelling power, in the Gospels, is the same as Jesus' power in the classical Reformed view of the atonement that is capable of influencing a transformation in a believer. Therefore, the Reformed Christians in Malawi cannot resist the call for participation with Jesus in his life, in the Gospels, for their new life in Jesus, but that they will emotionally respond in wonder and gratitude to God for their justification by grace through faith in Jesus – leading to their works of love and care for others in society. Hence, it affirms that where Jesus' call for our participation with him, in the gospels, is used for the renewed life of the Reformed Christians in Malawi, the resultant is an emotional response in wonder and gratitude to God - leading to a different view concerning their relationship with others in society, and hence, the Reformed Christians in Malawi will resort to protection and upholding of human dignity, human rights and freedoms in the society they live.

For the CCAP in Malawi, such implications of the Reformed doctrine of atonement will provide a more inspiring, persuasive and instructive theological justification for a culture of human dignity and rights than many of the theological foundations provided over the past decades in ecumenical discussions and documents. That is, instead of being a challenge, this classic Reformed doctrine of atonement will definitely become a tool for the cultivation of human rights culture in the contemporary Malawi.

CHAPTER 5

CONCLUSION

INTRODUCTION

In this concluding chapter, the research study will restate in a more condensed form the central issues discussed in the foregoing chapters. The chapter is organized in two sections. The first section reviews a summary of findings. The second section deals with the contribution of new knowledge by the research.

SUMMARY OF FINDINGS

The research thesis' argument, in Chapter 1, is basically that the Reformed Christians in Malawi want to support a culture of human dignity and rights, but there is a widespread sense that the doctrine of the atonement, at the heart of the Reformed faith, does not assist them in doing that, but rather seems to contradict such a sense of "rights" with teachings as "Centred on God's glory alone", "Based on God's Word alone", "Justification by Faith alone".

"Centred on God's glory alone" is whereby Reformed theology affirms the sovereignty of God over every aspect of the believer's life. This is to say that believers must allow God himself to sanctify their works unto his glory, and therefore, believers must refrain from sanctifying their own works unto their own glory. "Based on God's Word alone", is whereby the Bible is entirely sufficient in all matters of believers' faith and practice in society as Christians, and therefore, anything else cannot be of equal value with the divine Scriptures. "Justification by Faith alone", is whereby faith alone in Jesus is the only substance or matter of what believers must do in order to be saved, and not good works.

In recent works, also in Chapter 1, particularly in the ecumenical Reformed documents on human rights (WARC, Reformed Ecumenical Synod), the research study finds that they use other doctrines to support human rights, but not the atonement that is central to the Reformed faith. The ecumenical Reformed documents basically support a vague feeling of human dignity, but not the notion of specific rights. It has something about human beings created in the image of God to mean that man and woman are equally created in the image of God, and that our being created in the image of God does affirm our equal dignity and interdependence of the present generation and the future generations in the stewardship of creation. Also, our being created in the image of God makes us stand in covenant relationship with God in our stewardship of creation, and vocation.

In the recent works in Chapter 1, the research study, also, mentioned of John Calvin that he did include a theology of revolution in his theology, which sought to reform theology, church and society of his time. However, Calvin's point of departure was, overall, the Holy Scriptures, and not the "atonement" as such. Calvin paid so much attention to the Law of God. He made expositions of the Ten Commandments as the moral Law, as best framework for understanding the Christian life. But others see Calvin's depiction of the Christian life as dying of oneself and rising from the dead with Christ, of discipleship and sanctification.

Again, in the recent literature in Chapter 1, the research thesis mentioned Karl Barth, who finds the Christian life in "the command of God the Reconciler". In so doing, Barth finds the heart of the Christian life in Prayer, Invocation and Calling upon God through reflection on the different petitions of the Lord's Prayer - and not necessarily in the Reformed doctrine of atonement..

It is this research study's belief, therefore, that it does contribute something in the regard of the Reformed doctrine of atonement, for the Reformed Christians in Malawi to be capable of supporting a culture of human dignity and rights. Indeed, it is the research study's argument that the Reformed understanding of the atonement is capable of supporting convictions regarding human dignity and even specific rights.

The argument is two-ford. Firstly, it was argued in the hypothesis of this research study that the Reformed understanding of the atonement is much broader than just the "cross and the resurrection of Jesus", to include such notions as election, calling, covenant, image of God, justification, regeneration, sanctification, work of the Spirit, community in the church, and others. Such a broader and more faithful understanding of the atonement, also amongst Reformed churches and believers, could help the Reformed Christians in contemporary Malawi to see the importance of a culture of human rights for the faithful practice of their own Reformed faith and piety more clearly.

A broader and more faithful understanding of the atonement - the restoration of the broken relationship between God and human being – is broader than the cross and the resurrection and should comprise everything about believers' justification and their connectedness with society. As such, the dissertation has repeatedly said right from the beginning of the research that a number of components in Jesus' salvation work like incarnation, covenant, adoption, election, creation in the image of God, sanctification, and others – which are popularly understood as involving believers' inward renewal - should be included in the broader view of the atonement, basing on the fact that they also are very much connected with transformation of human persons in society. With such in mind, the research conducted an exploratory study.

The results in Chapter 2 about a broader and more faithful understanding of the atonement show that the making of the covenant was recognition that, if a society is to work, it requires a common structure of law to give framework for living. The covenant, therefore, was produced to give a pattern for life. It is as if God is saying, "You belong to me; this is how I want you to live" - "Pattern your life on mine" – "You belong to me, and I want you to live like Jesus my Son."

Again in the covenant, Jesus caught up all humanity into his life and was himself caught up into God's equation of justice, by his becoming a human being. Jesus was the bridge in the reconciliation between God and humanity, and therefore, the findings reveal that this is a great impression - by the power of the Holy Spirit - on Christians, such that they are made into people who will welcome other human beings into their lives.

There is, in the covenant, God on one side that does not will to be God without humanity, and on the other side there is humanity that is failing to receive the covenant with God. Therefore, in the incarnation Jesus comes in and addresses the situation with the love from God in him. With the love from God Jesus comes to be with humanity, and hence, when human beings come to be with Jesus they find themselves in love with one another.

The incarnation meant that it was crucial for Jesus not to remain above humanity, up in heaven. Neither as God alone could Jesus feel death, nor as man alone could he overcome it. The findings reveal that as Jesus stooped onto human beings, despite his being God, he impressed on Christians with his Spirit for them to do likewise and to stoop down onto others in society, especially the poor and the vulnerable.

In the incarnation, also, God's Son Jesus Christ, though divine, did bear humiliation and weakness of the human body, and identified with us sinful humanity, satisfying what we humans owed God. Jesus, thus, was very humble to the point of identifying with human beings and their problems and sufferings, and in turn, Christians as followers of Christ should be willing to do something about the problems and sufferings that other people in society are experiencing.

Also, Jesus acted as God when he acted as a human being in the incarnation. He was the very God and the very humanity. Here, Jesus did unite human essence with his divine essence in order that he addresses the two – one on the other, especially the divine to the human – and therefore, Christians should be willing to uplift the lives of the poor, needy and vulnerable, which shall always require an expense on their part.

Hence, Jesus Christ was capable of perfectly satisfying the justice of God his Father by his perfect obedience and sacrifice of himself unto death in the incarnation, and hence, he purchased reconciliation and everlasting inheritance in the kingdom of heaven for human beings. Therefore, Christians as followers of Christ should be impressed and empowered by what Christ did and the Holy Spirit, and should take every opportunity of mediation in human conflict, and sacrifice themselves in that struggle, even unto death as Jesus did for us.

Jesus had to suffer and die on the cross in order that he makes a proper, real and full satisfaction of his Father's justice on behalf of humanity. As followers of Jesus, Christians, too, should assist in doing justice among fellow human beings in society because all human beings need justice for the society to function well. It took so much courage, endurance and love for humanity for Jesus to die such a terrible death on the cross. Moreover, Jesus did not violate God's justice himself, but human did. Christians, too, should not to turn away from doing justice toward other human beings society - even though they have not violated any justice themselves – and no matter such a mission is or looks dangerous.

Some people do not understand how a good God would target wrath toward his people because of their sinfulness. However, even though God had wrath against his sinful humanity, but he also had his mercy for his people such that he saved them his Son's death on the cross - and hence God gave humanity room for their rehabilitation in Jesus. As Christians we ought to be concerned about the violence, crime or injustice that affects other members in our society as Jesus did for us, and indeed let the law take its course. But at the same time, as societies we need to have laws that will give room for rehabilitation of those criminals and evildoers amidst us in society.

On the cross, it was not humanity that died, but Jesus. Jesus deeply humbled himself by suffering human beings' punishment of sin and died on the cross, and hence, he redeemed them of their sin, once for all. Jesus struggled for God's justice in his suffering and dying on the cross. He thus did suffer God's judgment – humiliation – in humanity's place, but also at the cross he did receive exaltation together with humanity. Christians, by the power of the Spirit of Jesus will not to turn away from struggle for justice for all in society on account of any humiliation, suffering, trials or even death they may experience, because as community of human beings, we stand together dignified.

Again, the results in Chapter 2 show that if there should have been death of Jesus only, then we should have not been talking about hope or new form of existence of human beings in the resurrection of Jesus. However, the resurrection is not only the exaltation of Jesus, but is also the exaltation of human beings. The resurrection is the new creation of human beings' or the new form of existence in Jesus Christ, and therefore, Christians are made capable to look beyond every struggle for justice in our human society, with a hope for a new and better world or society for all. By looking beyond life struggles, it makes a vision or a goal real, and hence, it is very encouraging.

Indeed, Jesus underwent humiliation in his perseverance in suffering and death on the cross, which he did so successfully, and hence, God made him rise up from the dead – in his exaltation – to become the head of his church and believers were capable of receiving new life. The findings affirm that Jesus encourages Christians by his Spirit to persevere the many hardships that come into their lives as they struggle daily for a better world for everyone.

The results in Chapter 2 have it that Christ unites us, under-dignified as we are, onto him in a spiritual union in such a way that all that Christ is becomes ours. The findings affirm that in our union with Christ as Christians, the Holy Spirit turns us into people who will accommodate others, in their lives, in the society that they live.

Also, in his union with believers, Jesus is capable of effectually applying and communicating his graces onto them by the Holy Spirit, and at the same time, Christians find themselves uniting with others in the society they live - supporting each other and sharing in the benefits or gifts that the society may offer. Moreover, the benefits in a society equally belong to all members. In this direction, because of union with Jesus Christ, we now can claim that what belongs to Jesus belongs to us, too. In our union with Jesus, he did take onto himself human sinfulness and punishment by God and shared the pain therein, of which he so persevered unto death on the cross in anticipation of the benefit of being exalted by God. Such leaves a good impression on Christians for them to suffer with the oppressed and suffering around them in society, in a bid to uphold justice in that society, and also in a bid to uplift the lives of those oppressed and suffering people for them to fully and equally enjoy the privileges that society offers, just like every other member of that society.

Again, the results in Chapter 2 show that in the fullness of time Jesus Christ died for human beings' sin and rose again for their justification. Therefore, human beings as believers, and by power of the Spirit of Jesus, must be determined in the struggle toward the liberation of those of their people that are under oppression of some kind, and even give up their lives in the struggle.

Justified human beings are those who are righteous by faith to the exclusion of all works, but at the same time, justified human beings are those who have set up righteousness in their life. Therefore, human beings can and must do good works because they are now at peace with God (justified) out of God's justice, mercy, love and grace in Jesus Christ.

In our justification, Jesus Christ sets an ethical example of compassion and mercy according to our nature as human beings – that of sparing the wicked, and therefore, save the wicked that in justice might be destroyed. Christians, too, must to forgive and spare other human beings, around them in society, from condemnation resulting from the wrongs they have done, who in justice they would sue and take to court to be judged and sentenced. After all, Christians are forgiven sinners in Jesus Christ.

The results in Chapter 2 show that Jesus does elect human beings to become his companions - even though human beings do not deserve it because of their sinfulness. This explains why human beings were not created lonely creatures right away from the beginning of their existence, but were created social animals. Therefore, as the elect human beings, Christians will freely share their lives with other fellow human beings, despite who they are, and because they all are equally human.

Jesus does elect human beings as his companions by living a life acceptable to God his Father. However, as much as Jesus did live a life acceptable to God his Father, even so he did it for human beings' election and human beings' redemption from all unrighteousness by his application of his righteousness onto them. In so doing, Christ impresses upon believers a life of being there, in this world, for others.

The results in Chapter 2 also show that Jesus freely and willingly acted on human beings' behalf when he suffered and died on the cross to reconcile them to God and share his benefits with them, and hence, Jesus calls Christians to discipleship, makes them ready to suffer for the liberation of those of our people in society who are in pains, oppression and other inflictions.

In the calling to discipleship, moderation serves to guide believers in the proper use of creational gifts, given them freely by God, with a humble spirit - and hence, such moderation make Christian believers capable of loving their neighbours from the heart. How tempting are creational gifts that we may discover to possess, which are given us freely by God, and hence, one tends to feel full of esteem as frequent use of such gifts grows. Nevertheless, Jesus as a human being had recreational gifts that he used in his life to care for others around him.

The results in Chapter 2 have it that God in Jesus Christ redeems human beings from being outsiders in God's family, and hence, God make them partakers of his grace of adoption in Jesus Christ. As adopted children of God in Jesus Christ, therefore, believers are entitled to enjoy the liberties and privileges of the children of God.

The liberties and privileges comprise of their putting on of God's name as God's children, their receiving the Spirit of adoption, their having access to the throne of grace with boldness, their being pitied, protected, provided for, and chastened by God as a good father, and inheriting God's promises as heirs of everlasting salvation. Moved by the power of Jesus' Spirit, Christians, too, must be willing to adopt those of our needy and orphaned children in society because these orphaned children deserve parental guidance and support as every other child in society. When adopted into families, such children should not at all be ill-treated, but should be given the liberties and privileges of children born in those families. In the same direction, Christians, also, must sympathize with those of our people who have been socially, economically and politically displaced in society – a kind of adoption - and to uplift them to their rightful place or level in society because they equally deserve dignity as every other member of society.

The results in Chapter 2 have it that faith originated from God himself when in Jesus Christ he chose himself for human beings. Indeed, Jesus willingly and with love chose himself for other human beings such that we can trust and depend on him as our Lord and Saviour. Likewise, Christians must be willing to choose themselves for others around them in society with love. Every human being does need trust and dependence from other in society for support and security.

The results in Chapter 2 have it that Jesus is the true image of God to which believers are called to conform. Here, there is the outward aspect of believers' imitation of the death of Jesus Christ in bearing the cross, which involves accepting the hardships, and difficulties that God brings into our lives, both the afflictions we share with all human beings and those undergone for the sake of the gospel and the cause of righteousness.

On his becoming a human being, Jesus restored humanity's broken relationship with God, inasmuch as he participates in and shares in humanity's creation in the image of God. As much as

Jesus restores human beings' relationship with God, at the same time, human beings find themselves restoring broken relationships amongst themselves.

The results in Chapter 2 have it that the incarnate Jesus Christ, as a sharer of everything with God, is a participant in the communion of the Holy Trinity, such that he incorporates human beings into communion with the Holy Trinity of God by his Spirit (the Holy Spirit). In so doing, human beings find themselves members of one of another with other human beings, in their daily lives.

Only those that are united with Christ does he gather to form the "Communion of Saints", and therefore, they find themselves uniting to one another in love, having communion in each other's gifts and grace and being in solidarity in times of suffering and need – hence such is solidarity of the Spirit.

In our solidarity through the Spirit, the Lord's Supper produces a life together in our mutual sharing and love as Christians. Here, our lack of love in our human society as believers may contradict our participation in the Supper.

Secondly, the research thesis argues that within this Reformed view of the atonement, the notion of Jesus' active obedience, in addition to the passive obedience, is of central importance. The hypothesis, here, involves the claim that a broader appreciation of the life and ministry of Jesus as integral to his work of atonement could contribute to a more positive view of human rights and dignity. Thus, the hypothesis involved the relevance of the life and ministry of our Lord Jesus Christ to such a more positive view of human rights that was aimed at correcting many of the misunderstandings created so often and easily in the light of Reformed convictions. Indeed, the research study did come up with the notions about Jesus' active obedience to God in light of the broader view of the classic Reformed understanding of the atonement, in Chapter 2 of the research study. Hence, it used atonement views by Anselm of Canterbury, John Calvin, Karl Barth, and the Westminster Confession of Faith to seek and explain such notions. The atonement views by Anselm, Calvin, Barth and the Westminster Confession were used because of their relevant historical or theological connections with, and/or contributions to the classic Reformed view of the doctrine of atonement.

To find the impact, difference and implications, the classic Reformed understanding of the atonement makes in the lives of the Reformed Christians in Malawi, the research study examined the active obedience by Jesus to God his Father, in light of the affirmations on the broader Reformed view of the atonement. The results showed that, by his active obedience to God his Father, Jesus by his Spirit invites believers to enter new life in him, in the sense that it is a revelation of the kind of renewed life that Jesus calls them to participate in. Here, Jesus Christ is the measure with which believers are capable of relating appropriately to God and others in society. Hence, the study affirmed that Jesus' transformational power onto believers for their new life does stem out of Jesus' active obedience to God on their behalf. That is, as much as Jesus obeys his Father in order that he cares for human beings, at the same time, Jesus by the Holy Spirit impresses his character and behaviour upon believers, and therefore, Jesus makes them capable of obedience to God and care for one another as human beings in society. Based on these two claims above - the broadening of the atonement and the addition of Jesus' active obedience into the atonement – the research study, therefore, went on to argue for human dignity and rights.

Regarding the second argument, the problem has been that normally Jesus' active obedience is also forensically reckoned "as if" we did it ourselves. For example, Jesus suffered the penalty for us (Jesus' passive obedience) and Jesus positively fulfilled the law for us (Jesus' active obedience) – both of these we receive without having to do it ourselves. Indeed, we thus fulfil the moral law, but we do not have to do it ourselves – is the classical understanding. The research study interprets this to mean that because we freely receive the successful passive and active obedience by Jesus as our own, we therefore should do it, follow it and even practice it. The research study, here, finds very strong quotes in the Christologies of John Calvin, Karl Barth and the Westminster Confession of Faith to support this argument. In the Christologies of these people Jesus Christ is referred to as the "pattern" for our life; justification and sanctification as merely two sides of the one double grace; and that through the Holy Spirit's "transformative power" we are renewed. Hence, such is so powerful material to argue for human dignity and rights amongst Reformed Christians in Malawi.

But before doing that, the research study did set out to find out whether the Church of Central Africa Presbyterian in Malawi has received or has not received the classic Reformed view of atonement above. To do so, it needed to examine and analyse the Church of Central Africa Presbyterian's views about God, Jesus Christ, humanity, sin, reconciliation between God and humanity, and human salvation in Jesus Christ. Therefore, a study about the Church of Central Africa Presbyterian's Constitution, confession of faith and catechisms was made in Chapter 3. The results in Chapter 3 show that the Church of Central Africa Presbyterian has received the Reformed views of the atonement, as evidenced by its Constitution, Confession of Faith and Catechisms. Thus, the Church of Central Africa Presbyterian does affirm that God, in his covenantal faithfulness, willed and intended to save human beings from their sins, in his Son Jesus Christ, and therefore, in the fullness of time God sent his Son Jesus Christ to save all humanity from their sins in his covenant of grace. In the incarnation, therefore, Jesus humbled himself by stripping off himself the divine glory and was born and lived as a true human being, and hence, was capable of fulfilling the Law of God on behalf of human being.

The Church of Central Africa Presbyterian, also, has it that humanity's violation of the Law of God led to its sinfulness, and hence, all humanity deserved the curse and punishment of the law, which is death. However, God took the death punishment on to himself in Jesus Christ, who died for human beings on the cross, taking upon him all their sins – and hence saved and justified them. Jesus Christ did die on the cross for us in order that he takes upon himself all humanity's iniquities, for their salvation and justification. When Jesus Christ died on the cross he was buried, but he rose again from the dead. On his resurrection, Jesus destroyed the power of Satan, death and sin.

Again, the Church of Central Africa Presbyterian believes in the Holy Spirit of God who works faith in us, and thus unites us with Jesus Christ, and hence, brings about salvation in us. This faith is a gift from God, who, by the Holy Spirit in Christ convicts human beings of their sin - and hence, enables them to recognize God's love for them in Jesus Christ.

For the Church of Central Africa Presbyterian in Malawi, Jesus does convict human beings of their sins by his Spirit, and hence, adopts them into children of God by new birth. Again, Jesus Christ by his Spirit sanctifies human hearts by turning them away from sins that are visible. These sins are very much connected with a negative human's life toward others in society. Here, the Church of Central Africa Presbyterian in Malawi affirms that believers do know the Spirit of Jesus because they can see its work and signs, which are works of love, works of happiness and works of peace in and among them.

Again the Church of Central Africa Presbyterian says that those united with Christ do receive his life of grace, which cleanses them of all weaknesses of their lives and encourages their new reborn life. The image of God in human beings was totally defaced, except for a very small remnant. The remnant in human beings assists Jesus by his Spirit to work rebirth in them. Jesus, here, is the true image of God.

However, the study found out that there is relatively little emphasis on the deity and humanity of Christ in the contemporary preaching and practical life of the Church of Central Africa Presbyterian, in spite of this Malawian church's receipt of some of the views from the Reformed tradition. Instead, there is but more emphasis of the works of Christ, which feature higher in Malawian preaching than Christ's deity and humanity. Again, the fact that Matthew, John, Luke, Acts, Mark, are amongst the top five most commonly chosen in the whole of the New Testament, seems to indicate that they are chosen in order that they substantiate the sermons that put more emphasis on the works of Christ. Also, the fact that "practical" James and "moralistic" 2 Timothy are the more commonly chosen than the more doctrinal Ephesians and Colossians seem that sermon themes on the works of Christ (mentioned above) are very much prevalent in the church in Malawi, with Jesus' call upon the Reformed Christians in Malawi for participation with him in his life, in their renewed life. Definitely, Jesus' invitation to participate with him in his life, in the gospels, is consistent with the Reformed view of atonement's proclamation of God's grace in Jesus and gratitude on the part of human beings in their renewed life. Here, the Reformed Christians in Malawi do respond to Jesus Christ's works in the Gospels, in the sense that the works are a true and genuine reflection of the kind of life they are called for by Jesus - leading the Reformed Christians in Malawi to doing Christian duties of love of God and to love of neighbour. However, the extreme strong emphasis on law-keeping and good works by the Reformed Christians in Malawi does give the impression that by good works they do contribute to their salvation. The research study, hereby, recommends that the Reformed preachers in Malawi need to be aware that, on one hand, there is Jesus Christ who fulfilled the Law for us, and on the other hand, we need to do good works not to our credit but out of our gratitude to God for his grace and mercy.

The Reformed view of the atonement in the notion of Jesus Christ's active obedience that calls for believers' participation in Jesus' life, in their renewed life, in Chapter 2, and Jesus' invitation to participate in his life, in the gospels, in the renewed life of the Reformed Christians in Malawi - in Chapter 3 - does provide a basis for human rights in Chapter 4. Chapter 4, therefore, affirms that the Reformed Christians' renewed life in Malawi may lead toward the protection and upholding of human rights and freedoms, findings that are not available in the recent works on Reformed faith and human dignity.

The results in Chapter 4 fills in the gap that the above-mentioned are not capable of filling up. Hence, the results in Chapter 4 show that Jesus, in the gospels, actively obeys God his Father through his caring for other human beings, and hence, he exerts a transformative power onto Malawian Reformed Christians for them to emotionally respond to God in wonder and gratitude for their justification in Jesus – leading them to a different view concerning their relationship with others in society, resorting into works of love and care for others around them. Hence, it points to and/or leads to their respect for rights and freedom of other human beings. Certainly, Chapter 4 demonstrated and affirmed that Jesus' acts as a human being on earth, Jesus' sayings or parables in the Gospel narratives are of much relevance as Jesus call to the Reformed Christians in Malawi to practice Jesus' pattern of life in their lives. Therefore, this pattern of Jesus' life is deemed as capable of leading the Reformed Christians in Malawi to a different view concerning their relationship with others in society, and leading them to their respect for human rights and freedom in society, as the findings, hereby, affirm.

The Gospels do reveal of Jesus as being very fond of welcoming other people into his life of a human being - no matter whether and how much these other people were different from him in their sinfulness. As a human being, Jesus thus did not discriminate against anyone. In Malawi, it is the person's right not to be discriminated against.

The Gospels describe Jesus as a mortal human being who lived on earth to experience sufferings and even death for the sake of delivering vulnerable human beings from their miseries and sufferings. Traditionally, problems that affect one member of society in Malawi, do affect all members of the same society, and hence, such is an encouragement to protect and support one another as members of same society. In Malawi, also, it is the person's or a group's right to claim, without fear, that a fundamental right or freedom (of self or another person) guaranteed by the Malawi Constitution has been infringed or threatened.

Again, the Gospels speak of Jesus as having died and shed his blood on the cross for human sin. Jesus, thus, rendered his life as a sacrifice acceptable and meaningful to God and sinful human beings. Jesus thus did exert a transformative power onto the Reformed Christians in Malawi for them not to turn away from struggle for justice for all in society on account of any humiliation, suffering, trials or even death they may experience – but to render their lives as a sacrifice acceptable and meaningful to God and their neighbours - because, as community, they all equally stand together as dignified human beings. In Malawi and through the assistance of the courts, the Ombudsman, the Human Rights Commission and other organs of the Malawi Government, it is the right of all persons in Malawi to seek the promotion, protection and redress of grievances in respect of human rights for all.

The Gospels tell us about the resurrection of Jesus that it is the new creation of human beings' or the new form of existence in Jesus. Hence, the Reformed Christians in Malawi would look on to Jesus and his resurrection as empowering them to look on beyond human struggles for justice and better society, to a new and better world for all. By looking beyond such life struggles, it makes a vision or a goal real, and hence, it is very encouraging. Moreover, everyone has a right to development in that better world. In Malawi, it is everyone's right to development and therefore to the enjoyment of economic, social, cultural and political development of all.

Jesus Christ willingly and intentionally unites with believers in order that he shares in their sin and its consequences and thereafter uplifts them from the agony of sin. Therefore, in uniting with believers and sharing in their sin and its consequences for their up-lifting, and hence, Jesus through the Holy Spirit thus influences and empowers the Reformed Christians in Malawi to sympathize with the oppressed and suffering around them in society in a bid to uphold justice in that society, and in a bid to uplift the lives of those people so that they may fully enjoy the privileges that they themselves enjoy in society. In Malawi, it is the right of all persons to development and therefore to the enjoyment of economic, social, cultural and political development, with the vulnerable such as women, children and the disabled given special consideration in the realization of the right.

Again, Jesus Christ's union with believers makes him mortal, and hence, a sharer in their misfortunes of sin and its consequence in the divine and human unity of being, enabling believers to partake of his graces in his suffering, death and resurrection. The Reformed Christians in Malawi ought to stoop down, and to accommodate in their lives the vulnerable in society – Jesus' way. In Malawi, the vulnerable have the right to experiencing power of social justice and equality. That is, it is the vulnerable persons' (especially women, children and the disabled) right to development, with measures taken to introduce reforms aimed at eradicating social injustices and inequalities in society.

In Gospels, Jesus Christ teaches us what it means to live our calling. Jesus loved us from the heart, such that he lived a sacrificial life of fellowship and service with us both men and women, in his union with us - vulnerable as we were in our corrupt condition and sinfulness. In our world today, women, children, the poor, the HIV positive or AIDS patients are among the vulnerable. Jesus thus teaches the Reformed Christians in Malawi that in their calling to discipleship they should participate with him in the suffering for the liberation of those people in society that are in pains, oppression and other inflictions. The people in pain, under oppression and other inflictions equally need freedom and joy as every other member of society. Women in Malawi are among those in pain and oppression resulting from exclusion from leadership in many sectors of life and violence against women. Nevertheless, it is women's right to full and equal protection by the law in Malawi, and the right not to be discriminated against because of their gender or marital status.

The Gospels speak of God as presenting his Son Jesus as a sacrifice of atonement, through our faith in his blood - demonstrating his justice – and hence, the Reformed Christians in Malawi have, here, Jesus as a pattern for their life of struggle toward the liberation of those people in society that are under oppression of some kind – whose dignity is threatened or rights violated. There are many people in Malawi who tend not to care what happens to others. All they care is, but, themselves. However, all people are called to respect the right to the dignity of all persons in the Malawi Constitution. The right protects everyone in Malawi from acts of injustice and indignity on one another.

By virtue of Jesus Christ's righteousness, and not good works, human beings are declared righteous before God, even though they are not righteous in themselves. The imputation of Jesus' righteousness into believers, does influence and empower Reformed Christians in Malawi to do others the same justice they freely received from God in Jesus, despite their sinfulness – leading to their protection and upholding of the dignity of other human beings in society, despite any undeservedness. In Malawi, it is the right of all persons to equal recognition as a person of dignity, before the law.

The Gospels say that Jesus, by his Spirit, willingly and freely called sinful human beings to become adopted children of God, in order that they become capable of experiencing and reflecting God's love in him - in which God the Father loves the Son, as God the Son loves the Father. Hence, with this knowledge that though sinful themselves as every other human being, but God in Jesus has been so gracious in adopting them into his love, the Reformed Christian in Malawi are thus made capable of adopting others in society into their lives. Many times, lack of accommodation into each other's life often results into violation of human rights among people. In Malawi, the law shall prescribe criminal penalties for violations of human rights, and hence, all persons in Malawi must respect the rights of other people as an obligation.

In his public ministry, as the first elect of God, Jesus felt compassion for people around him, and hence, he did works acceptable to God and looked to the cause of other human beings. Jesus through the Holy Spirit thus calls the Reformed Christians in Malawi to fulfil God's purpose of election through looking to the cause of their fellow human beings freely, in the midst of corruption and evil in society. Corruption and evil tend to restrict or limit exercise of rights and freedom in a person. In Malawi, by law and without prejudice, all persons should not place any restrictions or limitations on the exercise of any rights and freedoms provided for in the Malawi Constitution.

In the Gospels, Jesus reconciled us onto God, and hence, did not turn away from God's justice, but went through death and suffering in order that God presents us holy in his sight, without blemish and free from accusation. As followers of Christ, the Reformed Christians in Malawi are thus encouraged and empowered not to turn away from the justice they owe God because of any trials they can experience – leading to their protecting rights and freedoms of other human beings. Moreover, Malawian Christians have the support of the law in Malawi, which says that the courts shall have the power to make any orders that are necessary and appropriate to secure justice where the enjoyment of human rights and freedoms that have been unlawfully denied or violated.

The Gospels portray Lord's Supper as presented by Jesus to be a place of love. Jesus' introduced the Lord's Supper to exhort Christians to purity and holiness of life; and to love, peace and peaceful relations among human beings. Hence, Christians will not allow other human beings to be despised, rejected, abused or offended in any way because they are the same body of Jesus. In Malawi, it is all persons and peoples' right not to be discriminated against – leading to the passing of legislation to address inequalities in Malawi society, which is aimed at loving and serving one another as human beings equal in dignity.

CONTRIBUTION OF NEW KNOWLEDGE BY THE RESEARCH STUDY

In the research study's argument, it was stated that the Reformed Christians in Malawi want to support a culture of human dignity and rights, but that there is a widespread sense that the doctrine of the atonement, at the heart of the Reformed faith, does not assist them in doing that - but rather seems to contract such a sense of "rights", especially with teachings like "Centred on God's glory alone", "Based on God's word alone" or "Justification by Faith alone".

Again, it was stated that the ecumenical Reformed documents on human rights do not use the doctrine of atonement to support human rights, but rather use other doctrines. Basically, these ecumenical Reformed documents support a vague feeling of human dignity, but not the notion of specific rights as it were. They have something about "human beings created in the image of God" – man and woman equally created in the image of God and equal dignity and interdependence of different generations, "covenant responsibilities in our stewardship of creation", and "vocation". Hence, there is a strong belief that this research study does contribute something in this regard. The argument is that the Reformed understanding of the atonement does indeed support convictions regarding human dignity and specific rights.

Firstly, this research study argues that it does contribute something new to the academic circles in sense of its understanding the Reformed view of the atonement as being much broader than just "the cross and the resurrection of Jesus Christ", to include election, calling, covenant, image of God, regeneration, sanctification, work of the Spirit or community in the church. Secondly, the research study argues that it does contribute something new when it argues that within this Reformed view of the atonement, the notion of Jesus' active obedience, in addition to his passive obedience, is of central importance. That is why the hypothesis in Chapter 1 includes the call for a broader appreciation of the life and ministry of Jesus, as integral to his work of atonement that is capable of contributing to a more positive view of human rights and dignity. Based on these two claims (the broadening of the atonement and the addition of Jesus' everyday life on earth) about the atonement, therefore, the research study was capable of arguing for positive view of human rights and dignity.

Again, the research study argues that it does contribute something new when it is capable of making a case about Jesus' transformative power in the Gospels (Matthew, John, Luke and Mark), for the renewed life of the Reformed Christians in the contemporary Church of Central Africa Presbyterian in Malawi. Hence, the research study was capable of ascertaining that Jesus' transformative power in the Gospels does remain faithful to the proclamation of God's grace to humanity, in the sense that it does stem out of Jesus' active obedience to God, as evident in Jesus' own works, spoken words and parables. The research study, hence, affirms that in Jesus Christ's life, sayings or parables in the Gospels there is Jesus' active obedience toward God the Father for human salvation, which is truly consistent with the broader view of the atonement.

The research study, in light of the Reformed view of atonement, was able to make a case about the active obedience that is expected of Christians in their renewed life, resulting from Jesus Christ's atoning active obedience to God, in Jesus' life and ministry. The research study, also, argues that it does contribute something new when it is capable of affirming that Jesus' earthly life, sayings or parables in the Gospel narrative comprise of the atonement process as in the cross and the resurrection and are of much importance and relevance, and do possess Jesus' strong invitation for the Reformed Christians in Malawi to participate in his life, in their renewed life; and that such a strong invitation is capable of leading Reformed Christians in Malawi to a different view concerning their reception and building of human rights culture in Malawi. The research study, therefore, rejected the feeling that the Reformed notion of the atonement – grace alone, undeserving and sinful human beings without any claim or right, rejection of good deeds as being of any merit – does contradict the very foundation of a human rights culture. The classic Reformed doctrine of atonement and its broader meaning, thus, could deeply be inspiring and orienting with a view to a culture of respect for human dignity and human rights in contemporary Malawi. Such an understanding can be of great significance to the Christian population in Malawi. About eighty percent (80%) of Malawi's population is Christian, and therefore, the impact of this understanding of the Reformed view of the atonement towards human dignity and rights cannot be overemphasized.

Bibliography

Ambe, John. *Meaningful Celebration of the Sacrament of Reconciliation in Africa*. Aldoret, Kenya: AMACEA Gaba Publications. 1992.

Anselm. *Cur Deus Homo*. In Fairweather, Eugene R. *A Scholastic Miscellany: Anselm to Ockham*. Philadelphia: The Westminster Press.

Anselm. *Proslogion*. In Fairweather, Eugene R. *A Scholarstic Miscellany: Anselm to Ockham*. Philadelphia: The Westminster Press.

Aulen, Gustaf. *Christus Victor*. London: S.P.C.K. 1970.

Banda, Jande. *The Constitutional Change Debate of 1993-1995*. In Phiri & Ross. Eds. *Democratization in Malawi: A Stocktaking*. Blantyre, Malawi: Christian Literature Association in Malawi. 1998.

Barth, Karl. *Church Dogmatics*. Edinburgh, United Kingdom: T & T Clark. 1956.

Barth, Karl, *The Christian Life*. Grand Rapids, Michigan: William B. Eerdmans Publishing Company. 1981

Beeke, Joel R. *Calvin's Piety*. In McKim, Donald K. Ed. *The Cambridge Companion to John Calvin*. Cambridge, United Kingdom: Cambridge University Press. 2004.

Billings, J. Todd. *Calvin, Participation, and the Gift*. Oxford, United Kingdom: Oxford University Press. 2007.

Bizer, Ernst. *Reformed Dogmatics*. Grand Rapids, Michigan, United States: Baker Book House. 1978.

Brinkman, Martien E. *Justification in Ecumenical Dialogue: Central Aspects of Christian Soteriology in Debate*. Utrecht: Interuniversity Institute for Missiology and Ecumenical Research. 1996.

Bueta, G.G. *Christianity in Tropical Africa*. Oxford: Oxford University Press. 1968.

Busch, Eberhard. *The Great Passion: An Introduction to Karl Barth's Theology*. Grand Rapids, Michigan, United States: William B. Eerdmans Publishing Company. 2004.

Calhoun, David & Covenant Theological Seminary a. *Calvin's Institutes: Justification and Christian Freedom*. Online: www.covenantseminary.edu/worldwide/en/CH523/CH523_T_15.pdf. 07.09.2005.

Calhoun, David & Covenant Theological Seminary b. *Calvin's Institutes: Repentance*. Online: www.covenantseminary.edu/worldwide/en/CH523/CH523_T_13.pdf. 07.09.2005.

Calvin, John. *Institutes of the Christian Religion*. Philadelphia: The Westminster Press.

CCAP. Constitution. Lilongwe, Malawi. 8 December 2002.

Chirwa, Wiseman C. *Civil Society in Malawi's Democratic Transition*. In Ott. Ed. Et al. *Malawi's Second Democratic Elections: Process, Problems, and Prospects*. Blantyre, Malawi: Christian Literature Association in Malawi. 2000.

De Gruchy, John W. *Reconciliation: Restoring Justice*. Cape Town, South Africa. 2002.

Dzimbiri, B. Lewis. *Competitive Politics and Chameleon-like Leaders.* In Phiri & Ross. Eds. *Democratization in Malawi: A Stocktaking.* Blantyre, Malawi: Christian Literature Association in Malawi. 1998.

Fackre, Gabriel, *The Joint Declaration and the Reformed Tradition.* in Rusch, William G. Ed. *Justification and the Future of the Ecumenical Movement.* Collegeville, Minnesota, United States: Liturgical Press. 2003.

Fiedler, Klaus. *Christianity and African Culture: Conservative German Protestant Missionaries in Tanzania 1900-1940.* Blantyre, Malawi: Christian Literature Association in Malawi. 1999.

Forell, George W. *Human Rights Rhetoric or Reality?* Philadelphia: Fortress Press. 1978.

Forster, Peter G. *T. Cullen Young: Missionary and Anthropologist.* Blantyre, Malawi: Christian Literature Association in Malawi. 2003.

Gerrish, B.A. *Grace and Gratitude.* Minneapolis: Fortress Press. 1993.

Gorringe, Timothy. *Karl Barth Against Hegemony.* New York, United States: Oxford University Press. 1999.

Grudem, Wayne, *Systematic Theology: An Introduction to Biblical Doctrine.* Grand Rapids, Michigan: Zondervan Publishing House, Grand Rapids. 1994.

Gunton, Colin. *Salvation.* In Webster. John. Ed. *The Cambridge Companion to Karl Barth,* Cambridge, United Kingdom: Cambridge University Press. 2000.

Guthrie, Shirley C. *Christian Doctrine.* Louisville, Kentucky: Westminster John Knox Press. 1994.

Haas, Guenther. *Calvin's Ethics.* In McKim, Donald K. Ed. *The Cambridge Companion to John Calvin.* Cambridge, United Kingdom: Cambridge University Press. 2004.

Hancock, Ralph C. *Calvin and the Foundations of Modern Politics.* Ithaca and London: Cornell University Press. 1989.

Hara, Handwell Yotamu. *Reformed Soteriology and the Malawian Context.* Zomba, Malawi: Kachere Series. 2008.

Harvey, Van A. *A handbook of theological Terms.* New York: Collier MacMillan Publishing Company. 1964.

Heron, Alasdair I.C. ed. *The Westminster Confession in the Church Today.* Edinburgh, United Kingdom: The Saint Andrew Press. 1986.

Heron, Alasdair I.C. *Justification and Sanctification in the Reformed Tradition.* In Opocenskey & Reamonn. Eds. *Justification and Sanctification: In the Traditions of the Reformation.* 1999.

Heywood, Andrew. *Politics* (p.302). New York, N.Y.: Palgrave McMillan. 2002.

Hodge, A.A. *The Confession of Faith.* Carlisle, Pennsylvania, United States: The Banner of Truth Trust. 1978.

Human Rights Watch, Online: www.hrw.org/reports/1994/WR94/Africa-04.htm. 05.06.2007.

Hunsinger, George. *Karl Barth's Christology.* In Webster, John. Ed. *The Cambridge Companion to Karl Barth,* Cambridge, United Kingdom: Cambridge University Press. 2000.

Hunsinger, George. *Karl Barth's Theology of the Holy Spirit*. In Webster. John. Ed. *The Cambridge Companion to Karl Barth,* Cambridge, United Kingdom: Cambridge University Press. 2000.

Kamiruka, Jack, U. *A Luo Christian Perspective on the Role of the Holy Spirit in Sanctification According to John Calvin.* Stellenbosch, South Africa: University of Stellenbosch. 2007 (Unpublished thesis).

Kang, Paul ChulHong. *The Imputation of Christ's Righteousness from Reformation Theology to the American Great Awakening and the Korean Revivals.* New York, United States: Peter Lang Publishing. 2006.

Kanyongolo, Fidelis Edge. *The Limits of Liberal Democratic Constitutionalism in Malawi.* In Phiri & Ross. Eds. *Democratization in Malawi: A Stocktaking.* Blantyre, Malawi: Christian Literature Association in Malawi. 1998.

Kasambala, Ralph. *Civic Education in Malawi Since 1992: An Appraisal.* In Phiri & Ross. Eds. *Democratization in Malawi: A Stocktaking.* Blantyre, Malawi: Christian Literature Association in Malawi. 1998.

Kinneer, Jack D, *What is Reformed Faith?*:www.opc.org/new_horizons/NH99/NH9902b.html

Krotke, Wolf. *The Human Person in Karl Barth's Anthropology.* In Webster. John. Ed. *The Cambridge Companion to Karl Barth,* Cambridge, United Kingdom: Cambridge University Press. 2000.

Leith, John H. *Basic Christian Doctrine.* Louisville, Kentucky: Westminster/John Knox Press. 1993.

Life Application Study Bible. Grand Rapids, Michigan, United States: Zondervan Publishing House & Inc. Wheaton, Illinois, United States: Tyndale House Publishers. 1991.

Loonstra, Bertus. *Election-Atonement-Covenant.* Gravenhage: Boekencentrum. 1990.

Lutheran World Federation, Online: www.lutheranworld.org/LWF_Documents/LWI/LWI-EN-200408-low.pdf. 19.11.2007.

Machem, J. Gresham. *The Doctrine of the Atonement.* Online: www.the-highway.com/atone2_Machen.html. 11.10.2007.

Malawi Constitution. Online: www.sdnp.org.mw/constitut/chapter4.html. 23.05.2005.

Malawi Human Rights Commission: Online: www.malawihumanrightscommission.org. 12.10.2007.

Mayaya, Billy A. *Challenges for Democracy and Human Rights in Malawi*: Online: www.presbyterian.ca/assemblyoffice/iac/mayayaspeech.html. 07.04.2005.

Mbiti, John. *Bible and Theology in African Christianity.* Nairobi, Kenya: Oxford, United Kingdom: Oxford University Press. 1986.

McCormack, Bruce L. *What's at Stake in Current Debates Over Justification?* In Husbands & Treier. eds. *Justification: What's at Stake in the Current Debates.* Downess Grove, Illinois, United States: Inter-Varsity Press. 2004.

McCormack, Bruce. *Grace and Being.* In Webster. John. Ed. *The Cambridge Companion to Karl Barth,* Cambridge, United Kingdom: Cambridge University Press. 2000.

McCormack, Bruce L. *What's at Stake in Current Debates Over Justification?* In Husbands & Treier. eds. *Justification: What's at Stake in the Current Debates.* Downess Grove, Illinois, United States: Inter-Varsity Press. 2004.

McEwen, James S. *How the Confession Came to be Written.* In Heron, Alasdair I.C. *The Westminster Confession in the Church Today.* Edinburgh, United Kingdom: The Saint Andrew Press. 1986.

McGrath, Alister E. *Justification by Faith.* Grand Rapids, Michigan, United States: Zondervan Publishing House. 1988.

McGrath, Alister E. *A Life of John Calvin.* Massachusetts, United States: Basil Blackwell Ltd. 1990.

McGrath, Alister E. *Iustitia Dei: A History of the Christian Doctrine of Justification.* Cambridge, United Kingdom. 1998.

Migliore, Daniel L. *Faith Seeking Understanding.* Grand Rapids, Michigan: William B. Eerdmans Publishing Company. 1991.

Mijoga, Hilary B.P. *Separate but Same Gospel.* Blantyre, Malawi: Christian Literature Association of Malawi. 2000.

Miller, Allen O. *A Christian Declaration on Human Rights,* Grand Rapids, Michigan: William B. Eerdmans Publishing Company 1977.

Milne, Bruce. *Know the Truth.* Leicester, England, United Kingdom: Inter-Varsity Press. 1986.

Molnar, Paul D. *The Theology of Justification in Dogmatic Context.* In Husbands & Treier. eds. *Justification: What's at Stake in the Current Debates.* Downess Grove, Illinois, United States: Inter-Varsity Press. 2004.

Murray, Andrew. *Moyo Watsopano: Mau a Mulungu kwa Ophunzira Ongoyamba a Yesu Khristu.* Zomba, Malawi: Kachere Series. 2005.

Murray, Andrew. *The School of Obedience.* London and Edinburgh, United Kingdom: Marshall, Morgan and Scott Limited.

Musopole, Augustine C. *Need: a Theology Cooked in an African Pot.* In Fiedler, Klaus. *Theology Cooked in an African Pot.* Zomba, Malawi: Association of Theological Institutions in Southern and Central Africa (ATISCA). 1998.

National Coordinating Committee for UDHR50. *Questions and Answers,* Franklin and Eleanor Roosevelt Institute: Online: www.udhr.org/history/default.htm. 16.03.2006.

Nyamiti, Charles. *Christ as our ancestor.* Gweru, Zimbambwe: Mambo Press. 1984.

Nzunda & Ross, eds. *Church, Law and Political Transition in Malawi 1992-1994.* Gweru, Zimbabwe: Mambo Press. 1995.

Opocensky, Milan & Reamonn, Paraic. eds. *Justification and Sanctification in the Traditions of the Reformation.* Geneva, Switzerland: World Alliance of Reformed Churches. 1999.

Ott, Martin. *The Role of the Christian Churches in Democratic Malawi (1994-1999).* In Ott. Ed. Et al. *Malawi's Second Democratic Elections:*

Process, Problems, and Prospects. Blantyre, Malawi: Christian Literature Association in Malawi. 2000. p.122.

Parker, T.H.L. *Calvin: An Introduction to His Thought.* London: Geoffrey Chapman. 1995.

Paas, Steven. *English Lessons from the Bible.* Zomba, Malawi: Kachere Series. 2004.

Paas, Steven. *From Galilee to the Atlantic.* Zomba, Malawi: Kachere Series. 2006.

Paas, Steven. *The Faith Moves South: A History of the Church in Africa.* Zomba, Malawi: Kachere Series. 2006 (b).

Phiri, Isabel Apawo. *Women, Presbyterianism and Patriarchy: Religious Experience of Chewa Women in Central Malawi.* Blantyre, Malawi: Christian Literature Association in Malawi. 2000.

Phiri, Kings M. & Ross, Kenneth R. *Introduction: From Totalitarianism to Democracy in Malawi.* In Phiri & Ross. Eds. *Democratization in Malawi: A Stocktaking.* Blantyre, Malawi: Christian Literature Association in Malawi. 1998.

Princeton Theological Seminary. *Studies in Reformed Theology and History, Volume 1 Number 2, Spring 1993.* Princeton, New Jersey, United States: Bruce L. McCormack. 1993.

Reformed Ecumenical Council, Online: http://en.wikipedia.org/wiki/Reformed_Ecumenical_Council. 07.08.2007.

RES Testimony on Human Rights. 1983.

Rohls, Jan. *Reformed Confessions: Theology from Zurich to Barmen.* Louisville, Kentucky: Westminster/John Knox Press. 1977.

Ross, Andrew. *Blantyre Mission and the Making of Modern Malawi.* Blantyre, Malawi: Christian Literature Association in Malawi. 1996.

Ross, Kenneth R. *Church and Creed in Scotland: The Free Church Case 1900-1904 and its Origins.* Edinburgh, Scotland, United Kingdom. 1988.

Ross, Kenneth R. *Gospel Ferment in Malawi.* Gweru, Zimbabwe: Mambo Press, 1995.

Ross, Kenneth R. ed. *Christianity in Malawi: A Source Book.* Gweru, Zimbabwe: Kachere Series. 1996.

Ross, Kenneth. R. *Here Comes Your King.* Blantyre, Malawi: Christian Literature Association in Malawi.1998.

Schmiechen, Peter. *Theories of Atonement and Forms of the Church.* Grand Rapids, Michigan, United States: William B. Eerdmans Publishing Company. 2005

Sinclair, Margaret. *Salt and Light: Letters of Jack and Mamie Martin in Malawi 1921-28.* Blantyre, Malawi: Christian Literature Association in Malawi. 2002.

Smit, D.J. *On Social and Economic Justice in South Africa Today: A Theological Perspective on Theoretical Paradigms.* In van der Walt, AJ. Ed. *Theories of Social and Economic Justice* (p.225). Stellenbosch, South Africa: Sun Press. 2005.

Smit, Dirk. *Views on Calvin's Ethics.* In Asling, John P. *John Calvin: What is His Ligacy.* Geneva, Switzerland: World Alliance of Reformed Churches. 2007.

Smit, Dirk. *Justification and Divine Justice?* In *What is Justification About.* Weinrich, Michael & Burgess, John P. Eds. Grand Rapids, Michigan, United States: William B. Eerdmans Publishing Company. 2009.

Steinmetz, David C. *The Council Of Trent* in David Bagchi & David C. Steinmetz. Eds. *Cambridge Companion to Reformed Theology.* Cambridge, United Kingdom: Cambridge University Press. 2004.

Synod of Blantyre Larger Catechism. Blantyre, Malawi: The Christian Literature Association of Malawi.

Synod of Blantyre Shorter Catechism. Blantyre, Malawi: The Christian Literature Association of Malawi.

Synod of Nkhoma Catechism. Nkhoma, Malawi: The Council of Reformed Churches in Central Africa. 1968.

Tamburello, Denis, *Christ at the Center: The Legacy of the Reformed Tradition.* In *The Bulletin of the Institute for Reformed Theology,* Winter 2004, Volume 4, # 1. Online: www.reformedtheology.org/siteFiles/Winter2004/Essay_Christ_at_th e_Center.html. 13.09.2005.

Tengatenga, James. *Church, State and Society in Malawi: The Anglican Case.* Zomba, Malawi: Kachere Series. 2006

The Belgic Confession of Faith. Online: www.reformed.org/documents/BelgicConfession.html. 3.6.2005.

The Canon of Dort. Online: www.biblefacts.org/church/dort.html.

The New Interpreter's Bible, Volume 8. Nashville, TN, United States: Abingdon Press. 1995.

The New Interpreter's Bible, Volume 9. Nashville, TN, United States: Abingdon Press. 1995.

The Scottish Confession of Faith. Online: www.swrb.com/newslett/actualNLs/ScotConf.htm. 3.6.2005.

The Westminster Confession of Faith. Online: www.spurgeon.org/~phil/creeds/wcf.htm. 23.5.2005.

The Westminster Larger Catechism. Online: www.epcew.org.uk/wlc/index.html. 23.5.2005.

The Westminster Shorter Catechism. Online: www.Gracebpc.org/Westminster_shorter_catechism?PHPSESSID=cba2bc31e6469d4b. 23.5.2005.

Thomas, G. Michael. *The Extent of the Atonement.* London, United Kingdom: Paternoster Publishing. 1988.

United States Department of State Report of 2005: Online: www.state.gov/g/drl/rls/hrrpt/2005/61579.htm.12.10.2007

United States Department of State Report of 2006: Online: www.state.gov/g/drl/rls/hrrpt/2006/78744.htm. 12.10.2007.

Universal Declaration of Human Rights, Online: http://hrweb.org/legal/udhr.html. 30.11.2004.

Van Wyk, Jurgens Johannes. *The Historical Development of the Offices According to the Presbyterian Tradition of Scotland.* Zomba Malawi: Kachere Series. 2004.

VonDoeppi, Peter. *The Kingdom Beyond Zasintha: Churches and Political Life in Malawi's Post-authoritarian Era*. In Phiri & Ross. Eds. *Democratization in Malawi: A Stocktaking*. Blantyre, Malawi: Christian Literature Association in Malawi. 1998.

Vorster, J.M. Calvin and Human Rights. In *The Ecumenical Review*. April 1999. Online: www.findarticles.com/p/articles/ml_m2065/is_2_51/ai _56063944/pg_3. 13.09.2007.

Walzer. Michael. *Spheres of Justice*: *A defence of Pluralism and Equality*. Princeton, New Jersey, United States: Basic Books, Inc.1984.

Webster, John. *Barth's Ethics of Reconciliation*. Cambridge, United Kingdom: Cambridge University Press. 1995.

Webster, John. Ed. *The Cambridge Companion to Karl Barth*. Cambridge, United Kingdom: Cambridge University Press. 2000.

Webster, John. *The Ethics of Reconciliation*. in Colin E. Gunton. Ed. *The Theology of Reconciliation*. New York, United States: T & T Clark Limited. 2003.

Wendland, Ernst, R. *Preaching that Grabs the Heart*. Blantyre, Malawi: Christian Literature Association of Malawi. 2000.

Wendland, Ernest & Hachibamba, Salimo. Eds. *Galu Wamkota: Missiological Reflections from South-Central Africa*. Zomba, Malawi: Kachere Series. 2007.

Werpehowski, William. *Karl Barth and Politics*. In Webster. John. Ed. *The Cambridge Companion to Karl Barth,* Cambridge, United Kingdom: Cambridge University Press. 2000.

Williamson, G.I. *The Westminster Confession of Faith for Study Classes.* Philadelphia, Pennsylvania, United States: Presbyterian and Reformed Publishing Company. 1964.

Wikipedia: the free Encyclopaedia, Online:

http://en.wikipedia.org/wiki/Hastings_Banda. 05.06.2007.

Wikipedia: https://en.wikipedia.org/wiki/Natural_law

World Alliance of Reformed Churches, Online:

http://en.wikipedia.org/wiki/World_Alliance_of_Reformed_Churches. 07.08.2007.

www.ingramcontent.com/pod-product-compliance
Lightning Source LLC
Chambersburg PA
CBHW050530300426
44113CB00012B/2030